The Educator's Guide to Preventing Child Sexual Abuse

Editors
Mary Nelson and Kay Clark

Network Publications, a division of ETR Associates
Santa Cruz, CA ∼ 1986

Library of Congress Cataloging-in-Publication Data
Main entry under title:

The Educator's guide to preventing child sexual abuse.

    Bibliography: p.
    Includes index.
    1. Child molesting—United States—Addresses, essays, lectures.
2. Child molesting—United States—Prevention—Addresses,
essays, lectures. 3. Child molesting—Prevention—Study and
teaching—United States—Addresses, essays, lectures. I. Nelson,
Mary. II. Clark, Kay, 1942-
HQ72.U53E38 1986   362.7'044   85-29670
ISBN 0-941816-17-6   (pbk.)

For more information contact
Network Publications
1700 Mission Street, Suite 203
P.O. Box 1830
Santa Cruz, CA 95061–1830
(408) 429-9822

ISBN 0-941816-17-6

Contents

Part II: Prevention Programs at Work

Appendixes

Preface

"Someday, maybe, there will exist a well-informed, well-considered, yet fervent public conviction that the most deadly of all possible sins is the mutilation of a child's spirit; for such mutilation undercuts the life principle of trust, without which every human act . . . is prone to perversion by destructive forms of consciousness."

Erik H. Erikson

The National Family Life Education Network (coordinated by ETR Associates) has been providing information and services to member educators and other professionals since its inception in 1982. Child sexual abuse prevention education has merged as a natural extension of our involvement in family life education.

As family life educators, we believe individuals need accurate, adequate information about family life issues, a firm respect for and understanding of self, skills in decision making and communication, and a respect for family values and the values of others.

The same underlying principles apply to sexual abuse prevention education. Most people who are working to prevent child sexual abuse believe that in order to be less vulnerable, children need accurate, adequate information about what sexual abuse is. They need to understand and trust their own intuitive feelings and be able to act on those feelings. And they need to be able to communicate their feelings to a trusted adult.

Our commitment to child sexual abuse prevention education began with the expansion of our library at The National Family Life Education Network to include prevention materials published since 1980. Over 200 books, curricula and miscellaneous teaching aids were added to our collection. The next step was to share the information with our Network members. We compiled a comprehensive annotated bibliography of sexual abuse literature. Finally, since we are networkers, we strongly support the concept of pooling and sharing resources, information and ideas toward a common goal. Therefore, because the issue was timely and relevant for our members, we decided to compile a compendium of articles by experts in the field into a special edition of our quarterly journal, *Family Life Educator*.

We contacted authors, teachers, social service directors, medical and mental health professionals and various other authorities who work in the field of child protection. It soon became apparent that, while there was excellent information available from a wide range of experts, there was no single resource that presented a summary of current educational efforts to prevent child sexual abuse. Our plans for a special journal issue expanded to be that resource. *The Educator's Guide to Preventing Child Sexual Abuse* is the result. In it, we provide an overview so that professionals and parents can assess—and access—the larger picture.

The growth of prevention education has been rapid. The volume of information available is now staggering. So are the number of approaches to the problem. School districts, rape crisis centers, counselors, physicians, law enforcement agencies, theater and community groups, parent/teacher associations, universities and colleges, and various representatives of the media are involved in developing materials and programs, conducting research and exploring all possible ways to prevent and treat child sexual abuse.

Great strides are being made. Today, programs that teach children sophisticated concepts about touch and rights and feelings are incorporated into elementary and secondary school curricula with the support and cooperation of parents. Materials to inform children from preschool through adolescence about sexual abuse and prevention techniques are appearing in bookstores, supermarkets, and variety outlets across the nation.

In order to assess future needs and directions, it seems appropriate to pause for a look at how far we've come and where we are. We hope *The Educator's Guide* does that.

Finally, a word about prevention education as we see it. The current focus on supplying our children with sophisticated concepts about touch and rights and feelings, about abstract "good" and "bad" qualities, has raised some questions. Will they get it? Will they become afraid of normal, loving touch? Will we? Will they become suspicious and afraid of babysitters, uncles, neighbors and friends? How can we teach them to trust, when the problem seems to be in trusting too much?

The fact is that sexual abuse prevention programs are teaching children to trust. All over the country, concern about sexual abuse is taking the form of prevention programs designed to arm children with the truth about their rights and those who would take away those rights. They are being taught valuable lessons in assertiveness and communication. They are being taught to trust themselves.

Acknowledgments

The Educator's Guide to Preventing Child Sexual Abuse exists because of the many busy people who made time to share their knowledge, experience, ideas and concerns. We'd like to thank them here.

First, we want to thank the authors who address the myriad issues confronting prevention educators today. We feel fortunate to have gathered so much expertise about so many different aspects of child sexual abuse prevention between the covers of one book.

Second, our thanks to the people across the country who are engaged in prevention education and who share the elements that make their programs work. Many of these programs were developed before there was support for their efforts or acknowledgment that there was a problem. We're proud to record their success in these pages.

To compile the bibliography we needed the cooperation of authors, publishers, editors, film distributors and nonprofit organizations who are making materials about child sexual abuse prevention available to educators around the nation. We received invaluable assistance from these people, and we thank them.

Finally, our thanks to our colleagues, whose skills, perseverance, patience and cheerfulness allowed us to complete this book in record time. Thanks to Sarah Lamb for word-processing the many drafts needed to satisfy the perfectionists we are. Thanks to Francesca Angelesco for designing *The Educator's Guide*. Thanks to Elizabeth Warshaw and Julia Chiapella who, in painstaking detail, translated the design into the book we had envisioned.

PART I

Introduction

Chapter 1

Prevention Education in Perspective

CAROL A. PLUMMER

Child sexual abuse as a national problem of epidemic proportions has only gained the priority spotlight within the past ten years. Due in large part to national funding and sponsorship of treatment and research, increasing numbers of persons were identified as being affected by past or present incest and other forms of sexual abuse. Although it still constitutes a minority of the total official reports of child abuse, some authorities now consider sexual abuse to be the major form of child abuse (Finkelhor, 1981b).

Not until 1980, however, was federal money first appropriated specifically for prevention. Due in part to this national endorsement, there is now a wide variety of prevention programs for children. They range from children receiving a "stranger danger" talk from "Officer Friendly" to a three-week curriculum covering incest and physical abuse. A play may be performed for the entire student body or students may receive individualized instructions in basic self-defense moves. Some children have received a comic book about sexual abuse to take home and discuss with their parents.

The purpose of this book is to help educators

and community members ascertain the range of possibilities for prevention aimed at children, and pinpoint the factors that can facilitate the success of a program. First, to put the prevention movement in context, this chapter outlines a brief history of child sexual abuse prevention education. Secondly, what prevention education is and what it can accomplish is discussed.

A Brief History of Prevention

There was virtually no focus on the prevention of child sexual abuse until the mid-to-late 1970s. In fact, professionals were only beginning to see the magnitude of the problem of sexual abuse of children, particularly incest. A few programs had been funded to study the problem through the National Center for the Prevention and Control of Rape (National Institute of Mental Health) in the 1970s, but the results were not available until the late 1970s or early 1980s.

Most significant was work by two researchers, Diana Russell and David Finkelhor. In separate studies they showed that the sexual victimization of children had a prevalence far beyond previous assessments. Russell (1983) found over one in three females in her study were sexually abused before reaching age 18. Male children were also found to be at high risk for sexual abuse before manhood; one out of eleven self-reported victimization in another study (Finkelhor, 1981c).

Even before these statistics were commonly quoted, psychologists and social workers attested to the extent of the problem and cited gaps in services for victims as well as their entire families. Four major treatment centers were funded in 1977 by the National Center on Child Abuse and Neglect (NCCAN), to develop incest treatment programs. Probably the best known program to develop from this seed money was Henry Giarretto's model, involving the entire family in counseling and in self-help groups called Parents United and Sons and Daughters United.[1] All of these programs included therapists who were specifically trained in child sexual abuse theory and treatment techniques. The idea that distinct sexual abuse treatment programs were needed, complete with trained specialists, was popular in many communities by 1980.

Treatment programs flourished, often finding the need exceeding their capabilities, and grew very rapidly. This growth forced professionals to ask a very basic question. Since child sexual abuse is so widespread, what can we do to prevent it? This question was being asked simultaneously by people in the child abuse field and those in the sexual assault community.

As early as 1975, several rape crisis centers had designed prevention talks for adolescents, though most still focused on rape by strangers or dates (rather than relatives). (A program in Columbus, Ohio, the Child Assault Prevention Project (CAPP), was one of the first to begin direct work with pre-adolescents in this area. See CAPP in Part II, *Prevention Programs at Work*.) A major breakthrough came in 1977 when Cordelia Anderson, then at the Hennepin County Attorney's office in Minneapolis, piloted the Touch Continuum stating simply yet profoundly that touch could be good, bad or confusing. It is this concept of balancing talk about good and bad touches so as not to frighten children about all touch that undergirds most programs today. Though the ideas sound obvious now, I recall waiting eagerly for the release of Anderson's curriculum, the first printed guidebook for prevention education with children (Anderson, 1979). With the exception of a few coloring books such as *Red Flag, Green Flag* (Williams, 1980), it was the only guidance available when everyone was uncertain about what to do and how to do it.

The topic of prevention first received attention in 1979 at a national conference sponsored by NCCAN in Los Angeles. During this conference, the presentation of "Touch," a play written and performed by Illusion Theater, represented a landmark attempt to address children in an entertaining yet informative way about sexual abuse. (See Illusion Theater in Part II, *Prevention Programs at Work*.)

In 1980 the fledgling child sexual abuse prevention movement got an encouraging push from the federal government through NCCAN. Six sites were chosen as demonstration projects, to test and refine methods of presenting sexual abuse information directly to school children. (The demonstration projects were in Goshen,

Indiana; Burlington, North Carolina; Minneapolis, Minnesota; New York City; Tacoma, Washington; and North Hampton, Massachusetts.) What was particularly innovative about these grants was the requirement that they be used for educating children in schools, rather than for community awareness, parenting classes or professional trainings. As importantly, it implied federal-level endorsement for this approach. These projects were chosen, in part, for the regional, ethnic, racial, age and program diversity represented. For example, the Massachusetts project focused primarily on a preschool program for the children of Hispanic migrant workers (See Personal Safety Curriculum in Part II, *Prevention Programs at Work*.), whereas the Minneapolis project was funded to write, pilot and perform a play for junior and senior high school students in public schools. (Further information about these projects can be obtained through writing: Illusion Theater, 528 Hennepin Avenue, Minneapolis, MN 55403.)

In 1980, few communities had even heard of school prevention programs for children. In fact, in many areas no effort had been made to heighten community awareness about child sexual abuse, let alone its prevention. It is largely to the credit of Kee MacFarlane, then at the National Center on Children Abuse and Neglect, that federal dollars were designated for this problem area. The impact of this endorsement should not be underestimated. First, the six funded projects had a ripple effect, inspiring new programs in surrounding towns and states. For example, within the two-year grant period the project in Massachusetts prompted the creation of similar programs in a three-state area. Secondly, the national recognition of the enormity of the problem paved the way for communities to begin programs. The fact that officials in Washington said child sexual abuse existed and that programs for children were needed opened school doors more quickly to Bridgework Theater's prevention plays in Goshen, Indiana. (See Bridgework Theater in Part II, *Prevention Programs at Work*.) All prevention programs, whether or not they were initiated with federal dollars, benefitted from the national endorsement of the need.

Today there are sexual abuse prevention programs for children in every state in the United States and a growing number in other countries (Canada, Puerto Rico, South Africa, Sweden, Australia). Illusion Theater, which served as the National Clearinghouse for Prevention Programs from 1983-84 is now aware of programs in thousands of communities (prompted by Children's Trust Funds in 25 states), about forty plays on the topic, between 400-500 curricula, and hundreds of coloring books.[2] In five short years, the combined efforts of all prevention programs have reached over one million children with sexual abuse prevention messages. Still, this movement is young and is now in need of a focus more on quality than on quantity.

Defining Prevention

One of the initial confusions about prevention education, and a problem that persists today, is agreement on what prevention programs are really all about. One definition is, "Prevention is an active intervention plan comprised of various components with the ultimate goal of averting or avoiding a negative outcome, in this case, sexual abuse" (Plummer, 1984). If sexual abuse is considered to occur whenever a child is forced or tricked into sexual contact, our aims become clearer. Prevention advocates need to have an *active plan,* which is, in part, to inform children of the problem and ways to prevent or solve it.

Most child sexual abuse prevention experts agree that our long term goal is the elimination of sexual abuse. Our shorter term goals have to do with reducing the chances for abuse by intervening in the "preconditions" for abuse to occur. David Finkelhor has delineated four distinct preconditions necessary for child sexual abuse to occur: (1) sexual attraction to a child, (2) lack of internal controls, (3) lack of external controls, (4) availability of or access to a child (Finkelhor, 1981a). School prevention programs clearly speak to the fourth precondition. If we inform children about sexual abuse (i.e. bad touch, having an older person touch your private parts when you don't want them to) and ways to prevent it (run away, tell someone, say no, yell, use self-defense) we adults believe children can be empowered to *help* avoid or interrupt their own victimization *sometimes.* This limitation must be acknowledged. We cannot always prevent sexual exploitation or abuse of children by giving them information or skills. The three other preconditions must also be addressed.

In attempting to address the other three preconditions, deeper societal ills are blatantly apparent. In fact, societal norms often perpetuate the existence of child sexual abuse. Certainly, objectification of people in the media,

selling with sex, rules to respect and obey all adults, pornography, low conviction or even identification rate for sex offenders,[3] etc., all help to perpetuate abuse and encourage the preconditions for abuse. To ignore these factors only focuses responsibility on children for preventing abuse and, even if inadvertently, inherently blames children if abuse does occur.

Still our responsibility must be to empower children so that if all other prevention methods fail, they have a last defense against sexual abuse. Those who are given knowledge, a sense of personal power, and a list of community resources, will be enabled to assist in their own self-protection.[4] Adults owe children all the safety we can possibly provide from this most victimizing of all crimes.

Prevention is not, however, a process of trying to identify past or present victims in a classroom or audience. As Cordelia Anderson chastised at a 1979 conference, "We are not on a headhunt for victims." Indeed, this becomes the goal of some prevention programs. Perhaps it is because we are more convinced that sexual abuse really is a problem when children report. Maybe reports prove to us that we're really doing something.

The fact is, however, that the *total* effect of prevention is not quantifiable and measurable. Prevention education relies upon the faith of those of us who work, planting seeds of information, tending young ones as they grow, with the long term effect being to create a safer world. Some of these children may teach and protect their children more adequately due to our efforts. Some, as adults, may control their own inappropriate impulses toward children. Some young children may feel empowered to say no ten years from now when dating often makes sex an unspoken obligation.

Prevention education is, in part, an act of faith. While we make attempts to justify and prove the value of our work, the bottom line is we must *believe* we are able to assist children in preventing their own sexual victimization.

Notes

1. Dr. Henry Giarretto's program, the Child Sexual Abuse Treatment Program, is located in Santa Clara, California.
2. Estimates provided by staff at Illusion Theater, June 1985.
3. For example, in the past year of providing outpatient therapy in sexual abuse and incest cases, I have seen very few convictions and the most severe sentence has been two years of probation and three weekends in jail (for a misdemeanor).
4. The concept of the need to help children equalize power, knowledge and resources between adults and children is borrowed from Linda Tschirhart Sanford. *The Silent Children: A Parent's Guide to Prevention of Sexual Abuse.* New York: McGraw-Hill, 1982.

References

Anderson, Cordelia. *Child Sexual Abuse Prevention Project: An Educational Model for Working with Children.* Minneapolis, MN: Hennepin County Attorney's Office, 1979.

Finkelhor, David. "Four Preconditions Model of Child Sexual Abuse." Paper presented to the National Conference of Family Violence Research, Durham, NH, 1981(a).

Finkelhor, David. "Sexual Abuse: A Sociological Perspective." Paper presented at the International Congress on Child Abuse and Neglect, Amsterdam, April, 1981(b).

Finkelhor, David. "Sexual Abuse of Boys." *Victimology* 6 (1981c): 71-84.

Plummer, Carol. *Preventing Sexual Abuse.* Holmes Beach, FL: Learning Publications, Inc., 1984.

Russell, D. E. H. "The Incidence and Prevalence of Intrafamilial and Extrafamilial Sexual Abuse of Female Children. *Child Abuse and Neglect: The International Journal* 7:2 (1983).

Williams, Joy. *Red Flag, Green Flag People.* Fargo, ND: Rape and Abuse Crisis Center, 1980.

Chapter 2

Thinking About Prevention Education
— A Critical Look —

SANDRA BUTLER

Since 1978 the sexual abuse of children has become a discrete field of research, analysis, treatment and public education. Experts in the field are trying to understand a number of issues: the different kinds of sex offenders and their motivation; generational repetition of abusive behaviors; developmental repercussions for the victimized child; treatment and intervention strategies that have been successful to date; and ways to understand the similarities and differences between intrafamilial and extrafamilial abuse patterns.

We are still learning the many ways sexual abuse can occur. From fathers to babysitters, from strangers to older children, from teachers to clergy, there appears to be no end to the permutations children encounter in their efforts to negotiate the often predatory world of adults and older children. We are beginning to discover the numbers of children who have been kidnapped, tortured, and used in pornography and for prostitution, both in well-organized rings and by individual adults.

In a recent random sample of 903 women, 28 percent reported being sexually abused before the age of 14 (Russell, 1983). Current estimates suggest that one boy is victimized for every three girls and that a quarter of all abuse occurs before the age of seven (Finkelhor, 1984). In 1983 there were 72,000 reported cases of child sexual abuse with 61,200 reports involving girls (85 percent) and 10,800 involving boys (15 percent) (Cohn et al, 1985). While this increase in reporting is heartening, most victims still remain unrecognized, untreated and silent.

These alarming statistics have generated another, even newer field—the prevention of child sexual abuse. There has been a massive proliferation of books, films, professional presentations, videos, live theater, puppet shows and classroom curricula, all directed at chil-

This piece acknowledges that everything we know about sexual abuse we have learned from the courage of children and adults who have persisted in speaking out with insistence and strength about their experiences. We owe them no less courage in our continuing effort to prevent further victimization by fighting back against those who would oppress and limit children's information, options, resources and potential power.

dren, parents, teachers, concerned community members and mental health practitioners. While this work is most welcome, very much needed, and often excellent, some issues have not been sufficiently addressed. This article will focus critically on them.

History

The field of child sexual abuse prevention education developed from two different sources. The first had its roots in the publication of *The Battered Child*, written by two physicians (Kempe and Helfer, 1968). This ground-breaking book clearly identified, with the use of the x-ray machine, that physical abuse was indeed a fact of children's lives and its authors focused national outrage on this issue. Nearly ten years later sexual abuse was added to the widening dimensions of child abuse and was typically seen to occur out of a confluence of factors. Intrapsychic or interpersonal deficits, dysfunctional family systems, stress related behaviors, alcohol or chemical dependencies and poor impulse control were seen to be at the roots of much abusive behavior. This analysis is based on abuse being a confluence of mental health factors and interventions were developed to reflect that perspective.

The second source of child sexual abuse prevention efforts grew out of a conference held in 1971 sponsored by the New York Radical Feminists. This was the first public declaration about women's experiences of rape and resulted in a series of public recommendations including the suggestion that schools provide psychological and physical self-defense education for children. These women defined the issue of sexual abuse quite differently than the child welfare professionals. To feminists, the sexual abuse of children, in addition to being dangerous, damaging and pervasive, is seen as an inevitable outgrowth of power and gender relations. Further, it is seen as a primarily male behavior, a consequence of male socialization that tacitly permits violence against those less powerful, namely women and children. The blurring of violence and sexuality in the culture is implicit in this view.

These fundamental differences of definition have generated avenues of prevention education that emphasize different outcomes and create different problems. Nearly all prevention programs stress the importance of saying no to unwanted touch, telling an adult, getting away from the abuser or situation, and understanding that a person is not to blame for the behavior of others. But these messages have different meanings and limitations depending on how they are taught. Many mental health professionals and prevention educators teach children that it is possible to avoid being sexually abused if the child has mastered the responses mentioned above. However, in my view, this is merely a first step. New strategies are necessary to equalize the inherently unequal relationship between children and adults. Adults must remember that it is often frightening to be a child in a world populated by powerful giants who are in charge and sometimes behave in unpredictable and confusing ways.

Protection versus Empowerment

Much as we would like, parents and educators cannot always be available to children. Nor are all adults able to empathize with a child's experience. One irony is that adults known to children constitute a high percentage of the sources of their potential abuse and danger. Common sense tells us that children should trust parents and adults as only one resource—they need to learn to trust themselves as well.

Children must be allowed to feel more powerful in the world. Thus it is important for prevention education programs to expand the boundaries of children's lives, not reduce and limit them. Teaching children to use each other as potential allies in dangerous situations is an important addition to prevention education. Programs that teach prevention within the framework of empowerment are premised on the belief that one primary reason children are abused and molested is because they are powerless. Children are potential victims because they are small, vulnerable, without many resources, and with insufficient information or skills to protect themselves. Prevention programs should offer children of all ages information about sexual abuse, personal safety, self-defense and their bodies. Prevention programs should discuss ways to assess and strategize about possibly dangerous situations and teach young people to turn to each other for support. These skills will help children deal with a wide range of life situations.

For example, after a prevention workshop for children, Jennifer came to ask for help because her father had been sexually abusing her for years. With her came her best friend, Luisa, who knew all about the abuse. As Jennifer told her story she frequently cried so much she couldn't go on talking. Each time Luisa picked up the story, explaining what had happened and encouraging Jennifer to go on. With the help of her friend Jennifer was able to do something she might not have been able to do alone.[1]

Groups of children acting collectively are a powerful and important prevention technique. It is testimony to the logic and wisdom of bonding.

Colao and Hosansky, in *Your Children Should Know,* have outlined their suggestions for the "Child's Bill of Personal Safety Rights." It is a foundation of any prevention education program no matter what the emphasis or variation might be.

1. The right to trust one's instincts and feelings.
2. The right to privacy.
3. The right to say no to unwanted touch or affection.
4. The right to question adult authority and say no to adult demands and requests.
5. The right to lie and not answer questions.
6. The right to refuse gifts.
7. The right to be rude or unhelpful.
8. The right to run, scream and make a scene.
9. The right to bite, hit or kick.
10. The right to ask for help.

It is important to remember that these guidelines are specifically for children's personal safety if they find themselves in potentially dangerous or threatening situations. This information needs to be presented in age-appropriate ways with careful illustrations and discussion. It does not frighten children and is comprehensive. Best of all, it has been consistently successful. To the degree that we, as caring adults, provide children with techniques and skills for interacting with their world is the degree to which we have a far greater chance of preventing their victimization.

Self-Defense Techniques

Teaching children that they have a right to say no to an adult or older child is the primary mission of most programs. For too many educators the word no has assumed a magical quality. The word itself is imagined to be enough to surround a child with a protective mantle. While no may be sufficient to ward off assaults by offenders who are timid, cowards, or not expecting any resistance, surely one word will not deter a molester who is determined and persistent. Other programs incorporate a self-defense yell thereby providing children with another defensive resource that may serve, in its unexpectedness, to scare off an attacker, bring other potential allies to the scene, and create in the child a sense of being powerful and effective.[2]

Even preschool children can recognize warning signs, can be taught to break secrets and can give a self-defense yell. It is easy and fun to teach children a positive self-defense skill. Children handle it quite responsibly and it has been shown to be an effective and simple technique in the prevention repertoire. Recently a three-year-old was kidnapped from her parents' car while sitting with her brother in a parking lot outside a crowded store where her parents and hundreds of other adults were shopping. Imagine the different outcome if she and her brother had simply given a series of loud and strong yells.

Trina was playing in her yard when a man came over and attempted to drag her to his car.

She immediately gave her self-defense yell and five other neighborhood children ran toward her and joined in the yell. The man, unable to believe what was happening, let go of Trina, ran to his car, and drove off.[3]

Colao and Hosansky define self-defense as "anything that enables someone to safely escape a dangerous situation." That can range from complying with the assailant until an opportunity for escape presents itself to saying no; from screaming and yelling to physically resisting. It is the "knowledge that one's physical and emotional well-being is in one's own control and is not controlled by others." This leaves room for the child to make a judgment in her/his own interest.

Some prevention educators are concerned about the reticence teenagers (even those well-trained and well-versed in martial arts) have shown in using defense skills against those they know who are behaving in threatening ways. These educators feel programs for teens should emphasize assertiveness skills, values clarification and early recognition of the subtle coercion and/or peer pressure that commonly precedes acquaintance and date rape. Self-defense training that incorporates information about physical strategies, psychological techniques and provides skills in the early recognition of potentially abusive situations uses a broader definition of self-defense than merely a series of punches, kicks or jabs.

The more information and resources we offer children the more possibility for a successful outcome of a menacing situation. For example, a six-year-old was visiting her friend. Her friend's father asked her to accompany him to the woodshed and help him carry wood. Once inside the woodshed he locked the door and started to molest the little girl. She kicked him in the shins, climbed out the window and ran home.[3] Such an experience would increase any child's sense of power and effectiveness in her/his own defense and develop a strong sense of body image and self-confidence. This is an important part of sexual assault prevention education.

Multi-Cultural and Multi-Racial Programs

What about the children whose lives are not reflected in the skits, the images, the plays or the books? What of the Black child whose older brother was beaten by a policeman? Or the Chinese child who lives with her grandmother, an undocumented worker whose presence at home must be kept from white authorities? Or the Latina whose family shows affection in more expressive ways than traditional white families? Or the Japanese child whose family does not physically express their deeply felt love? Prevention education programs must find ways to incorporate all the children who need information in ways that are culturally sensitive and reflect a full spectrum of life experiences.

Not all children live in a world in which authority figures—policemen, principals, counselors, teachers—are either concerned or respectful of them or their lives. This sad fact makes it even more necessary for prevention education programs to provide a full complement of sizes and shapes, varieties and colors, histories and language skills in their approach. The more children see their lives mirrored in powerful leadership roles, the more self-esteem

and positive self-worth can develop.

Some programs have made the important beginning of translating prevention information from the "original" (English) into other languages. Yet the multi-cultural realities of family living represented by those languages are often overlooked. A white prevention educator speaking fluent Spanish is certainly a welcome addition to a classroom of Hispanic children, but she/he is not Hispanic and the children will not see her/him as one of them. A program's staff, community outreach and educational materials must reflect the community's multi-cultural, multi-racial balance. Otherwise it is as vulnerable to charges of racism and classism as is the society as a whole. This is a glaring omission in nearly all of the programs I reviewed, with the exceptions of SAFE and CAPP, both of whom do classroom presentations. (See Part II, *Prevention Programs at Work,* for descriptions.) Sally Cooper's words are still critical: "Every child in every community deserves to have prevention information that is culturally sensitive and in their primary language."[4]

Sexual Abuse Prevention and Family Life Education

What are the sex-negative messages we give when a six-year-old is told that certain parts of her body are "private" and shouldn't be touched? What does it mean to teach about sexually abusive touching without teaching sexual information? We are walking a tightrope, talking about sex without really talking about sex. In most programs words for genitalia are not used or defined, nor are explanations of sexual behavior given. While information about personal rights, personal safety, self-care and self-protection is provided, there is no teaching about sex. It is an omission with far reaching consequences.

One reason for this silence about sexual matters is that, as a society, we have felt it is the parents' job to teach children about sex. Human sexuality is laden with family values, religious beliefs and lifestyle choices. For those reasons, family life education is usually entrusted to the adults in the child's life who can transmit those values and beliefs most directly.

In an effort to study what parents tell children about sexual abuse and sexuality, 521 parents in the Boston area were surveyed (Finkelhor, 1984, p. 134). Several patterns became clear. Parents were uncomfortable with telling their children about sexual abuse and, to a great extent, they were uncomfortable precisely because it meant talking about sexual matters. Sexuality and sexual abuse are potentially anxiety-producing subjects that can remind parents of their own childhood feelings and bring back memories of their personal unease with the subject. It creates fears of "doing it wrong," of a lack of information, as well as a natural desire to protect their children from needing to know about dangers in the world and their own developing sexual selves. But at the same time that parents are confused and anxious about discussing sexual matters with children, schools have been reluctant, for obvious reasons, to provide this education. One consequence of these fears is that for many children the only family life education they receive will be limited to prevention education about sexual molestation. Clearly we need to do a more thorough job of teaching than that.

While the field of prevention education is still in its infancy, family life educators have been at work for decades developing a vast range of resources that include books, pamphlets, films, audiovisual aids and curricula. Resources are geared to specific populations with unique concerns (including the hearing impaired, blind, spinal cord injured, people with mental retardation) as well as a full complement of multi-racial, multi-cultural materials for children from preschool through adult. While many of these resources are excellent, they are not yet incorporated into prevention or personal safety education for political as well as pragmatic reasons.

Whose Job Is It?

An understanding of sexual information can help children recognize impermissible sexual touching. This can be particularly important since trickery and misrepresentation are often used to get a child to accede to unwanted sexual behavior. Both prevention and family life educators are clear that only professionals who have themselves been trained to teach sexual information and abuse prevention should teach them. However, issues of sexuality and sexual abuse need to be discussed by *all* the caring adults in a child's life because each is important in the child's experience.

Some prevention educators feel the current media attention on sexual abuse has marked a shift in outreach away from parent involvement and toward more focus on professional presentations in classrooms. Presumably, the argument goes, if parents are molesting children in such large numbers they are not a useful resource for prevention and education. This presumption is both shortsighted and unnecessary.

Programs that have included parent education in their outreach have reported much enthusiasm and success for their efforts. And, as author Jennifer Fay reports, even children who are being molested by a male family member find their mothers consistently available and responsive when sensitive outreach is made to include them. In addition, parents are the biggest supporters of prevention programs in schools. Parents are the major socializers of their children, the primary transmitters of family and religious values and attitudes. They can provide the daily, consistent teaching children need if abuse prevention education is to be effective. Parents are the most valuable resource educators have. Together parents and educators can be allies in a shared effort to keep children informed and safe.

Policy Questions: Where Do We Go From Here?

Since prevention is a young field with new programs springing up across the country, we are still operating on our best "hunches" about what works and what doesn't. Educators must move beyond hunches to more rigorous assessment and program development. The following questions deserve further research and investigation.

1. How can we better assess and evaluate primary prevention education? How can we further understand what is effective and empowering for children?
2. What are positive ways to teach sexuality education and healthy sexuality to children and adolescents that incorporate male and female sex roles?
3. What is the relationship between attitudes learned through prevention education and altered behavior in children?
4. What is the role of the educator in intervening to avoid generational replication of abusive behavior?
5. How can we target particularly vulnerable segments of the population for special outreach and prevention education?
6. How can we identify and intervene with potential molesters? What signs of aggressive behavior require more proactive intervention?
7. What is the role of law enforcement in prevention education?
8. What legal reforms need to be made, both civil and criminal, to incorporate child advocacy into the disposition of child sexual abuse cases?
9. What is the role and responsibility of the media with its increasing sexualization of children in advertising, films and pornography?
10. What are the successful ways to mount public education campaigns about the dimensions of child sexual abuse and the need for prevention?

Building Bridges

For prevention education to be thorough, for children to be truly safe, the communities in which they live must be safe. Churches, synagogues, law enforcement, community and social service organizations need education and encouragement about the importance of their role in providing children with a safe environment. Businesses need information about the crucial importance of well-supervised day care for their employees since there have been many attacks made against this invaluable resource for working parents. In his article, "Protecting Child Care," author and prevention educator Rich Snowdon reminds us that child care workers have historically been child advocates and parent supporters. They work with children because they care about and respect them, and they are as anxious as the rest of the community to rid centers of abusive people.

The prevalence of sexual violence in our culture needs to be challenged, thereby raising the level of consciousness about the issues prevention education encompasses. The media, which has emphasized sensational stories about abuse, must change its focus to publicizing the successes that children educated in self-defense and prevention techniques have enjoyed.

There are some who would use the issue of sexual abuse as a way to further control children's lives—to threaten, intimidate and undermine their innate sense of self-reliance. Any effort to insist on old-fashioned ideas of "good kids" is a dangerous one. We have learned beyond any question that "good kids" are endangered kids. Respecting authority without question, never challenging those in power, remaining silent and isolated in life situations keep children vulnerable and victimized. *Unquestioning obedience is not good or safe for children.*

Providing children and adolescents information about their bodies and their right to personal safety is entering unfamiliar territory— that of empowering our children while making

ourselves available to them as allies. It is providing them with the intellectual, emotional, physical and strategic resources that will allow them to realistically assess a variety of potentially dangerous situations and decide how to handle them. It is having the confidence that children can and will use good judgment in dealing with each other and with adults and knowing that children who are treated with respect do, in turn, treat those around them with respect. It is understanding that keeping children safe is the responsibility of all adults in that child's world. And that in order to fulfill that responsibility we must educate ourselves so that we can join in partnership with them to create an environment that is safe, supportive, strengthening and joyful.

Acknowledgements: I particularly want to thank Jennifer Fay, Tamar Hosansky and Richard Snowdon for their willingness to share their experience and concerns. A special thanks to Barbara Rosenblum whose rigorous thinking informs my own.

Notes

1. Reported in the Child Assault Prevention Training Center of Northern California newsletter, 1983.
2. Child Assault Prevention Program begun in Columbus, Ohio in 1979. First multi-cultural, multiracial self-defense program for children nationally. SAFE (Safety and Fitness Exchange), Tamar Hosansky, President. For descriptions of both these programs, see Part II, *Prevention Programs at Work.*
3. Reported in Child Assault Prevention Training

Center of Northern California newsletter, occurred in Columbus, Ohio, 1980.

4. Sally Cooper. Child Assault Prevention Program National Training Center, Columbus, Ohio.

References

Cohn, Ann, David Finkelhor and Christine Holmes. "Preventing Adults from Becoming Child Sexual Molesters." Working Paper #25. Chicago: National Committee for the Prevention of Child Abuse, 1985.

Finkelhor, David. *Child Sexual Abuse: New Theory and Research*. New York: Free Press, 1984.

Hosansky, Tamar and Flora Colao. *Your Children Should Know*. New York: Bobbs-Merrill, Co., 1983.

Kempe, Henry and Ray Helfer. *The Battered Child*. Chicago: University of Chicago Press, 1968.

Russell, D. E. H. "The Incidence and Prevalence of Intrafamilial and Extrafamilial Sexual Abuse of Children." *Child Abuse and Neglect* 7 (1983): 122-146.

Chapter 3

A History of the Touch Continuum

AN INTERVIEW WITH CORDELIA ANDERSON

There are myriad materials available today to help teach sexual abuse prevention skills to children. Books, pamphlets, puppets, plays, curricula, films and programs for children from preschool to high school abound.

Many of these materials use some form of the Touch Continuum© to explain sexual abuse to children. Cordelia Anderson (formerly Kent) coordinated the development of the continuum in 1977—years before the data reflected and the public acknowledged that sexual abuse of children was a problem. Her work and that of other professionals in the field with adult victims and offenders had convinced her that children were being abused (and generally weren't reporting the abuse) by people who were known to them. The only information available at that time focused on abuse by strangers. She determined to create a program "beyond Officer Friendly" to make children less vulnerable to abuse by acquaintances—a harder task than warning children not to take candy from strangers.

A grant to the Sexual Assault Services division of the Hennepin County Attorney's Office enabled Ms. Anderson to begin the Child Sexual

Cordelia Anderson

Abuse Prevention Project (CSAPP). The Illusion Theater and the Minneapolis Public Schools collaborated with Ms. Anderson and Sexual

15

Assault Services to pilot a program in the schools to prevent sexual abuse of children.

The result was the Touch *play and an elementary curriculum that focused on the Touch Continuum. The continuum was designed as an educational tool to teach young children the differences between good, confusing and bad touch. Listening to what children already knew, Ms. Anderson developed the scale with lack of touch at either end of a spectrum that includes good, bad and confusing touch. Exploring the touch continuum with children, especially the large area of confusing touch, opens the way to present information about intuition, rights and assertiveness—the other essential skills to make them less vulnerable to abuse.*

Ms. Anderson is currently Director of The Illusion Theater's Sexual Abuse Prevention Program in Minneapolis, where she spoke with our interviewer about the past, present and future of child sexual abuse prevention education.

Some see you as a pioneer in the area of child sexual abuse prevention education. How did you first become involved in the field?

Anderson: Well, I had actually worked in 1975 and 1976 more in the field of sexuality, and I'd worked on a statewide sex offender research treatment program. We were researching backgrounds—a lot of these were convicted offenders, so obviously, especially in the early 1970s, that's a pretty biased sample—and many of their prison sheets showed that they were victims of abuse as children. That is now, of

course, common knowledge. It wasn't then. I was also doing sexuality education therapy with adult women convicted of crimes, and it was very clear that many of their issues were related to the fact that many of them were abused as children. Sexual Assault Services in the Hennepin County Attorney's Office had a program for adult rape victims and was very interested in expanding advocacy and educational programming for children. What came out of this was a pilot program out of the Hennepin County Attorney's Office, where I was hired in 1977 to work with child victims in court and to coordinate and develop a prevention program for children.

With the prosecutor's office?

Anderson: Right, through the prosecutor's office. Now, this was somewhat problematic for us since people did not consider prevention necessary because they didn't understand there was a problem. So we were a little ahead of our time. The only other prevention programs that we knew of anywhere in the country were geared toward adolescents. There were programs for younger children, but they were the "dangerous stranger" and scare tactic types—the ones we all know about.

How did you plan to reach the children?

Anderson: We tried to reach the schools—which was not easy because they did not think there was a problem—and convince them that child sexual abuse was something that happened, even though it did not show up in the data, even though people didn't talk about it. We tried to say that we felt the need to teach children about sexual abuse beyond strangers.

Actually, the way we got into the first school

was nothing magical now that I look back on it because two women I worked with had children who went to that school. So the principal knew and trusted them and allowed us to pilot the program.

There were no model programs at that time?

Anderson: That's right. So, since I couldn't go anywhere and talk to anyone and say what do you tell kids, I did this very much experimentally. I just went out and started talking to children about what they knew about sexual abuse, what they thought it meant. In listening to their answers—this is kindergarten through sixth grade—over and over I kept hearing the fact that they certainly did know a lot about it but not necessarily accurately. Most of the concepts they had in their minds were very scary. They thought about strangers jumping out of bushes, they thought about people grabbing them up and chopping them into little pieces when they were kidnapped. I find it rather ironic that we were afraid of scaring children, when the information they already had was scary. They were very much in the stranger mode and a lot of them had experiences they had talked to no one about. It also became clear that they had no idea they could question adults or say no to touch that they didn't like.

Would you say you were the first to deviate from the traditional dangerous stranger approach?

Anderson: As far as I know, we were. With young children, yes.

And this was in 1977?

Anderson: 1977 was when we started in the schools. 1976 was when we were planning. Now there were other programs at that time working with adolescents, but they weren't working with younger children.

And they were using the touch approach?
Anderson: No.

Was there any particular moment in your own mind when it clicked that touch was the way to go?

Anderson: You know, I don't remember a specific moment or incident. It was early on that the director of Sexual Assault Services and I talked generally about differences in touch. It didn't take much talking to children to know that the right way to approach the subject was to talk about touch because they understood touch. I remember so often I heard the children talking about "yucky" and "icky" touch and realized that we really needed to balance that. They talked about "icky" touch or bad touch or not liking certain touch. And again, that's how the balance concept came up. I didn't want to just talk about don't and watch-out-fors. We didn't need to scare them away from touch because they were already too afraid of touch. We needed to make sure we were talking about what was good and what was nurturing as well. Many programs have used these concepts and oversimplified it to just bad touch. That oversimplification is dangerous because what we know is that much touch indeed is confusing. It's not clearly good or bad. It just mixes you up for some reason. You don't like it and you're not sure why. If you don't like the touch, at least that's clear. But when you like some of the touch or attention or the touch changes—it started out being good, which is how much of it does—and all of a sudden you get an uncomfortable, yucky feeling like you want to move or you want it to stop. Then what do you do?

What are the dangers of oversimplifying the continuum, say in a curriculum?

Anderson: Good and bad is only part of the message. Using only the two concepts misses some real critical intricacies—like the fact that someone's touch might feel good and that would be okay, but a lot of touch is confusing and you can't say exactly why. Critics say, well but you can't name what is confusing and therefore your continuum doesn't work. That is precisely the point. We can't say this is good, this is bad and this is confusing or it wouldn't be confusing. The reason it is confusing is *because* it's not clear and any touch can change from something that was good to something that is confusing or not okay. I think that is the part people may not grasp because it has been oversimplified. It's very frustrating.

Our program is sometimes interpreted as only being about touch and yet we've always talked about other key concepts such as children's rights, how to communicate about touch, whether or not the touch is sexual abuse, your right not to be touched and your obligation to not force or trick someone into touch. We've also always talked about who to tell, assertiveness and the range of types of sexual abuse and exploitation. These other concepts have been included from the beginning.

It all goes together.

Anderson: That's right. And needs to because you've got to know how to talk about it and what "it" means. What do you do when you don't like touch, what do you do when you're mixed up, who do you talk to, what if the first person you tell doesn't believe you or doesn't listen to you, then what do you do? We might have definite ideas about reporting—talk to protective services and/or the police department. Yet that's probably not who children are going to talk to first. If you ask children who "should" you talk to, most know they're supposed to say the police or mom or dad and they all say that. That doesn't necesssarily mean that's who they are going to go to. In fact, many children are going to talk to a friend. And that friend probably isn't going to know what in the world to do. So always in the program we've talked about how would you help a friend, what would you do if this happened to someone, how would you react. And all of these things are very important.

As important as the touch?
Anderson: Yes.

How did your program expand to a national level?

Anderson: We'd been developing the program for a couple of years in Minneapolis when Seattle became very interested in what we were doing. So, we did trainings in Tacoma, Seattle, various areas around Washington. This was in 1979. Then we started doing trainings at national conferences and it just took off like wildfire. I should add that the theater became much more involved at this point. Also, quite a few people were starting to be pretty visible working with children therapeutically, and incest was being talked about a lot more. And it didn't take much time in schools before we were hearing about babysitters and teachers—you know, the stuff that just didn't show up anywhere in the data.

The law and the theater is an intriguing combination. How did that merger come about?

Anderson: We hadn't originally intended to work with theater, but that was just because we had never thought about it. We were very much aware that a lot of children were already victims and we wanted to be sensitive to that. Although I was vehement and still am vehement that prevention programs should not be used as victim hunts to identify current victims. But initially a lot of our focus wasn't just prevention—we had no idea of the demand for that—but to learn more about how to talk to children and what children's perceptions were so that we could better prepare them when they came through the court system. And the court system just was not, and still isn't, really set up for children. I was in a sexual assault unit and our role was helping attorneys prepare the children. And it was so clear that we, as adults, didn't know how to talk to children. Parents wanted to know how to explain court to their children, how to talk to their children about what had happened. So the requests started coming and that's what really led us to knowing that we needed to do something.

Because nobody knew what to tell them?

Anderson: That's right. And we pulled together an advisory group, what I call our Board of Credentials, that included psychiatrists and child development experts and they told us their ideas of what children needed to know. Again, nobody knew much about child sexual abuse then and when push came to shove we listened to what the children said.

You got your information from the children?

Anderson: Yes. And from our own experiences that we remembered while doing improvisations to develop *Touch*. I had my own biases about content but we knew we had to say things in a way that made sense to children. We could use great legal definitions or medical definitions but it wasn't going to make any sense if children couldn't understand.

How did Illusion Theater get involved?

Anderson: They made the contact. We had been piloting the program in the schools when they came into it. The theater was interested in doing something educational for children. They were going to do that either in the area of violence or nutrition. They worked with children but they wanted to do something that would be more meaningful, not just entertaining. And they heard about our prevention program in Sexual Assault Services. We decided to experiment together and have them be the "media" for our project. They knew nothing about sexual abuse. They all had to go through training sessions and feelings like, "this doesn't really happen," "it never happened to me," they had to go through their own memories and lo and behold, some of them did remember some of their own experiences. And even those who didn't have their own experiences—we all have had times when we've been forced or tricked into touch. In some cases forced or tricked into sexual contact. Although, we may not have called it sexual abuse. Our awareness was that sexual abuse was not something a friend or a loved one would do to us, and that anything a friend or loved one did to us was not abusive.

Even if it had happened, it wasn't identified as abuse?

Anderson: Yes. And I think this is true of a lot of people. We didn't even have a framework for defining abuse. That doesn't mean people liked it or you put it in their minds. It just means yes, this is really crummy but I never thought of the fact that my boyfriend or girlfriend or father or babysitter pressured me or forced me or threatened me with abuse. The false concept we have of what consent means is also part of this.

Can you explain that?

Anderson: This is somebody you're supposed to listen to and do what they say, an authority person or somebody you look up to in your life. It must be *your* problem, not theirs. Because you didn't somehow stop it. You got caught in the threat or the trap or the trick or the pressure. Then it's your fault. Instead of saying, hey, wait a minute—part of the force is the fact that this person kept pressuring and pressuring me and just because I eventually gave in doesn't mean I consented.

These are complex issues to teach children. Even adults have trouble grasping some of the subtleties.

Anderson: You're right. And that's important. Because we are talking to children, we have to use language they understand when talking about their rights—not to be tricked or to say no. We're also talking about obligations. It is *not* okay to force, trick or pressure somebody into touch or sexual contact. And that has been a message that is not clear. So much of our media and socialization makes it seem like we are really condoning violence and abusive use of sex.

So an early message is, you may want to touch Suzie or George, but it is not okay to *force* the person to touch you.

Something we didn't tell children in the past.

Anderson: Yet we certainly told them the opposite—that you have to touch and kiss and hug your uncle or your aunt or your grandmother or your grandfather or your mom or your father or my ten best friends at this party here in order to be cute and nice and good. The reason we have to work with parents is they have to realize the messages they give children when they make them touch people even if they are scared or uncomfortable.

A lot of adults are guilty of that one.

Anderson: Oh, we've all done it—I am so embarrassed when I think about the things I used to do to children. Just the whole line of come and kiss me or you'll hurt my feelings. We are manipulating them. And if you can't say no to Aunt Suzie, how do you say no to something more confusing and more threatening?

Prevention education has come a long way since you began.

Anderson: It has. Our main goal has been to be a catalyst—to use theater, to use our curricula, to use our concepts, to encourage other people to do something about prevention whether they use our exact program, whether they use theater or not. We believe that after a training session or after seeing a show, people should be able to walk away and use the concepts. That indeed is what has happened. The unfortunate part is that we don't always get credit. The other unfortunate part is that we haven't even been able to keep track of all that has happened. Prevention has grown so far, so fast, that now part of our challenge is just trying to keep on top of who is doing what. It's grown from nothing to new booklets, new brochures, new films, new pamphlets coming out all the time.

Sexual abuse prevention as we are talking about it is almost an essential part of many school curricula today. In the beginning, did you encounter resistance from parents and the community in discussing the subject of child sexual abuse?

Anderson: Interestingly enough it wasn't as much the parents or the churches.

Where was the resistance?

Anderson: Our resistance by and large was from school administrators who were afraid of how parents would respond. And indeed parents were desperate—and are still desperate—to know how to protect their children, how to talk about abuse. Yet they don't want to scare their kids so we get a lot of questions from adults. Their concern is how we are going to talk about abuse because in their wildest imaginations they can't understand how you could do that in a nonthreatening way. Are you going to scare my child away from touch? All those fears were there and we knew it. And we knew when we explained to parents our balanced approach, we could work through those concerns. They are valid concerns. As a parent, I would want to know how this topic was going to be approached. A lot of approaches I wouldn't want used.

The frightening ones?

Anderson: Or the inaccurate ones. One of the biggest areas of controversy has been and still is around explicitness. Many places do not want you to use explicit language. They want you to say private parts or underneath your swimsuit. I am very much opposed to that. I can understand people's concerns and we need to talk about them, but I want people to realize that when we don't say breast, penis, vulva, vagina, we are giving children a double message. What we are saying is, you can talk to me about sexual abuse, it's not your fault, there's nothing wrong with you. But your body is so bad that I can't even say what is underneath your swimming suit.

How have you dealt with that in your program?

Anderson: Well, we say this is safety education and that's completely true, and our program from the beginning was able to operate in places where sex education was banned. That was because even if you didn't want sex education you could be convinced that safety information was important. Although in the truest sense talking about communication, touch, rights and obligations is part of comprehensive sexuality education.

Even though sex education and sexual abuse prevention information often overlap?

Anderson: Oh, certainly. And I'm a sex educator. But I didn't think the program needed to be blocked because of the fears. I knew once we got in the door we could say what needed to be said. The thing I really learned is that as soon as *I* got comfortable saying penis in front of a group of first or sixth graders *they* were comfortable. The crux of the communication problem is that adults are uncomfortable. Adults say well, the kids giggle, the kids are embarrassed so we shouldn't talk about this. But the children are uncomfortable because no one ever said the words before and because the adults are uncomfortable. So we role model. The first time I say penis there's probably going to be laughing and all I do is say, "I noticed a lot of people laughed. How come?" The response is, "Well, we're not used to saying these words." Or, "Mommy told me not to say penis." I tell the class, "I know we aren't used to saying words like penis and we're not comfortable but I am going to be saying these words a lot more." And you know, the second or third time you say penis there is no more laughing.

And then they can say the words?
Anderson: Then they can say the words. One of the early lessons I learned is that children can handle the information if we adults can handle giving it to them. And I think it is ridiculous, I think it is dangerous for us ultimately if we talk about abuse and don't use the proper names for the body parts. The reason I think it is dangerous is that prevention means we've got to have a healthier understanding of what is appropriate sexuality. If we are so fearful of sexuality, of our bodies, that we can't say breast, penis, vulva, vagina, anus, we are perpetuating the fear at the same time we are going full force talking about what's abusive and what's unhealthy.

Some critics contend prevention education teaches children to be suspicious of everyone. What is your opinion about this?
Anderson: Well, first of all I prefer to think of it differently. My belief is that we have *rights*

with *everyone.* Whoever the person is, whether we love or trust them or we don't know them, we have rights to ask questions, to say no. That's what we need to learn.

That's a much more positive approach.
Anderson: The other basic premise of our program is balance. When we talk about exploitation, we talk about nurturance. When we talk about people who might hurt you, we say that most people aren't going to. We also, for that matter, say the person who hurts us, or touches us in ways we don't like, or makes us feel bad about ourselves, might be someone that we love very much. So we've got to have a balanced approach to every single aspect. And as you mentioned, some people are saying we're teaching people to be afraid of everyone. No, we are teaching people they have rights with everyone.

Do you think kids really believe it when we say abuse is not their fault?
Anderson: I think there are a couple of concepts that need a lot of repetition. This is my other soap box. People will so often say children are confused about this or that—after one session. We'll say, please don't ever expect that one or even two or three sessions are going to be ample. We don't expect to teach a child how to tie their shoes in one session. Why do we expect we are going to teach something as complex as sexual abuse prevention in one session? These concepts need repetition. They need clarification. Education needs to be ongoing because you teach by repeating and you add concepts as the child gets older. One of the hardest things for children to learn is that it's not their fault. It's one thing to nod and say

you believe it, it's another thing if it happens. The other difficult one is the concept of assertiveness. Children will learn right away they have a right to say no, which they probably hadn't thought of before because they have been told just the opposite. They've been told to mind. They'll get it, but they have to practice learning how to say no. And then use that skill.

They have to have support from adults.

Anderson: They have to have support and that takes time. That's an ongoing process. Even if you know how to say no in class, that's like a laboratory. Then you need field study and practice. That means you need to be able to say it and try it and hear your voice. I want to add a caution here. People tell children to say no and say no and say no and sometimes I see this exaggerated in a dangerous way that puts all the responsibility on children. The implication is, if you couldn't say no it's your fault. Or if you said no and it didn't work there's something wrong with you. There again we need balance. Like I'm going to be assertive 99 percent of the time, but I know for whatever reasons there are times when I'm not. I didn't say what I wanted to say. Children need to understand that it's not their fault if they didn't say no, if they couldn't say no, if they were too scared or too confused, it's not their fault. They just need to know they have the right to say no.

How would you present what you just explained to me to a class?

Anderson: You can say something like, how many of you think you would scream if someone tried to force you into touch? They all say they would scream. How many of you have been so scared or so surprised that you haven't

screamed? And they all say they have done that. Kids are always great at saying I'd kick them in the balls, even five-year-olds are saying I'd beat 'em up. And I say, I'll bet almost everybody in this room would want to do that but sometimes as much as you think you might want to, there might be times when you just can't or you just choose not to. And then what are you going to do? The analogy we use with children to translate a lot of these complexities is bullying. How many of you have been bullied or picked on? What does that feel like? They'll say, crummy, sad, no one likes you and there is nothing you can do. Everyone's been bullied, everyone's been called names. You might act tough and you might act like it doesn't bother you but what does it feel like when someone calls you a name because of your color? What does it feel like when someone calls you a name because you are tall or short or you don't have money?

They understand this?

Anderson: They get it. They get how crummy or helpless it feels. And we can use that to lead into understanding whether or not you've been a victim, forced or tricked into touch or sexual contact. You've all been bullied and when you're bullied those feelings are probably what you're going to feel and these are like the feelings people have when they are victims of sexual abuse. And how many of you have been bullied and felt like you should have done something about it? You feel like you should have stopped it but you didn't. You didn't know how. Or you tried and it didn't work because sometimes you might do things and it just doesn't stop it. Just because you couldn't stop the bully it doesn't mean the bullying was your fault. They can get that. And then, counterbalance that with how many of you have been the bully? A lot of them have. And why do people bully? And what does it feel like when you bully? Why do people bully? People bully to get power. Because someone picked on them. They bully to get attention. We can point out that these are some of the same reasons why people are offenders.

So from your work with children, you feel they're understanding the concepts?

Anderson: I think so. We are challenged—as educators are and always have been—to talk in a way that makes sense to children. How we teach children helps adults understand, and what we have to find in these tough issues are the simple basics underneath the complex issues. At Illusion Theater we are doing a new piece called *For Adults Only*, which looks at our confusion as adults about what is appropriate sexuality and what is abusive sex and violence. We can't sort out for our children why they can't watch certain things or MTV or cartoons or movies when we don't know why ourselves, or when we don't know how to talk about it.

What future directions do you see for child sexual abuse prevention education?

Anderson: I think our immediate problem and the way we need to go in prevention is separating sexuality from violence. This has been escalated so much in the last decade. Television, movies, the way we interact—we are more and more confused about what is healthy and what is abusive and we are not getting any counter information to balance

that. People aren't learning how to separate it. So the images and messages are confused from a very early age.

Can you give an example?

Anderson: Well, for instance there is a trend in advertising to picture children in adult roles. I don't want people to look at these images and say isn't that cute. I want them to be outraged that we have six-year-olds acting like adults with very sexualized language. One way, besides censorship, to combat pornography is to create erotica that is nonviolent, nurturing, respectful, pleasurable and mutual. Again, this is a question of balance. I think many of us are programmed to accept or be turned on by what I would call pornographic images. They are violent, they are objectifying, they are not realistic and we haven't seen anything to counter that. That's what we call sex. It also takes away from most humans because most of us don't look like that. It's racist. It's sexist. We need to get people to start understanding that we've been trained to be turned on to things that are violent and unrealistic. And certainly exploitative if not violent. The fear for a lot of people in taking away pornography is that they don't know the alternatives.

You're saying as a society our attitudes about sex have to change. That's a big order.

Anderson: It is. But I think it's approachable. It's going to take time, but this is where we are going. We need to look at prevention of violence. It's been great and necessary to talk to kids because they've needed to learn. But we've got to come back to the larger factors—society's roles and rules. Children are not responsible for stopping sexual abuse.

Although that was a place to start. You probably couldn't have talked about the larger factors in the beginning.

Anderson: We'd have been locked up. Another way we're going with prevention involves using the media in a positive way, reaching large numbers of people. We recently presented a model called Project Abuse in Minnesota, Michigan and New Mexico. This was two-weeks of intensive programming on TV. The programming included public service announcements around the clock, a documentary during prime viewing hours, and spots on news shows. *Touch* and *No Easy Answers* were aired during the day in classrooms. Teachers, protective services and churches received information that this was happening. The night before the childrens' programs were aired in the schools, a parents' program was shown to let them know what was going to be happening in their child's school and how to talk with their children about it. The schools received discussion guides. If teachers didn't feel comfortable or qualified doing the discussions, a pretaped show offered a teacher discussion. We had a 24-hour hotline staffed by crisis counselors throughout the entire show. In Minnesota, we had 6,000 attempts to get through to those lines. Fourteen hundred people received referrals.

All of this was supported by massive community organizing. This series won a national Emmy award for community service. I'm very excited about working with the media because media has a huge power that's primarily not used positively. I know it can be used positively when it is combined with community efforts. We reached almost 500,000 children in one day and up to that time we were very, very proud that we had reached over 500,000 people nationally directly through programs. And it's clear we can be reaching even more.

Issues in Child
Sexual Abuse Prevention

Chapter 4

Myths, Fairy Tales and Films

FLORENCE RUSH

When Florence Rush wrote The Best Kept Secret *in 1980, child sexual abuse was hardly acknowledged to be a problem beyond the occasional deviant act by a stranger. Rush was one of the first theorists on the subject to suggest that (1) child sexual abuse is a commonplace event and not an isolated incident; (2) a child victim of sexual abuse is not in any way to blame for the abuse; and (3) sexual abuse of children is not a new phenomenon but has been a part of our history from Biblical times to the present.*

As the chapters in this Guide *attest, the sexual abuse of children is no longer a secret. And Florence Rush's theories and documentation have constituted an important contribution to the prevention effort. The following excerpt from* The Best Kept Secret *is a reminder of the beginnings of prevention education.*

Since it is the function of a society to shape the motives and energies of its members, each social structure leaves as little to conscious behavior and thinking as possible but tries to direct individuals to comply with and even find gratification from the standards established by each society. And since our Western society wishes females to conform to sex roles and stereotypic symbols of femininity, Simone de Beauvoir (1968) comments on the unnoticed but nevertheless powerful effects of legends, songs and stories upon the impressionable female child:

The songs and legends with which she is lulled to sleep, are one long exhalation of man . . . children's books, mythology, stories, tales all reflect the myths born of pride and desires of men; thus it is that through the eyes of men the little girl discovers the world and therein her destiny.

Snow White, in order to merit her Prince Charming, had to cook, clean and care for seven dwarfs. Rapunzel suffered the pain of providing access to the tower by her long hair; the miller's daughter was challenged to spin straw into gold; and Cinderella, maid of all work, hardly idled in luxury before she was matched to her glass slipper and her prized prince. Some fairy tale heroines put up with loathsome dragons and animals before being granted their reward. Beauty catered to a beast, the sisters Snow

White and Rose Red took care of a huge bear and the King's daughter ate and slept with a repulsive frog.

Unlike Sleeping Beauty, who lay passively until activated by a kiss, or the obedient, hard-working Cinderella, some more spirited hero-ines rebelled; but each familiar tale tells us that rebellion is improper and must be punished, whereas obedience is rewarded. In the tales of *King Thrushbeard and the Swineherd,* for example, a haughty daughter who spurned all suitors was finally given in marriage by her exasperated father and taken in hand by a seem-ingly cruel and repellent husband. After the husband had labored, abused, insulted and humbled the proud daughter, he revealed him-self a rich, handsome, kindly king and, grateful and subdued, the daughter finally realized that both husband and father had acted in her own best interest (Olcott, 1968). "The Frog King" is a variant of this theme.

While playing outdoors, the story goes, the King's daughter became exceedingly distressed when her golden ball rolled to the bottom of the fountain. A frog offered to retrieve it if she would in turn agree to feed, sleep with him and become his companion. She agreed but never intended to keep her promise. "How silly the frog does talk! He lives in the water with other frogs and croaks and can be no companion to any human being." So as soon as she received her ball, she ran off. During dinner that night there was a loud knock at the castle door. "King's daughter, youngest! Open the door," the frog ordered. The King wanted to know the cause of the commotion and when the Princess told him of her venture with the "dis-gusting frog" he commanded, "That which you

have promised you must perform. Let him in" (Olcott, 1968). The Princess obeyed and the frog insisted she keep her word. He enjoyed eating from her plate but, repelled, she almost choked on each mouthful; and at bedtime, she carried him with two fingers at arm's length to her bed. Her father scolded, "He who helped you in trouble ought afterward not be despised " (Olcott, 1968). It can be argued that eating and sleeping with a frog is a high price to pay for a retrieved ball, promise or no promise, but the King's daughter, caught between her father and frog, nevertheless performed her hateful tasks. Just as it all seemed most unbearable she was happily surprised when the frog, who was really under a spell, changed into a handsome king with "kind eyes," and because she had heeded her father the Frog King became her dear companion and husband.

Several theories have evolved to explain this popular tale. Some students of folklore suggest that a frog wooing a maid exemplifies the an-cient belief in kinship between humans and animals; others, that the girl who resists the frog is filled with anxiety at the thought of separation from her mother; and those under Freudian influence see the frog as "a penis," with the resisting maiden overcoming her initial aversion to sex as she finally "transcends her anxiety and hatred changes to love." Bruno Bettelheim (1976), of the last school, has said:

> The fairy tale, by agreeing with the child that the frog [or whatever animal it might be] is disgusting, gains the child's confi-dence and thus can create in him [sic] the firm belief that ... in due time the disgust-ing frog will reveal himself as life's most charming companion. And this message is

delivered without ever directly mentioning anything sexual.

The assumption that the female initially resists sex and must be persuaded to relinquish her aversion is one man's conjecture. Little girls do not have a natural aversion to sex and do not need to be persuaded into sexual activity with their peers; they do understandably fear the coercion implicit in a relationship with a male adult (or a frog). And since coercion, no matter how seductively employed, can never magically transform a frog (or a man) into "life's most charming companion," it only reinforces rather than eliminates sexual anxiety.

The popular fairy tale, in fact, rarely advances the welfare of the female child. It instructs, rather, that each little girl suppress any healthy manifestation of individuality, strength and independence and urges her to blindly and humbly deliver herself to a man no matter how old, repulsive or unsuitable he may be.

Fairy Tales Are Made, Not Born

I do not see that the traditional tales from which most of our current fairy stories are derived represent collective unconscious or universal truths. Their implication and meanings stem from a particular geography, history, economy and place in time. They lack uniformity, consistency and logic, and any overall theory implying one credible interpretation can be extremely misleading. Norse mythology, for example, claimed that only ice existed before there was life, while in America the Ottawan Indians believed that first there was only earth, and the Navaho decided that originally all was fire (Stadford, 1972). Myths, the traditional tales of gods, kings and creation, not only vary from one society, but from one generation to the other, and in this process the sex of deities and other mythical characters changed over time. In the Assyrian-Babylonian accounts, Tiamat, the female creator of all life, was replaced by the God Marduck, who was later hailed as the sole progenitor. The Goddess Ishtar, embodiment of all creation, was ousted when the "theologians of ancient Israel came to see Yahweh as the creator of all fertility" (Harrelson, 1969).

And since so many of these tales were orally transmitted, details depended also upon the personality and inclinations of the storyteller. In the seventeenth century, Charles Perrault refined the peasant tale for the amusement of the French court. The classical renditions of "Bluebeard," "Beauty and the Beast," "Puss in Boots," "Hop O' My Thumb," "Little Red Riding Hood" and "Cinderella" came to us from his editorial pen. As Susan Brownmiller (1975) has noted, "Bluebeard," patterned after the fifteenth-century Giles de Tais sex murders of countless little boys, was converted into a more pleasing version:

> It is almost as if the truth of Bluebeard's atrocities was too frightening to men to survive in the popular imagination, but turned about so that Bluebeard's victims were acceptably female, the horror was sufficiently diminished (not of course to women). Charles Perrault who included the heterosexual version of Bluebeard in his tales of Mother Goose, deserved credit for the turnabout of the Bluebeard legend, which had its most recent incarnation in the form of a Richard Burton movie, widely

advertised with pictures of seven pretty young women, each in the throes of a different and violent death.

During the Christmas season of 1812, German booksellers presented their customers with *Kinder und Hausmarchen,* later known in English as *Grimm's Fairy Tales.* The brothers Wilhelm and Jacob Grimm, founders of the science of folklore, scoured the countryside for thirteen years to gather authentic peasant tales. Some modern folklorists, however, have been critical of their Germanic "chauvinism" and the undue liberties taken in transposing the stories from their oral to written form:

In their methods the luster of the brothers has dimmed. Through the successive editions of the Marchen, Wilhelm steadily veered from the concept of fidelity to the spoken text toward a synthetic tale adapted from the available variants and refined with his editorial hand. Consequently he abandoned the Volksmarchen or true folktale collected exactly from the lips of the storyteller for the Buchsmarchen or literary version shaped by the editor (Ranke, 1968).

Subsequently others who transposed the *Buchsmarchen* imposed further changes. One editor who could not bear to have Gretel (of Hansel and Gretel) push the wicked witch into the fire disposed of her less aggressively by having her simply disappear. And by the time Cinderella, Snow White and Sleeping Beauty reached the Disney studios their docility and passivity were reduced to a state of semiconsciousness. And nothing could better illustrate manipulation than the current selection of "fairy tales" for popular consumption.

The Grimm brothers gathered about two hundred and ten tales, and of this number about twenty-five are popularized in American and European markets and these are limited to stories with passive heroines. Those who make the selection do have a much wider choice. For example, in "Rumpelstiltskin," a miller gives his daughter to a king with the pledge that she can spin straw. She accomplishes the task with the aid of a mysterious little man and promises him her first-born child in return for his help. The king marries the miller's daughter and a year later a child is born. When the little man comes to collect, the queen cries and pleads to be permitted to keep her child. The little man allows that if she can guess his name he will release her from her word. Fortunately, the queen obtains the answer from a bird and when she announces it as "Rumpelstiltskin" the little man, furious, dies of excessive rage. Excluded from common editions, however, is another version entitled "The Three Spinners." Here a widow turns her lazy daughter over to a queen with the assurance that she is a prolific spinner. The queen's son is offered in marriage if she can produce but the daughter is miserable because she cannot spin. Three elderly "spinsters" hear of her plight and come to her assistance; they do the job for her. The daughter insists that her three friends remain in the royal household after her marriage, and at dinner one night the prince asks one spinner why her thumb is so thick:

She answered, "It comes from picking" [picking the flax]. The second one had a thick nose. When he asked about it, she said that it came from the dust. The third one had thick lips. He asked her too and she said that it came from licking. Now he called out, "My wife has been spinning so much! She must never do it again! I do not want her to have a thick thumb, thick lips and a thick nose." So she was relieved (Ranke, 1968).

And so the story ended.

If we consider the influence of sex stereotyping, moralizing and values featured in children's literature, the disparity of these takes is of great significance. One gets a totally different impression regarding the relationships, character, capabilities and cleverness of women if rescue comes from other women, and certainly if a female by her own wit exposes an occupational hazard while simultaneously relieving herself of a damaging and hateful task.

What is more, many tales from around the world illustrate female heroism, positive mother-daughter relationships and evil fathers, but these are kept from public view. According to Kay Stone in her contribution to the *Journal of American Folklore*:

> Among the Ozarks tales collected by Vance Randolph we find women who destroy the threatening male villains and also a girl who does not need her father to convince her that frogs make interesting bedfellows ... In "The Little Girl and the Giant" a mother and daughter cooperate in escaping from a giant and destroying him, etc. (Stone, 1975).

From other parts of the world we have "Cantenella," where a father-king forces Cantenella to marry a vile husband. She flees from him and finally the wicked man is killed by her loyal friends. There is no suggestion here that blind obedience to her father is a virtue or that a hate-

ful spouse will be transformed into a Prince Charming (Lang, 1900). The moral is, rather, that a wicked man, husband or not, should be punished. And in contrast to the many wicked mother stories, in "Sunchild" a brave and clever twelve-year-old girl, without any male assistance, escapes an evil spirit and returns to her mother, where they both live in "happiness and contentment" ever after (Land, 1900). "Nix Nothing and Naught" is a sex reversal of both "Jack and the Beanstalk" and "Sleeping Beauty." A giant's daughter rescues a prince from her father and later, when the young man, under a spell, cannot be stirred out of a trance, she awakens him with a kiss (Corcoran, 1968). But most surprising is the little-known English tale of "The Marriage of Sir Gawaine."

One day as King Arthur was walking in the forest, he was overtaken by a wicked knight who would free him only if he could answer the riddle: "What is it every woman desires?" Permitted to search for the answer, the king consulted with his knights. Some suggested that what a woman most desires is "jewels" or a "rich husband," but Arthur somehow knew they were incorrect. He sadly returned to the wicked knight without an answer, but on the way he met the "ugliest lady he had ever seen" who offered the answer if he would grant her wish. He agreed. She whispered the answer in his ear and Arthur quickly whispered it into the ear of the wicked knight. Since it was correct, the wicked knight was compelled to release him.

Later, however, the king was horrified to learn that the ugly woman wished for a hand in marriage to one of his young knights. Arthur was prepared to die rather than subject one of his loyal men to such a union, but Sir Gawaine, handsomest and bravest of all, stepped forward and offered himself as the groom. After the wedding it was all Gawaine could do not to turn from his bride's ugliness but when he saw tears in her eyes he pitied her. He took her in his arms and kissed her, and suddenly, to his amazement, he held a beautiful young girl. But his kiss did not entirely free his wife from her ugliness for she was under a spell cast by the wicked knight. She explained that she would continue to be ugly for half a day. The young bride asked her husband to choose which half, night or day, he would prefer her to be beautiful. Gawaine thought for a moment and then answered, "Choose for yourself, my dear. I give you your own way."

> The fair young girl laughed with joy and threw her arms around the handsome knight. "You have broken the spell! Now I shall always be as you see me at this moment. By both day and night I shall be fair to look upon for you have answered the riddle which the wicked knight asks for all strangers, 'What is it a woman most desires?' It is *her own way*."

> And from that day forward Sir Gawaine and his lovely lady rejoiced in happiness forever after (Corcoran, 1968).

> This story must have escaped the attention of Sigmund Freud, I think, for he too asked, "What does a woman want?" Had he been exposed to tales such as these, rather than the *Frog King* variety, he might have avoided much confusion.

Media experts today have a much wider influence than those who displayed the works of the Grimm brothers. Current technology can evoke such vivid images that they are often substituted for reality.

The Walking, Talking Image

Over an expanse of seventy-odd years, from Mary Pickford and Shirley Temple to Tatum O'Neal, the little girl of the silver screen may have changed her costume, cut her curls, straightened her hair and learned to smoke, but her relationship with men remained unaltered. Whether she was a woman made into a child or a child made into a woman, or no matter how updated, she still sacrificed for, pursued or reformed a father figure. The little girl/grown man combination proved so successful that *Daddy Long Legs,* in which an orphaned child grows up and actually marries her rich, middle-aged benefactor, was adapted for film four times and successfully performed by Mary Pickford, Janet Gaynor, Shirley Temple (in a film renamed *Curly Top*) and Leslie Caron. Whether thirty-five-year-old Mary Pickford was reduced to infancy or five-year-old Shirley Temple was propelled beyond her years, the welfare of the celluloid child-woman, who never associated with peers or female adults, rested with men only.

Hollywood found the combination of childishness and sex extremely popular and lucrative. The independent screen female (as the assertive fairy tale heroine) was reduced in roles played by Richard Burton (*The Taming of the Shrew*), John Wayne (*The Quiet Man*) or Clark Gable (*It Happened One Night*) to proper infantile status. Any man worth his salt could bring the "little girl" out in any uppity woman. The popular Hollywood sex goddess, however, did not have to be cut down to size. Her neurotic anxiety, uncertainty, childishness and inability to cope as illustrated by Hollywood's image of Marilyn Monroe and Jayne Mansfield were satisfyingly synonymous with the helpless, needy woman-child. Monroe and Mansfield were appreciated not for their mature bosoms alone but because their childlike fragility in a well-developed body was exceedingly appealing. Innocence in a child or woman is sexy not because it evinces the vigor of integrity but because it betrays the weakness of dependency. For the man who enjoys a sense of power over female companions, whether childishness emanates normally, from a little girl or abnormally, from a grown woman is only a matter of personal taste.

And since yielding compliance is preferred, the strong screen woman is usually presented in her negative aspects. A woman with power is a shrike (June Allyson in *The Shrike*), a demented killer (Bette Davis in *Whatever Happened to Baby Jane?*), a rapacious cruel mother (Shelley Winters in *A Patch of Blue*), or an obsessively possessive wife (Rosalind Russell in *Craig's Wife*). The witch and stepmother of the fairy tale become the shrike, the shrew and the destructive "mom" of the silver screen. And since little girls, no matter how bossy, assertive and "fresh," are obviously powerless, these traits in them can be safely "cute" and nonthreatening.

Mary Pickford and Shirley Temple

In 1909 Mary Pickford, age sixteen, began her career under the tutelage of D. W. Griffith.[1] As America's Sweetheart her actual age increased as her screen age declined; at twenty-eight and thirty-two she played twelve-year-old Pollyanna and twelve-year-old Little Annie Rooney respectively. And since America did not want her to grow up, she cut her curls and retired at forty. We did not remain long, however, without a little girl; Shirley Temple, at age four, moved in to fill the vacuum. Although Pickford's career spanned twenty-five years and Temple's flashed and dimmed during six years between age four and ten, Temple and Pickford supplied the same dream. Both were seen in *Poor Little Rich Girl, Daddy Long Legs, Rebecca of Sunnybrook Farm, The Little Princess* and *Little Annie Rooney*. Whether the fantasy was filled by a woman who acted as a child, or a child who acted as a woman, mattered little—the result was equally satisfying (Windeler, 1974; Lee, 1970).

In 1932, four-year-old Shirley Temple strutted seductively in several shorts entitled "Baby Burleskes," and by 1934 she had completed small parts in five feature films with a notable role in *Stand Up and Cheer*. From 1934 to 1938 she outranked most adults and starred in nineteen record-breaking box-office hits. In addition to her talent for mimicry, her confidence and poise, her success was also due to an extremely reliable story format: a child whose mother died or otherwise disappeared was rescued by a father, grandfather or other male benefactor and in this process the child often saved or reformed her rescuer who was most often a grumpy old man, tycoon, gangster or even a simpleton. Rarely veering from this formula, Temple hugged, kissed, sang to, danced with, admonished and scolded (when necessary) an impressive number of male adults.[2]

In *Curly Top*, Shirley, at age seven, was too young to decently supply the love interest, so a big sister was created for the job. With romance properly allocated to Rochelle Hudson (the big sister) and John Boles (rich, middle-aged benefactor), Hudson, who served her purpose, was made as insignificant as Lolita's mother. With Hudson out of the way (until she married Boles at the end) the film freely focused upon exquisitely dressed little Shirley Temple and John Boles, who was the recipient of her hugs, kisses and fondling.

Motherless, eight-year-old Shirley in *Poor Little Rich Girl,* whose governess was struck dead by a car, lavished her sunshine on Henry Armetta, grumpy Claude Gillingwater and "puddinhead" Jack Haley, in addition to her daddy, Michael Whalen. Both Armetta and Haley had perfectly fine film wives, but Shirley's attention was riveted upon the male adults only. Carole Lombard and Gary Cooper were equally billed in *Now and Forever* but Lombard had scarcely a chance as Temple and Cooper mutually indulged in sorrow, joy and other such attention-getting pastimes (Basinger, 1970).

This persistent, little girl/grown man combination exclusive of women cannot be dismissed as harmless entertainment. With a regular weekly movie audience of over sixty million people, Hollywood set the styles in clothes, hairdos, morals and daydreams. The Shirley Temple model was so successful that parents invested in Temple hair permanents so that their little daughters could acquire those coveted corkscrew curls; they arranged for dancing, elocution and acting lessons so that they could learn to charm men and skip along the same road to fame and fortune. The image was further

perpetuated by other attractive young performers. Edith Fellows was paired with screen father Richard Dix who kidnapped her from the clutches of a demanding mother in *His Greatest Gamble* (1934); five-year-old Sybil Jason in *Little Big Shot* (1935) sported with ne'er-do-well Edward Everett Horton and Robert Armstrong; and Jane Withers joined her disreputable uncle in *Keep Smiling* (1938). Before Baby Sandy could walk, she was protected by singing taxi driver Bing Crosby in *East Side of Heaven* (1939); later in *Sandy Gets Her Man,* she shared Stu Erwin and Jack Carson; she was in the company of Billy Gilbert and Mischa Auer in *Sandy Is a Lady* (1940), and in *Bachelor Daddy* (1941) was adopted by Edward Everett Horton, Donald Woods and Raymond Walburn (Best, 1971).

Occasionally this precise formula varied, but no matter how it altered, Hollywood almost never focused upon children in a positive relationship to women.[3] When little girls were occasionally involved with women they were usually used as foils to a sacrificing mother as in *Imitation of Life* and *Stella Dallas*. Eight-year-old Patty McCormack was cast primarily with women in the film *The Bad Seed* (1956), but as a psychopathic child murderer, her relationship to her mother was, to say the least, terrifying. And though male children were prominent enough in films, the girl/man formula was not balanced by a boy/woman counterpart. Little boys, just as little girls, ignored women and related positively to men only. Long before Shirley Temple, young Jackie Coogan and Charlie Chaplin (silent films) and later Jackie Cooper and Wallace Beery were unbeatable teams. Subsequently, other popular child actors were paired with men[4] but unless some subtle homosexual message escapes me, mature and immature males were always friends and comrades. Furthermore, boys, given a wider berth, also performed in many tales of heroism, adventure[5] and animal stories.[6] But little girls never strayed from the straight and narrow. Shirley Temple performed in Rudyard Kipling's *Wee Willie Winkle,* a tale which focused on the rebellion-torn Khyber Pass and was written for a boy. And though she saved a regiment and prevented a war, eternally feminine, she was made to thaw out C. Aubrey Smith, Cesar Romero and Victor McLaglen. Graham Greene, who reviewed the film in England, found Shirley Temple so seductive that his review inspired a lawsuit for libel. His comments cannot be reprinted but he did say of Temple that "some of her popularity seems to rest on coquetry quite as mature as [Claudette] Colbert's and on an oddly precocious body as voluptuous in grey flannel trousers as Dietrich's" (Sayre, 1972).

Though Temple's early precociousness cannot be denied, I think her "coquetry" could be better understood in terms of her ability to imitate and take direction (before capable of mature discretion) rather than as an innate sexual characteristic. Shirley Temple's body was clearly that of a sturdy, healthy, chubby little girl. If her behavior was mature, her body was not. Looking younger rather than older, the description "voluptuous" is oddly inappropriate; at an age before she could establish an independent perspective she clearly mimicked the current styles in sex appeal.

But Shirley's strong personality, if not her imitative capacity, persisted beyond childhood and, unable to "act" or be other than herself,

she lost her appeal. The assertiveness and independence so attractive in the child was unattractive in the woman. Shirley Temple, however, was not alone. Irrepressible Deanna Durbin and cantankerous Jane Withers, also child stars, were similarly afflicted and met with the same fate, whereas the unchanged quivering uncertainty, timidity and high-strung sensitivity of child-stars Judy Garland and Elizabeth Taylor carried them to adult screen success.

In 1973 *Paper Moon,* advertised as a far cry from the sugared sentimental Temple productions, starred Tatum O'Neal and essentially followed the same formula as the Shirley Temple movies. It is the story of an itinerant con man, Long Boy, who is saddled with an illegitimate orphan, Addie Pray (her prostitute mother is dead). Making their way through the Depression-ridden flatlands of Kansas, they steal from widows and small shopkeepers, with wised-up little Addie Pray used to soften prospective victims. Addie, smarter and more practical than Long Boy, takes care of him, loves the scoundrel and even ruthlessly rids herself of an adult rival. After a series of shabby thefts and close brushes with the law, she has the opportunity to live in a comfortable stable household with an aunt (whom we never see), and though she yearns for a "home and piano," she chooses instead a transient, police-dogging twilight existence in order to be with Long Boy.[7] Here again the mother and all other females are eliminated. The message, loud and clear, is that for a girl a man, any man, is better than any woman. In *Bad News Bears* preteen Tatum O'Neal (with mother mentioned but never seen) is at first tough and feisty. She stands up to and resists Walter Matthau's attempts to use her as a pitcher on a Little League team. Eventually, however, she not only acquiesces but dissolves into complete compliancy toward this decidedly unattractive, unreliable alcoholic screen character as portrayed by Matthau. Just as the King's Daughter, who is at first assertive and strong, she yields to the repulsive frog.

Unfortunately these images and messages affect us beyond story and screen fantasy. Their pervasive projections have such powerful influence that persons of the stature of Helene Dautsch and Bruno Bettelheim confuse contrivance with reality. The painfully realistic poet Anne Sexton (1971) was singularly impressed by the influence of the fairy tale and in her collection of poems, *Transformations*, reminds us that the Princess who submits to a frog may soon learn that he never becomes a prince and is not so charming after all:

> *It's not the prince at all,*
> *but my father*
> *drunkenly bent over my bed*
> *circling the abyss like a shark,*
> *my father thick upon me*
> *like some jellyfish*

When the Princess finally awakens, what awaits her may be more terrifying than any nightmare.

Notes

1. Griffith collected other teenagers such as Lillian and Dorothy Gish, Blanche Sweet and Mae Marsh, but Mary Pickford climbed the highest cinematic peak as the eternal little girl.

2. Among others were Adolph Menjou (*Little Miss Marker,* 1934), James Dunn (*Baby Take a Bow* and *Bright Eyes,* 1934), Gary Cooper (*Now and Forever,* 1934), Lionel Barrymore (*The Little Colonel*), John Boles (*The Littlest Rebel* and *Curly Top*), Guy Kibbee (*Captain January*), Victor McLaglen, C. Aubrey Smith and Cesar Romero (*Wee Willie Winkle*), Jean Hersholt (*Heidi*), George Murphy (*Little Miss Broadway*), Ian Hunter, Arthur Treacher and Cesar Romero (*The Little Princess*), Randolph Scott (*Susannah of the Mounties*) and Michael Whalen, Henry Armetta and Jack Haley (*Poor Little Rich Girl*).

3. There are, of course, always exceptions, such as *I Remember Mama*.

4. Bob Watson with Lionel Barrymore in *On Borrowed Time* (1939) and with Wallace Beery in *Wyoming* (1940); Dean Stockwell with Dana Andrews in *Deep Waters* (1948) and Wallace Beery in *The Mighty McGurk* (1947); Brandon de Wilde and Alan Ladd in Shane (1953); Kevin Corcoran and Ernest Borgnine in *Rabbit Trap* (1959); Tommy Rettig and Richard Widmark in *Panic in the Streets* (1950); Peter Miles with Robert Cummings and Brian Donlevy in *Heaven Only Knows* (1947); Tim Hovey and Jeff Chandler in *Toy Tiger* (1956) and others.

5. Adventure films such as *Captains Courageous, Treasure Island, Kidnapped, Tom Sawyer, Huckleberry Finn, The Prince and the Pauper, Kim,* etc.

6. Animal stories such as *Old Yeller, The Shaggy Dog, Sign of the Wolf, Dog of Flanders, The Sad Horse, Misty, My Friend Flicka, Lassie Come Home, Goodbye My Lady, Buena Vista, Once Upon a Time, The Red Pony,* etc.

7. Though many of the films mentioned in this chapter are adapted from novels and stories, all references are to the screen versions.

References

Basinger, Jeanne. *Shirley Temple.* New York: Pyramid, 1970.

Beauvoir, Simone de. *The Second Sex.* New York: Bantam, 1968.

Best, Mark. *Those Endearing Young Charms*. New York: A. S. Barnes, 1971.

Bettelheim, Bruno. *The Uses of Enchantment*. New York: Pocket Books, 1972.

Brownmiller, Susan. *Against Our Will*. New York: Simon and Schuster, 1975.

Corcoran, Jean, adapter. *Folk Tales of England*. Indianapolis: Bobbs-Merrill, 1968.

Harrelson, Walter. *From Fertility Cult to Worship*. New York: Doubleday, 1969.

Lang, Andrew, ed. *The Grey Fairy Book*. New York: Longmans, Green, 1900.

Lee, Raymond. *Sweetheart*. New York: Praeger, 1974.

Olcott, Francis Jenkins, ed. *Grimms' Fairy Tales*. New York: Follett, 1968.

Ranke, Kurt, ed. *Folktales of Germany*. Chicago: University of Chicago Press, 1968.

Sayre, Nora. "Graham Greene on Film." *The New York Times Book Review,* December 17, 1972.

Sexton, Anne. *Transformations*. Boston: Houghton Mifflin, 1971.

Standford, Barbara. *Myths and Modern Man*. New York: Pocket Books, 1972.

Stone, Kay. "Things Walt Disney Never Told Us." *Journal of American Folklore* 88:374 (January-March, 1975).

Windeler, Robert. *Sweetheart*. New York: Praeger, 1974.

Excerpted with permission from *The Best Kept Secret* by Florence Rush. Englewood CLiffs, NJ: Prentice-Hall, Inc., 1980.

Chapter 5

The Child as Sex Object: Images of Children in the Media

JEAN KILBOURNE

'You're a Halston woman from the the very beginning," the advertisement proclaims. The model stares provocatively at the viewer, her long blonde hair waving around her face, her bare chest partially covered by two curved bottles that give the illusion of breasts and a cleavage.

The average American is used to blue-eyed blondes seductively touting a variety of products. In this case, however, the blonde is about five-years-old.

The ad ran in *The New York Times Magazine* in 1977. It was one of the first of what could be considered a trend in advertising to use young girls (and occasionally boys) in sexually provocative poses (and often featuring double entendre as well). Films such as *Pretty Baby, Beau Pere, Little Darlings, The Blue Lagoon, Manhattan* and *Taxi Driver* also capitalized on this theme.

Brooke Shields was fifteen when she gazed suggestively into the television camera and said, "What comes between me and my Calvins? Nothing." In another jeans ad, a young girl is mounted in a sexually suggestive pose on a boy's back. An editorial spread on perfumes in

Harper's Bazaar features a girl of about five, heavily made up and with her hair done in a variety of sophisticated styles. An ad for furs shows a girl of about eleven, with an ubiquitous sultry look, make-up, high heels, and above her

head the message, "Get what you've always wanted."

Women have long been encouraged by advertising and the popular culture to be like little girls. The classic Broverman study of 1970 demonstrated that it is the "male" traits that are considered "adult" in this society and that a woman cannot be an "adult" and a "woman" simultaneously (Broverman, 1970). According to Susan Sontag, "So far as women heed the stereotypes of 'feminine' behavior, they cannot behave as fully responsible, independent adults" (Sontag, 1972, p. 38).

The very traits considered most feminine in the culture are also considered most childlike, e.g. passivity, submission and dependence. (It is important to note, however, this is far more true for white women than for women of color.) Advertising slogans such as "because innocence is sexier than you think" and "sensual, but not too far from innocence" place women in a double bind. Somehow women are supposed to be both sexy and virginal, experienced and naive, seductive and chaste. There has been increasing pressure on women of all ages to be both sophisticated and accomplished, yet "feminine," in other words, fragile and childlike.

One alarming aspect of this message has been the increasing emphasis on extreme thinness for women, which in turn has led to what many consider an epidemic of eating disorders. It is interesting to note that anorexia, the most severe eating disorder, figuratively takes women back into childhood by halting menstruation and the development of the adult female body. Some experts consider anorexia to be the individual's unconscious effort to delay maturation (Bayer and Baker, 1984).

We have been surrounded for years by images of grown women acting like little girls, often playing with dolls and wearing bows in their hair. Erving Goffman demonstrated in *Gender Advertisements* that women are often shown as children in advertisements via their body language, in addition to the more obvious ways (Goffman, 1979). It is only recently, however, that the little girl herself has been presented as a grown woman, the sex object, the ideal.

Little girls are being sexually exploited today by everyone from Calvin Klein to the multibillion dollar pornography industry. Sexual abuse of children seems to be increasing dramatically (or perhaps is just more often reported). An estimated one out of four girls and one out of ten boys is sexually molested during their childhood. Is there a connection? Is there a link between the images of very thin women that surround us and the rise in eating disorders?

It would be foolish to suggest that advertising is *the cause* of eating disorders or the sexual abuse of children. The problems are complex and have many causes and contributing factors. There is no doubt that flagrant sexism and sex role stereotyping abound in all forms of the media. There is abundant information about this (Butler and Paisley, 1980; Courtney and Whipple, 1983). It is far more difficult to document the effects of these sex role presentations on the individuals and institutions exposed to them, because it is difficult to separate media effects from other aspects of the socialization process and almost impossible to find a control group.

The average American is exposed to over two thousand ads every day and will spend a year and a half of his or her life watching television commercials. Advertising is an over eighty-five billion dollar industry, and uses very sophisticated techniques for both research and production. The influence is pervasive, often subtle, and mostly unconscious (Fore, 1977; Gerbner, 1972; Leymore, 1975). The evidence indicates that the media perpetuate and reflect sex role stereotypes, but the precise effects are more difficult to determine. Research does show, however, that media users, especially children, are directly affected and influenced by media content (Comstock, 1978; Courtney and Whipple, 1983).

It is certainly safe to say that advertising is a powerful educational force in America. It is both a creator and perpetuator of the dominant attitudes, values and ideology of the culture, the social norms and myths by which most people govern their behavior (Ewen, 1976; Price, 1978; Williamson, 1978).

At the very least, advertising helps to create a climate in which certain attitudes and values flourish, such as the attitude that a woman's physical appearance is what is most important and valuable about her, that aging makes women unattractive and therefore less valuable, that women who are the victims of sexual assault "asked for it." This attitude applies now to females of all ages, as was evidenced by the recent remark of a Wisconsin judge that a five-year-old rape victim was "an unusually sexually permissive young lady" (*National Now Times*, 1982). This is a very dangerous attitude. The media do not cause this type of attitude but they do contribute to it by surrounding us with images of women and girls as passive, decorative, seductive and often as enjoying aggression

and violence.

Advertising is partially a reflection of the culture that has created it. Because of its power, however, it does a great deal more than simply reflect the cultural attitudes and values. It plays an important role in shaping those values. Far from being a passive mirror of society, it is an effective medium of influence and persuasion. Advertising performs much the same function in industrial society as myth performed in ancient and primitive societies, and with a similarly conservative effect (Leymore, 1975).

The myths of any culture are deep and powerful and difficult to change. The myth that women love and deserve to be beaten has made it difficult for the millions of women who are the victims of violence to get help and for the whole issue of domestic violence to be taken seriously. The myth that women ask to be raped and enjoy forcible sex has been perhaps the major factor in encouraging cultural tolerance, if not actual acceptance, of rape. The myth of Lolita, the seductive and manipulative child-woman, undoubtedly contributes to the abuse of children and the readiness of society to blame the victim. According to Florence Rush, this myth "is invented and perpetuated by people with highly commercial interests in promoting the fantasy of child sexuality" (Rush, 1981).

The deeply held belief that all women, regardless of age, are really temptresses in disguise, sexually insatiable and seductive, conveniently transfers all blame and responsibility onto women. This belief is so ingrained in our culture that it is only rarely questioned. We are all thoroughly conditioned to accept it. Recent research indicates that the media reinforce this belief and affect people's attitudes and behavior

(Malamuth and Donnerstein, 1984).

One possible explanation for the recent proliferation of images of sexy little girls in the media (and the enormous increase in child pornography) could be that it is a form of backlash against the women's movement of the past fifteen years. Certainly the traditional sex roles in this society are being questioned and examined as never before and this is challenging the very foundation of patriarchal society. Some changes are taking place, but there has also been some great resistance (Lindsey, 1980). The dominant culture, and the advertising

Mademoiselle Russian Raccoon. Or Beaver. Or Lynx. Or Fox. Or Sable. Or any fine fur. (Shown: Lu al Russian Raccoon.) Don't let another year go by without a Mademoiselle Fur. Furriers to bette

which reflects and perpetuates it, has responded to these changes in several ways, ranging from ignoring them to ridiculing them to capitalizing on them.

As women become more powerful and independent, they move away from the cultural ideal of femininity. To some extent, the popular culture reflects this change, generally by coopting and trivializing it, as in the Virginia Slims cigarette campaign, "You've come a long way, baby," which has the audacity to equate liberation with addiction, freedom with enslavement to tobacco. However, the media also reflect and exacerbate the fears and ambivalences that inevitably accompany such enormous changes. This need not be a conscious conspiracy. It is as likely the reflection of the mostly unconscious fears, desires, shared goals and values of those in power (and of what Carl Jung termed the "collective unconscious").

There is tremendous fear in the culture of any kind of power whatsoever in a woman, as if it would be inherently destructive (Brownmiller, 1975; Miller, 1976). No wonder there is such pressure today on women to be thin, to not take up too much space, literally or figuratively, to be like little girls. At the same time, there is pressure to succeed, to achieve, to "have it all"—in other words, women can be successful as long as they stay "feminine," i.e. powerless, enough not to be truly threatening.

As women are warned not to be too powerful, men are taught to fear powerlessness above all (i.e. being like a woman). Yet there are very few routes to power for most men in the society. The most common and available form has always been power over a woman. As this kind of power is threatened, it should come as no surprise that men are being encouraged to turn to little girls (and sometimes boys) in fantasy and often, tragically, in reality.

As is the case with rape, the issue is not sex but power. Men who have been conditioned to fear mature women (i.e. powerful women) have long sought to deprive women of power (legally, economically and politically, as well as through the sexual repression and violence that women have seemingly always been subjected to).

For all the cultural preoccupation with sex, there is in fact a real distaste for adult female sexuality. Women are considered desirable only if they are young, thin, carefully polished and groomed, made up, depilated, sprayed and scented—rendered quite unerotic, in fact. Men are conditioned to seek such partners and feel disappointed if they fail. The constant objectification of women in the media is part of this attempt to rob women of power and of their own real lives. As Nabokov has Humbert say of Lolita, "What I had madly possessed was not she, but my own creation, another fanciful Lolita—perhaps, more real than Lolita; overlapping, encasing her; floating between me and her, and having no will, no consciousness—indeed no life of her own" (Nabokov, 1955).

There are other problematic aspects of the sexual exploitation of children in the media, in addition to the symbolic and often literal danger it places them in and the impact of such exploitation on all of us, adults as well as children, men as well as women. Many theorists today have written about the loss of childhood in America (Elkind, 1981; Wynn, 1981). This is due partly to the widespread influence of the media. Children today are routinely exposed to

situations and information that in the past were solely the province of adults.

In addition, children are deliberately targeted by advertisers and are sold not only products, but also an assortment of values and attitudes. Advertising affects all of us throughout our lives. Children are particularly vulnerable, however, because they are generally impressionable and trusting and because they are new and inexperienced consumers. They are in the process of learning their values and roles and developing their self-concepts. Most children, especially adolescents, are sensitive to peer pressure and find it difficult to resist or even question the dominant cultural messages perpetuated and reinforced by the media. Mass communication has made possible a kind of national peer pressure that erodes private and individual values and standards. Margaret Mead once said that today our children are brought up by the mass media rather than by parents.

Advertisers are aware of their role and do not hesitate to take advantage of the insecurities and anxieties of young people in the guise of offering solutions. A cigarette provides a symbol of independence. A pair of designer jeans conveys status. The right perfume or beer resolves doubts about femininity or masculinity. Since so many anxieties revolve around sexuality and intimacy, and since advertising so often offers products as the answers and uses sex to sell, it is perhaps the concept of sex roles that is most deeply affected.

Children learn sex role stereotypes from a very early age. These stereotypes have existed for a long time and certainly have not been created or perpetuated solely by advertising. Sexism and sex role stereotyping exist in every aspect of our society and we receive these messages from birth. No messenger is more pervasive or persuasive, however, than advertising.

Young people are also affected by advertising in other more subtle ways—ways more indirect but perhaps more powerful than the stereotypes (which increasingly are being recognized and sometimes ridiculed). Advertising could be considered the propaganda of this society. It teaches us to be consumers, to value material things above all else, to feel that happiness can be bought, to believe there are instant solutions to life's complex problems, and to expect products to fulfill us and meet our deepest human needs. As a result, objects and things are given great importance and value, while people are often reified and objectified. This is particularly true for women but is increasingly true for men as well. Women, especially young women, are primarily depicted as sex objects and men as success objects. In both cases, the person becomes a thing, and his or her value depends upon the products used.

Girls and young women are primary targets of this message and are socialized to spend enormous amounts of time, energy and money striving to achieve the ideal image. They are made to feel very anxious and insecure about their appearances and their bodies. This preoccupation diverts energy and attention from more important pursuits such as the development of their minds and spirits. Children are encouraged to become prematurely sophisticated. It is a common sight today to see very young girls wearing heavy make-up and tight jeans.

This precocious sexuality can be used as an excuse by abusers and in some sense by the society in general. It cannot be repeated too often that no child asks or deserves to be sexually abused. The sexualized image of children and the inevitable mimicking of that image, however, does put real children at risk.

These images put children at psychic risk as well. Advertising's approach to sex is pornographic; it reduces people to objects and de-emphasizes human contact and individuality. This reduction of sexuality to a dirty joke and of people to objects is the real obscenity of the culture. Although the sexual sell, overt and subliminal, is at a fevered pitch in most commercials, there is at the same time a notable absence of sex as an important and profound human activity.

Sex in commercials is narcissistic and auto-erotic and exists apart from relationships. Models parade alone through the commercials, caressing their own soft skin, stroking and hugging their bodies, shaking their long, silky manes, sensually bathing and applying powders and lotions, and then admiring themselves at length in the mirror. Commercials depict a world in which there is pervasive sexual innuendo but no love and in which passion is reserved solely for products. This is the world our children are exposed to, a world of flagrant sexuality throughout the media but with very little sex education in our schools or homes.

On the deepest level, what must be done to prevent the sexual abuse of children (and adults, for that matter) is to work to eradicate sexism, to abolish these damaging stereotypes of women and men, and to create avenues to real power for all people. It is unrealistic to expect any radical changes to occur in advertising.

The purpose of advertising is, as Stuart Ewen described it, "to invest the laborer with a financial power and a psychic desire to consume" (Ewen, 1976, p. 25) and to articulate a world view which justifies the acquisition of things as the means to happiness and fulfillment (Cagan, 1978).

In the short term, it does help to protest the images but it is doubtful that authentic change will ever take place within the advertising. It can take place within the society, however. An essential step in creating that change is understanding and challenging the cultural myths and stereotypes. Above all, as always, we must break the silence.

References

Bayer, Alan E. and Daniel H. Baker. "Adolescent Eating Disorders: Anorexia and Bulimia." *Family Life Educator* 3:2 (1984): 4-9.

Broverman, I. K., D. M. Broverman, F. E. Clarkson, P. S. Rosenkrantz and S. R. Vogel. "Sex-Role Stereotypes and Clinical Judgments of Mental Health." *Journal of Consulting and Clinical Psychology* 34:1 (1970): 1-7.

Brownmiller, S. *Against Our Will: Men, Women and Rape.* New York: Simon and Schuster, 1975.

Butler, M., and W. Paisley. *Women and the Mass Media.* New York: Human Sciences Press, 1980.

Cagan, E. "The Selling of the Women's Movement." *Social Policy* 9:1 (1978): 4-12.

Comstock, G. "The Impact of Television on American Institutions." *Journal of Communication* 28:2 (1978): 12-28.

Courtney, A. and T. Whipple. *Sex Stereotyping in Advertising.* Lexington, MA: D.C. Heath & Co., 1983.

Elkind, D. *The Hurried Child: Growing Up Too Fast, Too Soon.* Reading, MA: Addison-Wesley, 1981.

Ewen, S. *Captains of Consciousness: Advertising and the Social Roots of the Consumer Culture.* New York: McGraw-Hill, 1976.

Fore, W. "The Role of Mass Communication in Society: A Theological Perspective." In B. Logan (Ed.), *Television Awareness Training.* New York: Parthenon Press, 1977.

Gerbner, G. "Communication and Social Environment." *Scientific American* 26:3 (1972): 152-160.

Goffman, E. *Gender Advertisements.* New York: Harper & Row, 1979.

"Judge Blames Sex Assault on 5-Year-Old Victim." *National Now Times.* January 2, 1982, p. 2.

Leymore, V. L. *Hidden Myth: Structure and Symbolism in Advertising.* New York: Basic Books, Inc., 1975.

Lindsey, K. "Towards a New Recognition of Reality." *Sojourner* (January 1980): 5, 22.

Malamuth, N., and E. Donnerstein. *Pornography and Sexual Aggression.* Chicago: Academy Press, 1984.

Miller, J. B. *Toward a New Psychology of Women.* Boston: Beacon Press, 1976.

Nabokov, V. *Lolita.* New York: Putnam Publishing Group, 1955.

Price, J. *The Best Thing on TV: Commercials.* New York: Penguin Books, 1978.

Rush, Florence. (Quoted in "Advertising and the Lolita Image.") *The Christian Science Monitor.* January 30, 1981, p. B4.

Sontag, S. "The Double Standard of Aging." *Saturday Review of the Society* 55:39 (1972): 29-38.

Williamson, J. *Decoding Advertisements: Ideology and Meaning in Advertising.* London: Marion Boyars Publishers, Ltd., 1978.

Wynn, M. *Children Without Childhoods.* New York: Pantheon, 1983.

Chapter 6

What Happens to Victims of Child Sexual Abuse?

LYNN B. DAUGHERTY

What happens to victims of child sexual abuse?

Our current answer to this question is shockingly simple. We don't know. Fortunately, we can also add, . . . but we're finding out.

Why We Don't Know

There are many reasons why we don't know what happens to victims to child sexual abuse. The difficulties of identifying victims; the lack of any systematic method for classifying, recording and reporting incidents of child sexual abuse; and limited efforts to follow the progress of former victims on a long term basis are among them.

At present, we don't really know how many children are being sexually abused in the United States or who they are. Many occurrences, probably the majority, are never reported. One estimate suggests that at least 50 percent of all sexually abused children never tell anyone about the abuse (Queen's Bench Foundation, 1977).

In a survey of professionals who work with child sexual abuse cases attending a workshop on the subject in 1981, 22 percent reported having been sexually abused as children. Not one had ever previously told of the abuse (Kepler, 1984). Sometimes the child victim says nothing to anyone about the abuse for many years. Often he or she never discloses the secret. And certainly the abuser rarely reports the abuse.

Even when the child reports being sexually abused, he or she often is not believed or is ignored. If the child convinces a parent or other adult that sexual abuse has taken place, the adult is often reluctant to report the abuse to any authorities. Embarrassment, fear of breaking up a family, or fear of legal proceedings can stop the adult from taking action.

When child sexual abuse is reported, it may be described with many different labels and be classified in many different categories. Sometimes abuse is recorded as a criminal charge. Often it is handled in other ways that may never reach statistical record keepers. The abuse may be recorded as a rape, child molestation, public disturbance, marital problem, domestic situation, child abuse, indecent exposure, prostitution, runaway, or a variety of other labels, all of which overlap with various other possible acts.

Estimating the Incidence of Child Sexual Abuse

Thus, it is not surprising that we cannot easily answer the basic question, how many victims of child sexual abuse are there in the United States today? According to the U.S. Department of Health, Education and Welfare, 360,000 cases identified as child sexual abuse are reported annually (1979). Estimates of unreported cases range as high as ten times that figure (Kepler, 1984).

In recent years many attempts have been made to estimate the true frequency, but estimates are only guesses and change as new information is obtained. One author reported that estimates of the frequency of incest have increased from one in one million cases in 1940 to one in one hundred cases in 1950 to one in 20 cases in 1970 (Woodbury, 1971). Another reported estimates increasing from 1.9 per million people per year in 1955 to 40 per million per year in 1968 to 53 reported cases per million children per year in 1980 (James, 1983). In Santa Clara County, California, a treatment program for incestuous families receives 200 referrals annually from a service area comprising approximately one million inhabitants (Giarretto, 1976). Estimates of the number of male and female prostitutes under the age of 18 in the United States range from "tens of thousands" to 2.4 million. The number of children who are the subject of pornography has been estimated at 3,000 (U.S. General Accounting Office; 1982).

The highest range estimates suggest that one girl in three and one boy in six become victims of child sexual abuse (Hart-Rossi, 1984) or that 30-46 percent of all children are sexually abused in some way before the age of 18 (National Committee for Prevention of Child Abuse, n.d.). Furthermore, estimates obtained from different sources differ widely in the numbers of victims they suggest exist in the United States. In many ways, estimating the incidence of child sexual abuse is akin to the proverbial group of blind men trying to describe an elephant. As each touches a different part, the description of the elephant changes drastically.

The major sources of figures for estimating the number of child sexual abuse victims are: (1) reports furnished by identified victims, (2) reports furnished by identified abusers, and (3) general surveys of the public.

Reports of identified victims may be direct or indirect. Direct victim reports are those in which the actual sexual abuse is reported to authorities at the time of the incident or shortly thereafter. Indirect reports of victims become known only when the abuse comes to light because of the victim's involvement with agencies or professionals for other reasons. For example, an adult seeking psychotherapeutic help because of chronic depression may report that she was sexually abused as a child.

One author has reported, "Several years ago when I first began working in this area, I was responsible for a caseload of 42 families, only two of which had been referred for sexual abuse. The other 40 cases were a combination of physical abuse, emotional abuse and neglect. And yet, within my first year as a caseworker dealing with these families, I became aware that sexual abuse had occurred within 27 of them!" (Kepler, 1984). So estimates based on direct or indirect reports of victims are probably lower than the actual incidence of child sexual abuse.

Estimates of the number of child sexual abuse victims in the United States based on reports of the abusers are usually derived from interviews with abusers who are incarcerated or who are in some type of therapy program after their offenses have been discovered. They represent only a small percentage of abusers. Such a sample is probably biased as well, in that individuals who abuse children in greater numbers probably have a greater chance of being caught, and thus have the opportunity to tell their stories. Therefore, in general, estimates based on this type of information probably lead to an overestimate of the numbers of victims, especially victims of brief incidents.

Conversely, the numbers of incest victims or numbers of children victimized in continuing but nonfamilial relationships are probably underestimated by using this method. These abusers are probably identified less often, as they abuse fewer children and run less risk of being reported. One extensive study indicated that the average abuser of girls abused 62 victims and the average abuser of boys abused 31 victims before being apprehended (Jenkins and McDonald, 1979).

General surveys of adults, the third method of estimating the number of victims, holds the most promise for providing accurate figures. Some problems still remain with this method, however. Most general surveys do not involve statistically random samples, but study preselected groups of individuals. There is no way of knowing whether the frequency of victims among these groups is greater, lesser or equivalent to that in the general population.

Such surveys also depend on the truthfulness of the respondent, although anonymity is usually provided, which would presumably encourage honesty. Still, some victims have difficulty discussing, or even admitting, their past sexual abuse in spite of anonymous conditions.

The pioneer studies of American sexual behavior indicated that one in four females and one in ten males are sexually abused before the age of 18 (Kinsey, 1948, 1953). Many other percentages of child sexual abuse have been reported in retrospective surveys: 17 percent of a group of middle and upper middle class university students (Walters, 1975); 10 percent of a group of adult male nonoffenders (Finkelhor, 1979); 35 percent of female and 30 percent of male members of a group of middle class college students (Landis, 1956); and 50 percent of a group of female college students who were stepdaughters (Finkelhor, 1979).

So, obviously, estimates of the incidence of child sexual abuse vary widely. Our best guess at present is that one in four girls and one in seven boys are victims of some type of sexual abuse before they reach the age of 18. The noticeable trend in estimates has been a strongly increasing one as more and more information comes to light.

Assessing the Effects of Child Sexual Abuse

The inability to identify most victims and then follow them throughout their lives limits what we know about the long term effects of child sexual abuse. Right now we can identify some victims. But we do not know whether the victims we identify and follow have the same outcomes as the victims we cannot identify, or those we do not follow.

Identified victims obviously receive different treatment than victims who are never identified. We do not know whether the turmoil that often results from identification or the treatment we may provide affects the outcome for the victims in significant ways. Would the outcomes be the same or different if these victims were not identified or treated?

Professional interest in child sexual abuse has only recently become widespread. At present, we have a few anecdotal descriptions of what has happened to former victims and we have some short term studies. The field is not yet old enough or large enough to provide us with detailed information about the outcomes for victims, even those we have identified and followed, especially over a long term period.

What We Do Know

The question of what happens to victims of child sexual abuse can really be divided into two specific issues. What happens to victims while they are still children? What happens to victims after they become adults?

Victims as Children

Our knowledge of the immediate effects of child sexual abuse comes primarily from descriptions of the problems encountered by victims identified as children. Retrospective reports of adults victimized as children also provide information.

What happens to children who are sexually abused appears to depend on a number of factors: (1) the prior emotional stability of the child and family; (2) the intensity, duration, frequency and nature of the sexual abuse; (3) the child's age and developmental stage; (4) the closeness and type of relationship between the abuser and victim; (5) when, how and if the abuse is disclosed; and (6) the reaction of other family members and of the community to the disclosure.

Some children suffer physical injuries or contract sexually transmissible diseases as a result of child sexual abuse, but such cases are rare. Behavioral and psychological effects are more often recognized in children, and include: (1) feelings of confusion, fear, anxiety, anger, shame and guilt; (2) disturbances in sleeping and eating; (3) nightmares; (4) increased minor physical complaints; (5) increased irritability or aggressiveness; (6) bedwetting or other disturbances of bowel or bladder; (7) regression; (8) behavioral acting out of feelings through rebelliousness, runaway or antisocial acts; and (9) lowered self-esteem.

Victims as Adults

Most available information about the long term effects of child sexual abuse comes from the retrospective reports of adults who were victimized as children. We are accumulating more and more clinical and statistical information about these former victims as more and more of them come forward. Although this will only give us a general idea of some aspects of the problem, it is at least an advance in our knowledge.

The field of psychology knows very little about how the victims of highly traumatic circumstances in their early years survive emotionally and manage to lead fairly healthy, normal lives. By far the majority of former victims of poverty, serious accident or illness, physical abuse, natural catastrophes, war, and even such drastic environments as concentration camps, go on to lead productive and in many ways satisfying lives. Fortunately this is also true for the majority of child sexual abuse victims, though we can't explain how or why.

This is not true for all victims, however. Many are later identified as having serious problems that interfere with their ability to adapt to the demands of adult life in society.

Other former victims who lead generally normal, healthy lives are definitely at risk for a variety of lesser problems that interfere with personal happiness. They are more likely than most people to suffer from lowered self-esteem, anxiety, depression, thoughts of suicide, difficulty in relationships due to poor social skills and problems in trusting others, distorted attitudes toward sex resulting in poor sexual adjustment, problems with independence and mature judgment, and difficulties in providing proper parenting to their own children. More extreme problems may include psychosis, drug abuse, suicide, physical abuse of children or spouse, and sexual abuse of children or adults.

High percentages of former victims have been reported among groups experiencing problems that interfere with personal happiness or bring them into conflict with society: 90 percent of a group of women being treated for sexual dysfunction (Baisden, 1971); 75 percent of a group of mothers in incestuous families (McCarty, 1981); 22 percent of a group of Seattle prostitutes and nearly 50 percent of a group of Chicago prostitutes (Justice and Justice, 1979); 60 percent of a group of incarcerated Miami prostitutes (Kepler, 1984); 75 percent of a group of female probationers (Martin, 1981); 80 percent of incarcerated sex offenders (Groth, 1982); 70 percent of a group of adolescents being treated for drug addiction and 44 percent of young adults in a home for drug abusers (cited in Giarretto, 1976); 50 percent of a group of Seattle teenage offenders (Clark et al, 1976); 40-70 percent of various groups of New York girl prostitutes (Sanford, 1980); and 80-90 percent of groups of mothers in treatment for child abuse (Finkelhor, 1979).

Why does one victim of child sexual abuse go on to become a member of Congress while another becomes a convicted felon? Does it depend on the type of abuse the individual suffered? The personality characteristics of the person? Whether the abuse was discovered or reported? How the report of the abuse was handled? What type of treatment the former victim received? How disruptive the abuse was to the family unit? The age at which the abuse occurred? Or any of a number of other factors? At the present time, the answer again must be, we don't know.

There are even those who suggest that sexual contact between adults and children can actually be beneficial, and should not be termed abuse at all. Clinical experience overwhelmingly refutes this, but again, no clearcut answer based on sound research is available.

What Do We Need to Answer Our Questions About Child Sexual Abuse?

This question is easy to answer. We need better information about the statistical aspects of child sexual abuse, more information about the specific factors of the situation that led to problems for victims, and better information about the effectiveness of various interventions. Progress in all three of these areas is interrelated.

First of all, we need better identification of the victims themselves. Encouraging victims and their families to report abuse or suspected abuse is an important step. Experience has shown this is most effectively produced when programs providing information about child sexual abuse, its prevention and its treatment are presented in systematic ways to the general public. Recent media attention to the subject has tripled or quadrupled reporting in many areas.

It is also important to continue to provide encouragement for physicians, social workers, teachers, counselors and others in a position to suspect child sexual abuse to report it. The mandatory reporting laws passed by many states are an important step in this direction, but must be coupled with continuing education programs to alert professionals to possible signs of child sexual abuse and to the importance of their duty to report suspected activity.

Reducing the trauma and uncertainty involved in the response of authorities to the report of child sexual abuse would further encourage its reporting. At present the response of agencies and authorities is often described as "a second rape" of the victim.

Additionally, it would be helpful if reporting were standardized in some manner so that cases of child sexual abuse were clearly identified as such for the purposes of keeping records and compiling statistics.

Developing effective treatment interventions and making their availability widely known are very important in encouraging the reporting of abuse. This process may be likened to that which has occurred with a variety of problems or diseases during this century. For example, as schizophrenia or sexually transmissible disease became better understood and the treatments more effective, individuals suffering from these conditions were less likely to be hidden away, and more likely to be brought forward and encouraged to participate in treatment.

Improving knowledge about factors leading to specific problems and developing effective interventions depend on research. At present, some cross-sectional studies and many retrospective reports provide us with the little information we have to answer our questions about child sexual abuse. Once victims can be identified reliably, longitudinal studies to follow groups of victims from the time the abuse is reported until well into adulthood can be conducted.

Certainly, as with all longitudinal studies of at-risk populations, both practical and ethical problems arise. Throughout the psychological literature, however, it has been demonstrated that the knowledge we have concerning human development is most valid when based on longitudinal studies. The advances in knowledge these studies provide far outweigh the difficulties involved.

Again: What Happens to Victims of Child Sexual Abuse?

As we have seen, we are gradually changing our answer from: we don't know into we are beginning to find out. What we are beginning to find out is that most victims of child sexual abuse, after some immediate problems, go on to lead normal, healthy, productive lives, but may experience problems in specific areas, such as relationships, trusting, sexual adjustment and lowered self-esteem.

The fact that most victims lead normal lives must be attributed to their own strength and determination, as well as to the inherent resiliency of the human being. Their lives may frequently be a struggle to overcome the difficulties they encounter, but they do go on to work, play, love, marry, raise children successfully, and feel satisfaction in their lives and accomplishments.

We do know that former victims of child sexual abuse are definitely at risk for a number of serious problems. On a level primarily of relevance to the individual are problems such as serious depression, suicide or psychoses. On a level posing a more direct threat to society are problems such as criminal behavior, physical abuse and neglect of children, and sexual abuse of other individuals.

While the numbers of former victims who develop these more extreme problems are low (compared to those who go on to lead normal lives) the numbers are certainly substantial. Former victims represent a significant proportion of the individuals experiencing such serious problems. These statistics should alert us to the need for intervention, not only as a benefit to the individual victim, but as a benefit to society as a whole.

Thankfully, we can give one further answer to the question, what happens to victims of child sexual abuse? Many of them are beginning to enter treatment for the problems they are experiencing, whether mild or severe.

There is much good news in the area of treatment today. What appear to be sound therapeutic approaches to the problems arising in former victims are rapidly being developed. For children, expressive approaches such as play therapy or art therapy provide opportunities for recognizing and mastering the difficult emotions involved in the experience of sexual abuse. Training the parents of these children to institute behavioral programs that help their children alter problem behaviors and develop new skills, thus allowing the children to increase their self-esteem, is also productive.

For adolescents, a variety of group therapy approaches are being developed that hold great promise. These capitalize on the importance of peer relationships in this age group to again deal with emotions, develop new skills, and increase self-esteem and coping resources.

For adults, individual psychotherapy using a variety of approaches can help individuals overcome the range of specific problems they may encounter. Group therapy can also be a powerful tool for adults in dealing with these problems.

Self-help approaches are also promising ways of recovering from the problems of child sexual abuse, particularly for those individuals who are leading basically normal lives, and only experiencing difficulties in some areas. General self-help books, of which there are many good ones available, focusing on specific problems such as assertiveness or depression, are useful. The lack of self-help books dealing specifically with the problems of child sexual abuse victims led to the publishing of *Why Me? Help for Victims of Child Sexual Abuse,* the first book of its kind available (Daugherty, 1984).

Worthy of special notice in the self-help field is the concept based on group sharing of experiences developed by Henry Giarretto in his California-based groups, Parents United (for parents in incestuous families), Daughters and Sons United (for children of incestuous families), and Adults Molested as Children United (for former victims now adults). These were organized through the Child Sexual Abuse Treatment Program in Santa Clara County, California, and excellent results have been reported by all involved.

Unfortunately at present, many former victims are simply "going on with their lives," struggling with, adjusting to, and occasionally overcoming, but often suffering unnecessarily with the problems they are experiencing. This last may be one final phase of their victimization. Many could lead much more rewarding and enjoyable lives if they were afforded the opportunity to become involved in treatment.

So, while our answers about child sexual abuse—its causes, its immediate and long term effect, and its treatment—are limited, we are moving in the right direction. "We don't know" is becoming "we are beginning to find out that ..." During the next few years we will be able to say more and more frequently, "Oh, yes, research and clinical practice demonstrate that..."

The problems of child sexual abuse will probably be with us, and with its victims, for a long time. But we are currently seeking—and gaining—the answers that will reduce its detrimental impact on our children and on ourselves.

References

Adams, Caren and Jennifer Fay. *No More Secrets*. San Luis Obispo, CA: Impact Publishers, 1981.

Baisden, M. J. 1971 (Cited in Giarretto, H., "Humanistic Treatment of Father-Daughter Incest.") In R. E. Helfer & C. H. Kempe (Eds.) *Child Abuse and Neglect: The Family and the Community*. Cambridge, MA: Balinger, 1976.

Baisden, M. J. *The World of Rosaphrenia: The Sexual Psychology of the Female*. Sacramento, CA: Allied Research Society, 1971 (Cited in Giarretto, 1976).

Clark, T., G. Wenet, B. Hunner and S. Sulzbacher. "Final Report: Development of Diagnostic and Treatment Programs for the Juvenile Sexual Offender." Seattle, WA: University of Washington Adolescent Clinic, November 30, 1976.

Daugherty, Lynn B. *Why Me? Help for Victims of Child Sexual Abuse*. Racine, WI: Mother Courage Press, 1984.

Finkelhor, David. *Sexually Victimized Children*. New York: Free Press, 1979.

Giarretto, H. "Humanistic Treatment of Father-Daughter Incest: A Psycho-Social Approach." *Children Today* 5 (1976): 2-35 (passim).

Giarretto, H. *Integrated Treatment of Child Sexual Abuse*. Palo Alto, CA: Science & Behavior Books, 1982.

Groth, N. and P. Linebaugh. Interview on *Today Show*. October 1, 1982 (cited in *One In Four*, 1984).

Hart-Rossi, Janie. *Protect Your Child From Sexual Abuse: A Parent's Guide*. Seattle: Parenting Press, Inc., 1984.

James, Beverly and Maria Nasjleti. *Treating Sexually Abused Children and Their Families*. Palo Alto, CA: Consulting Psychologists Press, Inc., 1983.

Jenkins, J. K. and P. McDonald. *Growing Up Equal: Activities and Resources for Parents and Teachers of Young Children*. Englewood Cliffs, NJ: Prentice Hall, 1979.

Justice, B. and R. Justice. *The Broken Taboo: Sex in the Family*. New York: Human Services Press, 1979.

Kepler, Victoria. *One In Four*. Mansfield, OH: Social Interest Press, Inc., 1984.

Kinsey, A. C., W. B. Pomeroy and C. E. Martin. *Sexual Behavior in the Human Male*. Philadelphia: Saunders, 1948.

Kinsey, A. C., W. B. Pomeroy, C. E. Martin and P. Gebhard. *Sexual Behavior in the Human Female*. Philadelphia: Saunders: 1953.

Landis, J. T. "Experiences of 500 Children with Adult Sexual Deviation." *Psychiatric Quarterly Supplement* 30 (1956): 91-109.

Martin, L. Personal Communication. Chief Probation Officer, Wayne County Juvenile Court, Wayne County, OH, October 17, 1981. (cited in Kepler, *One In Four*, 1984).

McCarty, L. M. "Investigation of Incest: Opportunity to Motivate Families to Seek Help." *Child Welfare* 10 (December 1981).

National Committee for Prevention of Child Abuse. "Basic Facts About Sexual Child Abuse." (cited in Adams and Fay, *No More Secrets*, 1981).

Queen's Bench Foundation. *Sexual Abuse of Children: A Guide for Parents*. San Francisco, 1977.

Sanford, L. T. *The Silent Children*. Garden City, N Y: Anc' or Press/Doubleday, 1980.

U.S. General Accounting Office. *Sexual Exploitation of Children—A Problem of Unknown Magnitude*. Washington, DC: HRD-82-64, 1982.

Walters, D. R. *Physical and Sexual Abuse of Children—Causes and Treatment*. Bloomington: Indiana University Press, 1975.

Woodbury, J. and E. Schwartz. *The Silent Sin: A Case History of Incest*. New York: Signet Books, 1971.

Chapter 7

Legal Intervention and Reforms in Child Sexual Abuse Cases

JOSEPHINE BULKLEY

Criminal Laws and Prosecution

All states have statutes providing criminal penalties for sexual offenses against children. Many of these statutes were changed during a reform movement in the 1970s to provide lower, more reasonable prison penalties and to provide degrees of offenses with the severity of the penalty based upon the child's age, and sometimes specifying that the offender must be a certain number of years older than the child (Kocen and Bulkley, 1981; this section is taken from the referenced chapter).

Based on a survey of all child sex offense criminal laws in 1980, the author found that most states provide for a maximum of between ten and twenty years' imprisonment for sexual intercourse with a young child (under 11 or 12 years). A number of states still allowed life imprisonment, and a few states provided a death penalty. (The Supreme Court, however, has held that it is unconstitutional as cruel and unusual punishment to impose a death penalty for rape.) When the victim is an adolescent, the most common maximum imprisonment is up to ten years, although some states provide penalties as low as one to one and one-half

years. Thus, penalties vary widely depending upon each state's philosophy of prison sentences and the age of the victim.

Many states also have passed separate provisions prohibiting sexual offenses of minors by persons in a position of authority, family members, or persons who have care, custody or supervision of the child. These provisions normally impose higher penalties. Sexual contact also is prohibited in most states, although the penalties are on the average lower than for sexual intercourse. Generally the maximum penalty is between five and fifteen years.

Penalties also vary depending on other factors. Thus, penalties are higher when: there is sexual intercourse or genital-oral sexual activity, rather than sexual touching; a young child is the victim; the perpetrator is a certain number of years older than the child (an age differential is more often used with older children, in part to abolish criminal liability for consenting sex between adolescents); there is a relationship between the perpetrator and child; force or threats are used; it is a repeated offense.

Whether child abuse and neglect should be criminally prosecuted, particularly if the offender is a parent or caretaker, is very controversial. The trend in the past five to ten years has been to prosecute sexual abuse of children and there has been growing advocacy from professionals and segments of the federal government to prosecute sex offenders (U.S. Dept. of Justice, 1984; Berliner and Stevens, 1980). In the past, criminal prosecution of child abusers was rare, and criminal penalties were sought only in egregious cases that generally received major media attention, in cases of severe or permanent physical injury or death, or if the perpetrator was not the parent. Thus, despite a longstanding belief by many child welfare professionals that criminal prosecution is unwise in these cases, child sexual abuse cases involving a parent today often are the subject of both a criminal and child protection investigation.

There are a number of problems with prosecuting a child sexual abuse case. First, in the criminal justice system, the state has the burden of proof and is required to prove the accused guilty beyond a reasonable doubt. These protections are based on fundamental concepts in the American criminal justice system. Individuals are presumed innocent until proven guilty, and constitutional due process requires a high standard of proof to ensure that innocent persons are not convicted.

The right to a fair trial and to be proven guilty only by reliable or trustworthy evidence also are benchmarks of our criminal system. Thus, there is a strict adherence to rules of evidence in criminal court, particularly the rule against admitting a declarant's out-of-court assertion to prove the truth of the matter asserted (called the hearsay rule). Finally, in a criminal trial, the defendant is entitled to a number of specific constitutional protections, the most important being the right to be free from unreasonable searches and seizures, right to a jury trial, right to a speedy and public trial, right to counsel, right to be confronted with witnesses against him (including the right to cross-examination) and right to have compulsory process for obtaining witnesses in his favor.[1]

There are also special problems in proving child sexual abuse in a criminal proceeding, including (1) the lack of eyewitnesses; (2) a child victim who may be too young to be a witness (i.e. an infant); (3) competency tests for children often leading to their being disqualified to testify; (4) a child victim who is competent but whose credibility may be questioned due to the child's cognitive and verbal limitations, or to misconceptions that a child cannot distinguish between fact or fantasy or is likely to fabricate sexual experiences with adults, or who may retract his/her story because of family pressures or insensitiveness by the legal process; and (5) lack of physical or medical evidence (MacFarlane, 1979; Finkelhor, 1979; Sgroi, 1978).

Moreover, prosecution may have a detrimental impact on the child and family, including the following: (1) possible incarceration of the abusive parent and splitting up the family, often making the child feel guilt and blame for the resultant loss and separation; (2) loss of social status and respect for the entire family and social stigma affecting all family members; (3) if there is an acquittal, a sense of hopelessness and guilt feelings on the child's part, and possibly reprisals by the offender; and (4) unavailability of treatment for offenders and families, when parental child abuse is a psycho-social problem involving complex family dynamics better handled by a nonpunitive, social service approach that can help and preserve the family.

Perhaps the greatest complaint about criminal prosecution is that it can cause additional trauma to children and families, since its primary objective is to convict and punish the offender. Many mental health and child welfare experts believe that juvenile court may be a more appropriate forum because its primary focus is to protect the child and help the family. Many believe that traditional legal intervention, particularly criminal prosecution, in child sexual abuse cases can cause more emotional damage to the child than the abuse itself (MacFarlane, 1979; Finkelhor, 1979; Sgroi, 1978). The problem is well-stated by Vincent DeFrancis, an early proponent of child victim/witness protections in sexual abuse cases. As early as 1969, DeFrancis, former Director of the Children's Division of the American Humane Association, indicated:

> Because sex crimes are so personal and because they relate to areas which in our culture are laden with taboos and strong emotional impact, child victims are exposed to serious emotional stresses and tensions . . .

The situation is compounded by the very real and urgent objective of criminal law—the immediate prosecution of the adult offender. Law enforcement personnel—police and prosecutor—are under pressure, and sometimes under fire, of public concern and public opinion to make an airtight case against "degenerates" who prey on children. The natural consequence is that what happens to children in the process seems of lesser importance, or is lost sight of, in the desire and rush to meet the clamor of public demands for retribution. Little thought is given by the community to the problems of the child victim and his/her parents whose needs and rights are often trampled in the pursuit of sanctions against the offender (DeFrancis, 1969).

The most often cited negative aspect of legal intervention is the subjection of the child to repeated questioning from preliminary investigation to the time of trial. DeFrancis states:

> The initial shock of the crime is heightened and tensions are increased and compounded under questioning by police in their search for evidence. A sensitive child may be subjected to an excruciating experience during efforts to elicit the sordid facts of the crime. Emphasis on the minutest details of the offense serve to magnify the act out of proportion and add to the child's sense of guilt and shame (DeFrancis, 1969).

The child often must repeat the details of the incident to several different police officers, doctors, social workers, counselors, the child's guardian *ad litem,* possibly the parents' attorney, and one or more prosecutors. Moreover, if the case goes to trial, the child will undergo direct and cross-examination in open court. In some felony cases, the child also may testify at either or both a preliminary hearing and a grand jury hearing.

Other aspects of the adversary judicial process also may have a negative impact upon the child's emotional well-being. These include facing the defendant, the jury and the public throughout a trial, and subjection to insensitive gynecological exams, polygraph tests, delays and long waiting periods in the legal process. Finally, the methods by which law enforcement personnel and prosecutors interview a child victim are too often insensitive and not adaptive to the child's level of understanding. For example, children often are subjected to legal and clinical jargon incomprehensible even to the average adult.

Advocates of criminal prosecution, however, cite a number of positive reasons for prosecuting child sexual abuse cases including the following (Davidson et al, 1981; Bulkley and Davidson, 1980). (1) Child sexual abuse has been designated a crime by society and should be treated like other criminal acts. (2) Unlike the juvenile court, the criminal justice system has control over the offender by being able to order the offender to vacate the home or stay away from the child, by sentencing the offender to prison in order to protect the child or society, or by providing a powerful authoritative incentive or leverage to secure the offender's participation in a treatment program as a condition of a guilty plea or deferred prosecution. (3) Criminal prosecution is a symbol to children that society will protect them and that their rights and welfare are valued. (4) Prosecution and some jail time is a necessary expiatory factor in the successful treatment or rehabilitation of some sexual offenders. (5) Criminal prosecution provides full due process and other constitutional safeguards to protect the offender's rights, and forces the state to prove abuse beyond a reasonable doubt, thus better protecting family privacy by preventing unwarranted state intervention that often occurs in a civil proceeding.

Child Protection Intervention and Juvenile Court Actions

The primary purposes of child protection intervention include protection of a child's and family's health and welfare and preservation of the family. The basic components of intervention may include the following: (1) immediate protection of the child through temporary stabilization of the home environment or, when a child is in imminent danger, taking the child into emergency or protective custody; (2) verifying the validity of the report and assessing the danger to the child; (3) assessing the need for and providing services to the family on a voluntary basis; and (4) instituting a civil court action if necessary to remove the child from a dangerous environment or to impose treatment or services upon the family (Besharov, 1977-78). Services range from concrete methods to relieve pressure for parents, such as a homemaker, day care or financial assistance, as well as psychological counseling and self-help groups with other abusive parents.

Generally, juvenile court action should be initiated only if the child is in imminent danger or services or treatment efforts for the parents have failed. A manual for protective services workers in Massachusetts states that a juvenile court petition is a serious step with significant consequences for the child and family and should not be filed except as a last resort (Davidson et al, 1981).

The civil court system has certain advantages and disadvantages over the criminal system (Davidson et al, 1980; Bulkley and Davidson, 1980; Davidson and Horowitz, 1984). The civil court offers: (1) swift protection of the child through the power of the juvenile court to remove the child or through the authority of police or protective services to take emergency custody of the child in certain circumstances; (2) greater access to services and treatment of abusive families and provision of long term monitoring of the child and family; (3) help to preserve the family and a nonpunitive approach; (4) a less traumatic investigation and trial and easier proof because of social casework investigative skills, lower burden of proof, relaxed evidence and constitutional requirements, and lack of a jury or public trial; (5) a guardian *ad litem* to represent the child's interests; and (6) sparing the child from testifying because parents are more likely to cooperate since penal sanctions cannot be imposed, and parents can receive "use immunity," which prevents their testimony in juvenile court from being used against them in a criminal prosecution.

Disadvantages of child protection intervention (MacFarlane and Bulkley, 1982; Bulkley and Davidson, 1980; Wald, 1975; Mnookin, 1973) include: (1) lack of direct control over the offender, thus requiring removal of the child from his or her home, making the child feel punished for disclosing or causing the abuse and displacing the child from his or her home; (2) lack of specialized treatment for sexually abusive families by many protective services agencies; (3) petitions against a nonabusive parent filed inappropriately resulting in the removal of the child from custody despite a desire and ability to protect the child and obtain treatment for parent and child; (4) lack of due process and other constitutional and evidence safeguards afforded defendants in a criminal prosecution; (5) risk of unwarranted invasion of family privacy or intervention be-cause of individual, class or cultural prejudice resulting from vague statutory definitions of child abuse and neglect, focusing on parental fault rather than specific harm to the child; (6) placement of children in foster homes for excessive periods of time, often involving multiple placements, inadequate care, and failure either to return the child home or terminate parental rights to free the child for adoption; and (7) power of the juvenile court to remove children for their protection resulting in unnecessary removals based on inaccurate assessments that the child is in danger or because the state does not attempt to first provide services to the family to enable the child to remain at home.

Reforms for Improving Legal Intervention in Child Sexual Abuse Cases

Beginning in the late 1970s, the increasing awareness of the trauma caused children by the legal system, the extreme difficulty of proving cases of child sexual abuse, the lack of treatment dispositions in a criminal proceeding, and increasing cases of child sexual abuse entering the criminal justice system all contributed to a movement to reform legal procedures and laws to improve the legal system's handling of these cases.

In addition, based on a survey of laws and evidence issues, prosecutorial practices and a program by the American Bar Association's Legal Resource Center for Child Advocacy and Protection, a set of *Recommendations for Improving Legal Intervention in Intrafamily Child Sexual Abuse Cases* was published in

1982 as a guide for states and local jurisdictions in improving legal intervention. The *Recommendations* suggest the need for innovative approaches in the legal system in three major areas: reducing trauma to children and families, improving successful legal outcomes, and providing treatment for the child, family, and where appropriate, the offender.

Victim advocates from a variety of child sexual abuse programs developed in the 1970s began to recommend that procedures in the legal system be modified to be more sensitive to children (Berliner and Stevens, 1981; Bulkley, 1981).[2] It is important to point out that the development of special procedures is also likely to result in more frequent and successful prosecutions. This has proven to be the case, for example in Seattle, Washington, where a pioneer program called the Sexual Assault Center (SAC) has been responsible for successfully implementing a variety of new and practical approaches for more sensitive handling of child sexual abuse cases by the criminal justice system. The SAC's data reveal that convictions are obtained in almost 90 percent of cases, and a high percentage of cases are resolved by guilty pleas.

The ABA *Recommendations* offer a wide range of suggestions for modifying state laws and procedures to make the legal system more sensitive to children including: (1) interdisciplinary teams; (2) coordination of juvenile and criminal court proceedings; (3) provision of a special advocate for the child in criminal as well as juvenile court; (4) preventing repeated interviews with children through joint interviews or one interview with a designated person, and possibly videotaping the interview and providing special interviewing rooms; (5) establishing special sexual abuse prosecution units and assigning the same prosecutor to all stages of the case (vertical prosecution); (6) developing methods (such as videotaping or closed circuit viewing of a child's testimony or closing the courtroom) to avoid a child's testimony at grand jury, preliminary hearings, or at a trial when necessary to prevent trauma without violating the defendant's constitutional rights.

One of the most popular state legislative reforms in recent years has been the development of alternatives to a child's testimony in open court in the presence of the judge, jury, public and defendant. At least seventeen states now have legislation allowing videotaping of a child's testimony before the trial, and many bills are currently pending. Five states allow the child's testimony to be taken by closed-circuit television in a room outside the courtroom and televised into the courtroom for the jury, public and defendant to see. Although a significant trend has developed among the states to adopt these reforms, some of them have been criticized from both a practical and constitutional point of view (Papers from a National Conference, 1985).

Witnesses normally are required to give testimony at criminal trials in a public courtroom in the presence of the defendant, judge, and jury, as well as be subject to direct examination by the prosecutor and to cross-examination by the attorney for the defendant. Any attempt to alter these requirements may violate a variety of constitutional rights, including the defendant's right to confront witnesses, the right to a jury trial, a public trial, and a fair trial, and the public's right to attend criminal trials.

The constitutional issue likely to be raised most often involves the confrontation clause of the sixth amendment of the U.S. Constitution, which requires that a criminal defendant be confronted with the witnesses against him/her. Some state constitutions use this language as well, although almost half require the witness to meet the defendant face-to-face.

Moreover, the U.S. Supreme Court in *Ohio v. Roberts* interpreted the confrontation clause as requiring the prosecution to: (1) produce the witness at trial or demonstrate the unavailability of the witness (for example, due to death, physical or mental disability including severe psychological harm from testifying; refusal to testify because of intimidation or threats by the defendant; total failure of memory) whose statement is offered; and (2) show that the statement possesses indicia of reliability by falling within a traditional hearsay exception or by possessing particularized guarantees of trustworthiness.[3]

Similarly, if closed circuit television is sought to be used, a showing of necessity or extraordinary circumstances must be demonstrated.[4] Possible grounds for the child's unavailability to testify in open court before the jury and defendant are: emotional trauma to the child or personal threats by the defendant against the child.

The reliability requirement may be met if a statute dictates an opportunity for direct and cross-examination of the child. Even if cross-examination of the child is required, however, the confrontation clause still may be violated if physical confrontation between the defendant and child is totally or partially eliminated. Some courts have found that the confrontation clause requires both witness and defendant to face each other.[5] Indeed, the Texas Court of Appeals and a trial court in Kentucky recently held their state statutes for videotaping a child sexual offense victim's testimony unconstitutional because the statutes prevent the child from seeing the defendant.[6] On the other hand, other courts have allowed a child victim to testify outside the defendant's presence as long as the child was subject to cross-examination and the jury could observe the child's demeanor.[7]

One method a court described as possibly satisfying the requirements of the confrontation clause is to provide for two-way closed circuit television.[8] The courtroom scene would be televised into the room in which the child is testifying, thereby projecting the defendant's image into the room with the child, as well as televising the child's testimony into the courtroom. California is the first state to adopt this approach by legislation.[9]

The *Recommendations* also suggest methods for improving successful legal outcomes, including: (1) evidence reforms such as hearsay exceptions for a child's out-of-court statement of abuse, elimination of competency tests for child witnesses, and abolition of the marital privilege and corroboration requirements; (2) legislative authority for a court's issuance of protective orders, (e.g., to order the offender out of the home) in any judicial proceeding; (3) reform of laws relating to judicial proceedings involving the nonabusive parent.

The need for a child victim's testimony in a sexual abuse case may be critical since the availability of other admissible evidence is often scarce or nonexistent. A trend is developing to abolish competency requirements for children, and more than twenty states now provide that "every person is competent to be a witness except as otherwise provided in these rules" (Whitcomb et al, 1985). This would establish a presumption of competency.

The majority of states, however, by statute or common law, still prescribe an age above which a child is presumed competent to testify. Below the specified age, usually 10 or 14, courts generally determine a child's testimonial capacity based upon the following four factors: (1) present understanding of the difference between truth and falsity and an appreciation of the obligation or responsibility to speak the truth (sometimes phrased as an understanding of the nature and obligation of an oath); (2) mental capacity at the time of the occurrence in question to observe or receive accurate impressions of the occurrence; (3) memory sufficient to retain an independent recollection of the observation; and (4) capacity to communicate or translate into words the memory of such observation and the capacity to understand simple questions about the occurrence.

Current research on children's memory, ability to distinguish fact and fantasy, appreciation of the obligation to tell the truth, propensity to fabricate, and suggestibility suggests that children's abilities are much greater than was once thought and not much different from adults (Berliner and Barbieri, 1984; Melton et al, 1981). One researcher testified before the U.S. Senate that children as young as four-years-old have the potential to give testimony as reliable as an adult's testimony (Melton, 1985).[10] Research also now shows there is little correlation between age and honesty, and that children's memory for events with which they are familiar is no worse, and sometimes may be better than adults' (Melton et al, 1981). Cognitively, young children have difficulty conceptualizing complex events, ordering them in time and space, and providing detailed verbal responses (Melton et al, 1981; Goodman, 1985). Further, although children often spontaneously recall less than adults, it can no longer be said that children are more suggestible than adults. In certain circumstances both adults and children are susceptible to suggestive information (Loftus and Davies, 1984; Johnson and Foley, 1984).

Another area of reform being adopted by state legislatures is a special hearsay exception to allow a person to testify to a child victim's out-of-court statement of abuse. In 1985 at least twelve states have enacted special exceptions (Bulkley, 1985; Whitcomb et al, 1985). Although other hearsay exceptions exist for admitting children's statements, some statements do not meet the strict or narrow requirements of these exceptions. Particularly in cases in which a child is too young to testify or would be severely psychologically traumatized by testifying, admissibility of a child's out-of-court statement may facilitate more prosecutions or convictions if the child victim is not a witness. Even in cases in which the child is a witness, the statement may serve to corroborate his or her in-court testimony.

Still, a state's adoption of a statute providing a new hearsay exception for a child abuse victim's statement does not guarantee its admissibility. The same requirements necessary for admitting videotaped testimony to satisfy the confrontation clause of the U.S. Constitution apply to statements of the child. First, in order to admit a statement, the child either must testify or must be shown to be unavailable as a witness. Then, if the statement does not fit within a "traditional" hearsay exception, it must be excluded unless it possesses particularized guarantees of trustworthiness.

Courts have cited various criteria for determining the trustworthiness of a statement. These include whether there is an apparent motive to lie, whether more than one person heard the statements, whether the child's young age makes it unlikely the child fabricated when the statement represents a graphic account beyond the child's experience, whether the statement has a "ring of verity" and terminology appropriate to the child's age, and whether the child was suffering pain or distress when making a statement (Bulkley, 1985).

With greater frequency, courts also are addressing the admissibility of expert testimony on the dynamics of child sexual abuse (or the sexually abused child syndrome), issues relating to a child's competency and credibility and offender characteristics. Expert testimony is routinely used in various types of legal proceedings. To qualify as an expert, an individual must possess skills, knowledge or learning in a field in which the average person has inadequate knowledge and which will aid the trier of fact in resolving an issue or reaching a decision.

The use of psychologists, social workers and other professionals as expert witnesses in intrafamily child sexual abuse cases has been approved by a number of courts around the country (Berliner et al, 1981).[11] Expert testimony in the areas noted above has indeed contributed to a greater understanding of the complex and sometimes paradoxical issues in these cases.

Common issues for expert testimony include the reasons why a child endures sexual abuse over a long period of time before disclosing the abuse, or why a child might retract. Another common issue is the nonoffending parent's ambivalence about supporting the child because of divided loyalty between spouse and child.

Some courts have prohibited the use of expert testimony on certain issues, such as the child's credibility or behavioral symptoms, and some commentators have criticized this type of testimony to show that a child is more likely to have been sexually abused (Roe, 1985). When, however, testimony is offered to rebut a defense attorney's attack on the child's credibility, it is helpful in showing that factors such as delay or retraction are not inconsistent with the abuse having occurred. Moreover, one court noted that the reliability of testimony should affect the weight not the admissibility of the testimony, and the defense may cross-examine the witness and present its own witnesses.[12]

As mentioned briefly, another area gaining increasing popularity is videotaping interviews with a child by a social worker, police officer or mental health professional. There are many advantages to videotaping interviews, including reducing multiple interviews with children and facilitating guilty pleas by showing the accused the videotape and demonstrating the credibility of the child. Videotaping interviews, however, can create many problems, including the right of the defense attorney to obtain a copy of the tape, which can then be used to impeach the child's testimony at trial by showing inconsistencies, disclaimers, and retractions, and to invalidate an interview if leading or suggestive questions were used (MacFarlane, 1985). Further, in most cases such videotaped statements cannot be used in lieu of the child's testimony at trial, because it probably will not satisfy the requirements of the confrontation clause.

Lastly, many community treatment programs for sexual abuse offenders and their families have been established since the mid-1970s. These treatment programs generally function within the legal system. If the offender acknowledges the abuse or pleads guilty, he often receives a short, work-release jail sentence, probation, or deferred prosecution conditioned upon treatment in a special program and separation from the family for a period of time. A program's involvement with the criminal justice system varies. Some incorporate the coercive authority of criminal prosecution into the treatment philosophy; others shun legal coercion as antithetical to the therapeutic process (MacFarlane and Bulkley, 1982).

Notes

1. These are guaranteed by the fourth and sixth amendments of the U.S. Constitution.
2. Long before jurisdictions began adopting innovative approaches, a 1969 law review article suggested proposals for minimizing the trauma of the legal system on child sex offense victims. See Libai, D., "The Protection of the Child Victim of a Sexual Offense in the Criminal Justice System." *Wayne Law Review* 15 (1969): 977.
3. *Ohio v. Roberts,* 448 U.S. 55 (1979).
4. *Hochheiser v. Superior Court,* No. 5005940 (Cal. Ct. App. Nov. 9, 1984 aff'd Cal. S. Ct.)
5. *U.S. v. Benfield,* 593 F.2d 815 (8th Cir. 1979); *Herbert v. Superior Court,* 172 Cal. Rptr. 850 (Cal. Ct. App. 1981).
6. *Commonwealth v. Willis,* No. 84CR346 (Ky. Cir. Ct. Feb. 20, 1985).
7. *State v. Strable,* 313 N.W. 2d 497 (Iowa 1981); *State v. Sheppard,* 484 A.2d 1330 (N.J. Super. Ct. 1984).
8. *Kansas City v. McCoy,* 525 S.W. 2d 336 (Mo. 1976).
9. S.B. 46, amending Cal. Pen. Code 1347.
10. Slightly revised version of testimony before Juvenile Justice Subcommittee.
11. *State v. Myers,* No. C8-82-1031 (Minn. S. Ct. Dec. 21, 1984); *Smith v. State,* No. 15309 (Nev. S. Ct. Oct. 4, 1984); *State v. Middleton,* 657 P.2d 1215 (Or. 1983); *State v. Kim,* 645 P.2d 1330 (Hawaii 1982).
12. *State v. Myers.*

References

Berliner, L. and M. K. Barbieri. "The Testimony of the Child Victim of Sexual Assault." *The Child Witness* 40:2 (1984). Special issue of *Journal of Social Issues.*

Berliner, L., L. Blick and J. Bulkley. "Expert Testimony on the Dynamics of Intrafamily Child Sexual Abuse and Principles of Child Development." In J. Bulkley (Ed.), *Child Sexual Abuse and the Law.* Washington, DC: American Bar Association, 1981.

Berliner, L. and D. Stevens. "Advocating for Sexually Abused Children in the Criminal Justice System." In B. Jones and K. MacFarlane (Eds.), *Sexual Abuse of Children: Selected Readings.* Washington, DC: DHHS, 1980.

Besharov, D. "The Legal Aspects of Reporting Known and Suspected Child Abuse and Neglect." *Villanova Law Review* 23 (1977-78): 495.

Bulkley, J., Ed., *Innovations in the Prosecution of Child Sexual Abuse Cases.* Washington, DC: American Bar Association, 1981.

Bulkley, J. *Recommendations for Improving Legal Intervention in Intrafamily Child Sexual Abuse Cases.* Washington, DC: American Bar Association, 1982.

Bulkley, J. "Evidentiary and Procedural Trends in State Legislation and Other Emerging Trends in Child Sexual Abuse Cases." *Dickinson Law Review* 89 (1985): 645.

Bulkley, J. and H. Davidson. *Child Sexual Abuse—Legal Issues and Approaches.* Washington, DC: American Bar Association, 1980.

Davidson, H. and R. Horowitz. "Protection of Children from Family Maltreatment." In R. Horowitz and H. Davidson (Eds.), *Legal Rights of Children.* Washington, DC: American Bar Association, 1984.

Davidson, H., R. Horowitz, T. Marvell and O. Ketchum, *Child Abuse and Neglect—A Manual for Judges.* Washington, DC: American Bar Association, 1980.

DeFrancis, V. *Protecting the Child Victim of Sexual Assault.* Denver: American Humane Association, 1969.

Finkelhor, David. *Sexually Victimized Children.* New York: The Free Press, 1979.

Giarretto, H., A. Giarretto and S. Sgroi. "Coordinated Community Treatment of Incest." In A. W. Burgess, A. N. Groth, L. L. Holstrom and S. Sgroi (Eds.), *Sexual Assault of Children and Adolescents.* Lexington, MA: Lexington Books, 1978.

Goodman, G. "Children's Memory and the Law." In Papers from a National Policy Conference on Legal Reforms in Child Sexual Abuse Cases. Washington, DC: American Bar Association, 1985.

Johnson, M. and M. Foley. "Differentiating Fact and Fantasy: The Reliability of a Child's Memory." *The Child Witness* 40:2 (1984). Special issue of *The Journal of Social Issues.*

Kocen, L. and J. Bulkley. "Analysis of Criminal Sex Offense Statutes." In J. Bulkley (Ed.), *Child Sexual Abuse and the Law.* Washington, DC: American Bar Association, 1981.

Loftus, E. and G. Davies. "Distortions in the Memory of Children." *The Child Witness* 40:2 (1984). Special issue of *The Journal of Social Issues.*

MacFarlane, K. "Sexual Abuse of Children." *Resource Materials.* Washington, DC: DHHS, 1979.

MacFarlane, K. "Diagnostic Evaluations and the Use of Videotape in Child Sexual Abuse Cases." In Paper from a National Policy Conference on Legal Reforms in Child Sexual Abuse Cases. Washington, DC: American Bar Association, 1985.

MacFarlane, K. and J. Bulkley. "Treating Child Sexual Abuse: An Overview of Current Program Models." *Social Work and Child Abuse* 1:1 and 2 (1982).

Melton, G. "Sexually Abused Children and the Legal System: Some Policy Recommendations." *American Journal of Family Therapy* 13 (1985): 61.

Melton, G., J. Bulkley and D. Wulkan. "Competency of Children as Witnesses," In J. Bulkley (Ed.), *Child Sexual Abuse and the Law.* Washington, DC: American Bar Association, 1981.

Mnookin, R. "Foster Care—In Whose Best Interest?" *Harvard Educational Review* 43 (1973): 599.

Papers from a National Policy Conference on Legal Reforms in Child Sexual Abuse Cases. Washington, DC: American Bar Association, 1985.

Roe, B. "Expert Testimony in Child Sexual Abuse Cases." In Papers from a National Policy Conference on Legal Reforms in Child Sexual Abuse Cases. Washington, DC: American Bar Association, 1985.

Sgroi, Suzanne. "Introduction: A National Needs Assessment for Protecting Child Victims of Sexual Assault." In A. W. Burgess, A. Groth, L. L. Holmstrom and S. Sgroi (Eds.), *Sexual Assault of Children and Adolescents.* Lexington, MA: Lexington Books, 1978.

U.S. Department of Justice, *Final Report of the Attorney General's Task Force on Family Violence.* September, 1984.

Wald, M. "State Intervention on Behalf of Neglected Children: A Search for Realistic Standards." *Stanford Law Review* 27 (1975): 985.

Guidelines for Prevention Education

Chapter 8

Child Sexual Abuse Prevention: Keys to Program Success

CAROL A. PLUMMER

Defining Program Success

In a field as new as child sexual abuse prevention, there is bound to be confusion about what constitutes program success. To assist those who are beginning or maintaining programs, this article will outline specific guidelines.

First, what program success *isn't*. One criteria inappropriate to prevention goals is counting the number of children who say "that happened to me." While this secondary outcome is a benefit in securing help for those victims, it should never be construed as a primary objective of a prevention program.[1] Don't stake your reputation on numbers of reports. Your program may well have great value without procuring many reports.

Other criteria also used inappropriately to sell a program to a community must be discarded for ethical reasons. Proponents may wish for a program that can be implemented quickly, easily, inexpensively, and is acceptable to all. Schools, for example, will often settle for buying a comic or coloring book for all students and be done with the issue. It's inexpensive, takes little time from academic subjects, re-

quires minimal or no training of teachers, can appease parents that the school has a "prevention program," and sounds like a beneficial but noncontroversial endeavor in the local media. The catch is, of what value is this to children? This must be the ultimate question when evaluating the success of any program.

In order to help assure program success, advocates are working hard to glean the needs of children by initiating research into program effectiveness. Although this article will not go into depth regarding the need for or outcome of prevention research, all prevention practitioners should be aware of some of the essential issues being grappled with, and the major findings of the research.[2]

When looking at how to evaluate the impact of educational programs for children about sexual abuse, most researchers focus on the following:

1. What knowledge is learned or attitudes changed by the program?
2. What skills have been acquired?
3. How long do the benefits of the program last? How often does the information need to be repeated?

4. What is the most effective method to disseminate this information to children (films, curricula, plays, puppet shows, books, TV, etc.)?

To highlight findings, there is significant learning of facts from preschool through high school with a variety of programs and approaches. Attitudes, especially those regarding victim-blaming, are more resistant to change. There may be, even at the elementary level, some differences between boys and girls in learning. There is a benefit to "booster sessions" to reiterate basic concepts since retention declines greatly by eight months (for 5th graders).[3] We know little about the differences seen by comparing the benefits of various programs or techniques. Actual skill acquisition has not been adequately examined by any program. (For more specifics on program evaluation/research, see "Evaluating Prevention Education Programs" by Dr. Jon Conte in this volume.)

Increasingly, those promoting prevention are beginning to consider what unexpected or unanticipated results may occur besides primary prevention of sexual abuse. Some programs, though certainly well-meaning, may actually be counter-productive, or even harmful for children's emotional development. Messages disseminated to children need to be clear and factually-based (or at least not inaccurate). Messages should not instill undue fear or anxiety, and, most importantly, they must be *understandable*.

Some examples of unintentional and inadvertent mistakes that create problems are[*]:

- A child leaves a program believing only mice can be sexually abused because that is what the slide show depicted.

- A child takes home a coloring book that says to tell a dog (or bear or other animal) if he/she is sexually abused. He/she hasn't identified one person as a resource.
- A child tries self-defense when approached and is severely physically harmed.
- A past victim (age 8) reads a book about "bad touch" and doesn't realize it is about sexual abuse.
- Children are given antitouch or antisex messages by a program and learn that all sexual expression is "bad."
- Graphic examples of "stranger danger" given by prevention instructions produce nightmares for some children.
- A child who says no, and says he/she will tell is abused anyway. Guilt and confusion result since he/she tried to do everything right and it didn't work.

Though these examples represent only a few of the actual or potential situational dilemmas, they point out the fragility of this direct education with children. Recognizing that we have collectively reached over one million children with school prevention programs, each of these pitfalls may have confounded dozens or even hundreds of impressionable children.

In essence, program success must consider the total effect of the intervention, assessing both anticipated and unanticipated results. First the program needs clear goals and objectives and must be taught by those who adhere to the content and process prescribed. Second, a

---

[*]NOTE: These examples are not necessarily critiques of the materials used or of the programs, but may reflect on *how* the materials were used or misused.

change in children's knowledge, attitudes and skills as a result of the program should be evaluated. Simply counting the number of reports generated is not adequate evaluation. Expedience, cost or ease should not weigh more heavily in consideration than the actual value of the program to children. To assess the value of programs, educators need to remain informed and keep updated on current research on child sexual abuse prevention. Finally, with prevention education so new and experimental, educators need to be aware that negative consequences could unintentionally occur. Programs must continually be monitored and improved to avoid pitfalls.

Success Check Points

The prevention programs this article addresses are those teaching sexual abuse prevention directly to children. (This is not to minimize the need for other prevention efforts including parent education and community awareness, but to clarify the scope of this article.) These programs may be in the school system or associated with clubs or extracurricular activities. They may be fledgling and new, or fairly stable but in need of clarification to maintain impetus. I address direct education programs because of their crucial role as the "last front" of prevention. These programs are needed in every area of the country, beginning with preschool children and continuing through to high school seniors. When we as adults and caregivers cannot insure safety round-the-clock, we owe it to children to arm them with tools for self-protection.

The recommendations included in this article are based on three sources. First, my own professional work with incest and sexual abuse victims since 1977 plus my involvement in the child sexual abuse prevention movement since 1979 are incorporated. As project director of Bridgework Theater's sexual abuse prevention program, I co-authored and piloted their plays, *Out of the Trap* and *Little Bear*, and wrote and piloted a curriculum, *Preventing Sexual Abuse*. Since 1980 I have provided consultation and training to many midwestern communities on initiating school prevention programs. Secondly, I have consulted with various colleagues who have also been working to prevent sexual abuse. For example, Cordelia Anderson from Illusion Theater has shared her extensive knowledge about successful and problematic prevention programs in every state in the United States as well as internationally. Third, an open-ended questionnaire was sent to sixteen prevention programs in Indiana, all in existence for two or more years, to determine their unique situations and solicit their advice to others.[4] The following "Success Check Points" are a compilation of major issues recognized by these three sources of information.

Check Point 1: Identify Leadership

Prevention programs are most often initiated by a person, or a few people, who get "fired up" about the atrocity of child sexual abuse and want to do something *now* to end it. These advocates may be parents of past victims or an energized social worker inspired by a conference. Their determination and drive spark the idea of educating children and may launch the whole community in the direction of program implementation. This impetus is essential, yet it will not sustain a program over time.

A cross-disciplinary task force or committee, organized to focus on the community's response to child sexual abuse, is often the necessary next step to turn the spark of an idea into a fire of activity. These groups, often comprised of law enforcement, medical, social service, and educational professionals as well as parents and community volunteers, may organize with a broad focus on child abuse or sexual assault. It is important, however, to make certain that the issues of children, sexual abuse and prevention are not lost in a committee with too broad a scope. For this reason, I recommend a distinctive task force be formulated to begin child sexual abuse prevention in a community. Once a program has been started, supervision, updates and maintenance may be accomplished as a part of a larger, more comprehensive committee (Child Abuse and Neglect Council or Committee on Family Violence, for example).

There are many jokes about the inefficiency of a committee in accomplishing any task. However, the value of committees is obvious. A committee implies broad-based support among professionals working together to impact on general community awareness. On the other hand, a committee or task force has weaknesses, one of which can be lack of leadership. Many community agencies can contribute to the effort, but only a few will give the commitment of staff time for program planning and implementation. It is often best to solidify task force leadership with the agency that is most centrally involved with direct prevention education.

Unless at least one agency or organization centrally organizes and commits to an area-wide prevention effort, the concern for prevention activity will soon diminish or die. For example,

one county-wide council developed and printed coloring books with prevention messages for elementary students. These books sat in a closet for two years because no agency had allocated time to determine guidelines for their use or to promote the idea of prevention with parents or school administrators. Without central leadership, endorsed by an interagency committee, territorial fighting may also hinder prevention progress. Often sexual assault centers, incest treatment centers or child abuse agencies may each feel that their particular organization is the most appropriate vehicle for channeling local monies and energy for school programs. Whoever takes organizing leadership for this cause must recognize that it is a long term project and that the support of Child Protective Services will be crucial to their success.

Check Point 2: Proceed Step-By-Step

When a sexual abuse television special or media blitz hits an area, there are bound to be people wondering, "Why don't *we* have a prevention program in our schools?" There may be a push to present a play, puppet show or film to school children *as soon as possible*. While the need *is* urgent, the process will determine the longevity of any prevention program. Certainly the energy behind this push is creative, but it must be tempered by the necessity of starting small and proceeding slowly. Focusing on presentations to children without the necessary groundwork will only backfire and can potentially disillusion people about the value of prevention.

An outline for building a solid program which has been tested in many communities and can serve as a flexible model is:

1. Create interest in child sexual abuse prevention
2. Form an interagency task force
3. Train area professionals in child sexual abuse dynamics and prevention methods
4. Identify prevention leadership
5. Contact schools to raise the issue and build support for school programs
6. Adapt prevention materials/programs to local needs
7. Introduce prevention programs to parents and incorporate their feedback
8. Pilot school programs
9. Evaluate and improve program
10. Train teachers and other school professionals
11. Implement prevention programs in ongoing fashion school-wide
12. Solicit ongoing feedback from parents, youth and professionals

The key to this process, using as much media coverage for public awareness as possible, is perseverance. Some steps will be easy in one locale but present a stumbling block in another. Realistically, this process may take five years or longer. Yet proceeding step by step will take the entire community with you and diminish the possibility of leaving some components behind as potential adversaries. For example, uninformed parents can be formidable foes, but informed parents are not only prevention advocates but have actually demanded such services from their school administrators. Starting small and proceeding slowly and methodically will build a strong foundation for a long term prevention plan.

Check Point 3: Maximize Community Awareness

Initially, prevention programs have sometimes purposely kept a low profile, believing that to publicize a program widely may activate the opposition. At one time, prevention initiators imagined the opposition to programs to be potentially both large and powerful. They feared opposition from parents, teachers, school administrators or anyone concerned with keeping children innocent. All programs with which I am familiar have found the contrary to be true. Community education efforts uncover more proponents than opponents by dispelling fears and misconceptions about program aims.

A study conducted at Bridgework Theater interviewed sixty community leaders about their perception of that prevention program after one year. Results showed that making individuals aware of *and* involved in the program made them overwhelmingly supportive despite initial reservations.[5] Again and again program directors have found that the closer people are to a high quality prevention program, and the more they know about it, the more they actively support it. What this means is that publicity should be sought rather than avoided to help nurture the growth of a community-based prevention effort.

One of the most effective tools for convincing communities of the need for sexual abuse education programs for children is to bring in an outside consultant. For some reason, as we all know, out-of-town people are often assumed to have more expertise. Even if people were not plagued with this bias, professionals are more convinced of program feasibility if someone with a track record of successful prevention experience elsewhere comes to share data and resources and confront apprehensions. A workshop by an outside consultant, even if she/he knows all the same facts as a local person, can be an invaluable door-opener. This training communicates not only that there is a need for prevention, but that such programs have been successful elsewhere.

Once professionals have a commitment to prevention, they usually cooperate to plan for general community awareness. If these professionals work from an interagency committee, they will have a natural network for spreading the information to their agency colleagues and supporters. In addition to this word-of-mouth advertising, many professionals have regular contact with local television and radio stations and newspapers. The use of the media locally should not be underrated, since on the national level, its impact has clearly been demonstrated (*Something About Amelia*, for example). In fact, the media often want to tie local stories to national media events, and thereby cover the local response to a global problem. Prepare simple news releases about your task force, pilot program or community awareness event. Better yet, personally contact media people to discuss your program and inject them with the enthusiasm that produces good articles. They may also be inspired enough to assist you in developing simple public service announcements for radio or TV as a free service to your cause.

Finally, try a kick-off event to introduce the public to the concept of prevention as a partial solution to the problem of child sexual abuse. A panel of speakers or the showing of a film proposed for use in the classroom are possible approaches. The use of highly publicized and creative theatrical presentations often generates maximal turnout and enthusiasm. Even should the audience size disappoint the organizers, the individuals who attend often join the prevention effort and work hard to institute programs for children in the schools. Illusion Theater has prompted the development of dozens of programs through a public presentation of their play, *Touch*, as a first step. Bridgework Theater has also found it to be an effective motivator to present *Out of the Trap*, their prevention play for adolescents and adults.

Check Point 4: Nurture Interagency Support and Involvement

When developing a program from the ground up, professionals in all agencies working with the problem of sexual abuse need to be involved in the planning. If this occurs from the beginning, ownership of the concept and program will be shared, as will the workload. In an era of limited resources, generating the energy and funds for a new, additional program can be difficult at best. Cooperation and coordination of efforts (both of individuals and agencies) is a must to avoid duplication of efforts or any sense of competition. A task force (as discussed under *Leadership*) is a valuable vehicle for such communication and can also serve to promote improved case management by delineating roles and problems in the service delivery system.

An additional benefit of involving the widest range of professionals in planning (police, schools, therapists, child protective services, volunteer agencies, physicians, etc.) is that we are all just learning about both sexual abuse and intervention strategies and can learn best together. Even professionals need training and updating on a regular basis. The task force can serve as a forum for self-education around these issues, thus helping professionals grow together, rather than apart, in their understanding of sexual abuse and how to combat it.

Check Point 5: Involve the Schools

Enlisting representatives from the schools to be part of the task force may take more effort than linking the social service providers, yet the payoff is worthwhile. Since one goal of prevention programs is ultimately to reach children with information, the school as an avenue for that information flow has obvious advantages. Education can occur through other channels, such as Boy Scouts, Camp Fire Girls,[6] or church youth groups, but public schools are the easiest route to the masses of young people. Having school representatives on the task force will give your group direct information about how best to work with the schools (who is likely to be most supportive, what issues will be raised, what is the proper procedure). Additionally, you will have inside advocates, who are perhaps more likely to be trusted by teachers or administrators than social workers would be.

Involvement of the schools will take investment on the part of community human service professionals. Principals, superintendents and teachers are unlikely to attend extra meetings to learn about your proposals. Most often school personnel must be contacted personally to convince them of the need for prevention in the schools. If principals are given the opportunity to preview and critique materials as well as discuss potential problems and their management, they may then allow you time at a teacher meeting or parent association gathering. Often times they will unlock the door for you, but will rely on a larger consensus of the school community to actually make a decision to open the door.

In some school districts, principals have had teachers vote on whether to implement sexual abuse prevention in the school. In others the decision has been shared with a parent advisory board. This is of benefit to the program since it increases community and parent awareness and implies a scrutiny to provide the best for children. So, in addition to the meetings with individual administrators to discuss the prevention concept, several other meetings to explain the program to parents, boards or teachers will demand further time investment. And this, by and large, is separate from trainings that will be necessary if (or when) the program has gained the needed approval to proceed.

Check Point 6: Have Well-Trained Presenters

A prevention presentation to children will only be as good as the people who teach it. So whether the program is a curriculum, play with follow-up or films with discussion, the instructors should be well qualified. This should not preclude use of volunteers, but sober us to realize the importance of this direct work with children, which has been the reason for all the previous groundwork. Difficulties with volunteers have been noted with other programs: burnout, feeling inadequate for the job, turnover (which requires replacement and more training), making the program seem like an "extra" rather than an essential.

Some agencies have designated staff full-time or part-time to actually present programs for children or to train others to present. This seems to be optimal, giving the job more stability and recognition for its importance to the community. In the long run, training regular classroom teachers to present the material makes it more like any other aspect of the child's education, not a special or fringe event, but a regular part of the curriculum (in health class, for example).

The training for teachers to actually use a curriculum with students needs to be a how-to workshop lasting at least four hours. This material is new to teachers and there may be considerable discomfort with the topic. The training needs to provide background information on child sexual abuse, a rationale for prevention, actual classroom objectives and activities, realistic expectations of youth's responses, child abuse reporting protocol, and help for teachers to deal with their own feelings about the topic. If training is short-changed or disregarded, the prevention program will be short-lived. Or perhaps even worse, as some researchers have found, the program given may not be the one intended. Inadequately trained teachers may pass on their own fears, biases or misunderstandings rather than the prevention concepts in the curriculum.

Check Point 7: Adapt Materials to Local Needs

The growth in numbers of films, coloring books, curricula, plays, etc. to help adults tell children about child sexual abuse has overwhelmed persons in the field. Today our problem is not in finding materials so much as selecting the best ones for our particular needs.

The problem of selection is exacerbated by the trend toward marketing. The private sector has kept the prevention movement alive when public monies were scarce for program development or dissemination of results/materials.

One lamentable example is that The National Center for Child Abuse and Neglect was unable to widely distribute the findings or materials generated from the six demonstration projects. (See Chapter 1, "Prevention Education in Perspective.") Private monies have promoted a particular play or approach but advertising to stay alive has sometimes made programs resistant to criticism or change and created a competitive spirit rather than the exploratory seeking and sharing that characterized early prevention work. What this means is that most programs promote themselves; indeed marketing has been the only way to stay alive to promote prevention at all.

The warning to those seeking to begin a program is to ask around, check the track records of programs, request proof of value or research results, scrutinize the overt and covert messages in the program/play/film/book. Remember that some programs were designed for or tested with, for example, third graders, yet claim to be useful with K-6. In my experience, however, a puppet show that works with first graders may bore fourth graders. What works well may even vary from one school to another. *Out of the Trap* works well with some schools' sixth graders but may be too sophisticated for another school.

Many prevention endeavors have "reinvented the wheel" partly due to lack of information and no network of communication among programs. As already stated, particularly with limited resources, we need to build upon the work of others rather than to simply rearrange their materials to create our own. For example, there are plenty of good coloring books, yet many groups spend time doing another rather than filling unmet needs (such as for a pamphlet for parents). When the materials available are adequate and already tested, there is no need to start again, only to adapt them for your particular needs.

To adapt rather than simply adopt a program, find what is available in prevention materials, select the most useful of these, and add to the original program's unique aspects based on local needs. This avoids the extreme of blindly accepting a program being marketed and the opposite extreme of re-creating an entire program when knowledge of the successes and failures of others could save time and mistakes.

Check Point 8: Seek Parent Endorsement and Involvement

Parents are the most powerful allies of a prevention program. Initially program developers were apprehensive that parents would not understand or support giving such explicit information to their children. The fact is that parents have seldom questioned and often welcomed the introduction of child sexual abuse prevention into the schools. Parents, more than anyone else, desire safety for their children and often feel a helplessness in the face of this problem. The helplessness they feel is twofold. Parents know they cannot completely protect and shield children from the world, and yet feel inadequate about talking to children themselves about child sexual abuse. For these reasons, parental support of prevention programs has been overwhelming.

The key to channeling parents' concern into support for prevention is education and involvement. Parent groups (PTA) should be contacted and presented workshops about the problem, solutions and roles they can play. Parent involvement has ranged from organizing a volunteer theater group to perform a prevention play, to PTA funding of a teacher training in the use of a prevention curriculum. In Indiana, through leadership of the Fort Wayne PTA Council, the entire state PTA organization may follow the Fort Wayne model of spearheading the local prevention efforts in the schools.[7]

Other ways to involve parents include parent trainings (in discussing prevention with their children), informational letters sent to parents before or after a program, inviting parents to presentations, or asking for feedback based on their children's responses to a program. The more active the parents are encouraged to be in prevention, the more successful the program.

Check Point 9: Develop a Long Term Plan

There is little point in expending all this energy for prevention if the program push is to get in the schools for a one-time only event. Since new children enter school every year, a program needs to get into the schools and stay in the schools. With the problem so widespread there is no chance we will eradicate a community's problem with a play for the entire school if we then do nothing more for three years. Yet this has happened all too frequently. The momentum for prevention should not stop with a one-shot program, but ignite a renewed investment toward implementation as a regular part of the school curriculum.

If the long haul is planned for from the beginning, many problems can be anticipated and momentum sustained because expectations will be more realistic. Careful planning requires both short term and long term objectives being accomplished side-by-side. While convincing a PTA council about the need for a puppet show for third graders, prevention proponents may also be working to draft a new health curriculum to place sexual abuse prevention in all seventh grade classes two years in the future.

It is a good idea to plan for data collection for research or evaluation purposes as soon as a program is established. One reason for this may be for program justification to funding sources. Another motivation is for feedback and improvement. Careful design of a pilot program for a school or classroom is recommended before widespread implementation. Finally, methodologically sound research on the impact of prevention programs is necessary to develop this field further and add to our collective knowledge base in order to more effectively prevent child abuse. If conducting program evaluation or research, practitioners must stay open to new findings in order to be ethical in our service delivery. This is especially true since prevention education is still experimental. Just in the past few years, for example, has come awareness that we must provide better prevention approaches for preschools and day care centers. One county reported a 200 percent increase in reports of sexual abuse one year after the prevention program. This may not prove that the program caused the increased reporting but does indicate a possible correlation as well as the need for additional intervention and treatment programs.

Communication with other prevention pro-grams also helps a community anticipate possible problems and borrow from successful endeavors, both essential for long term planning. Finding funds for program continuation is a common problem, yet one court has ordered offenders to pay "fines" to the local prevention program. This type of information can be shared and a professional camaraderie developed through newsletters and formal or informal gatherings of prevention workers at regional or national child abuse or sexual assault conferences.

Conclusion

In 1979 two progressive principals, colleagues as well as friends, sincerely questioned the need for school child sexual abuse prevention as I attempted to gain access to my first classroom. Today, only six years later, prevention programs are being introduced city-wide in places like Philadelphia, where they hope to train about 7,000 teachers in the use of a prevention curriculum. Individually, many of us have blundered our way through parent meetings, teacher trainings and embarrassing questions from children in classrooms. We have never had all the answers. Still, many of us have collected experience in prevention education; hands-on knowledge that we need to communicate with one another.

Communication is the greatest enemy of child sexual abuse. When parents and other caregivers brainstorm together about child sexual abuse prevention, their awareness levels and protective ability increase, and are one safeguard to children. When adults inform and listen to children, uncomfortable feelings can be discussed to prevent or intervene in potentially sexually abusive situations. When professionals nationwide share their ideas, research results and failures there will be constant improvement in our techniques and in the results of prevention efforts. When prevention programs are securely funded, regularly given and professionally monitored in every school in the country, we will be a formidable challenge to silencing the dragon of sexual abuse.

Notes

1. All prevention programs, however, need to have a clear commitment to and process for reporting all suspected child abuse. This necessitates a close relationship with local child protection agencies, who should minimally be informed in advance of all presentations to school children. Prevention proponents should anticipate that programs are likely to generate self-reports. At one school where Bridgework Theater performed for 1200 teens, six victims reported immediately after the play and within one month almost fifty reports were made from that school.

2. For an overview of early research on prevention, see Conte, Jon R. "Research on the Prevention of Sexual Abuse of Children." Paper presented at Second National Conference for Family Violence Researchers. Durham, NH, August 7-10, 1984.

3. Plummer, Carol A. "Preventing Sexual Abuse: What In-School Programs Teach Children." Paper presented at Second National Conference for Family Violence Researchers. Durham, NH, August 7-10, 1984. For more information contact Carol A. Plummer, P.O. Box 421, Kalamazoo, MI 49005-0421.

4. The programs from which advice was solicited were taken from the "Indiana Prevention Directory," which I compiled while at Bridgework Theater in 1983. They are located in the following Indiana communities: Fort Wayne, Goshen, Elkhart, South Bend, Gary, Anderson, Martinsville, Michigan City, Indianapolis, Columbus, Crawfordsville, Lafayette, Muncie, Rensselaer, and Vincennes.

5. It is interesting to note that whereas 78 percent of the interviewed community members claimed they had no initial reluctance to working with the prevention program, 76 percent felt that *other* members of the community would have hesitations.

6. For information on a program with Camp Fire complete with a comprehensive research study, contact Andrea Overvold or Yvonne Lutter, Sexual Victimization Prevention Project, Worcester Area Mental Health Center, 105 Merrick Street, Worcester, MA 01609.

7. For more information on the work of the Fort Wayne Parent Teacher Association, contact The Committee for the Prevention of Sexual Abuse of Children (PRE-SAC), Fort Wayne PTA Council, P.O. Box 5404, Fort Wayne, IN 46895.

Chapter 9

Training Teachers to Be Partners in Prevention

ANN DOWNER

The explosion of public awareness about the sexual abuse of children has affected public and private schools. In some cases, pressure for personal safety programs has resulted in quickly developed curricula and bewildered teachers. In other cases, schools have turned to community resources for help that was there all along, but never before welcomed.

The first to feel the pressure of public opinion, schools are in a dilemma. While attempting to respond to the educational needs of children, opinions about what children need change from person to person. Schools are left open to criticism from all sides. A program thought to be in the best interests of a majority of children is inevitably unacceptable to a minority of parents. Schools are often accused of responding to fads when they adopt curricula that reflect issues of public concern. Yet, lack of innovation yields the complaint that schools don't respond to changing times. In addition to these problems, financial support for schools is dwindling while expectations of excellence accelerate.

In the midst of the debates and confused expectations, the teacher is the ultimate target.

She/he feels the direct effects of changing policy, limited resources and curriculum pressure. Teachers are asked to do "more with less." They are asked to respond to decisions made by people several times removed from the classroom. They are asked to maintain an innovative yet basic educational program for thirty children from vastly differing cultural and economic backgrounds. Each year issues of topical interest to the general public filter down to the classroom in the form of new curricula, and each year teachers are asked to find time to add another curriculum to their already crowded day.

And yet, teachers are remarkably focused on the tasks of teaching and advocating for children. At a recent Committee for Children training on child sexual abuse prevention, several teachers paid for their own classroom substitutes in order to attend the three-day session.

Why do we still see this sort of commitment at a time when the public assumes teachers need inducements and public pressure to excel? Because teachers, better than any other group of professionals, know the real needs of children. They understand a simple truth: children who are struggling to just survive emotionally, physically or psychologically *don't learn* unless their situation changes.

The disputes over basic education, the role of schools, integration, educational excellence, test scores and family life education all fade in importance when a teacher faces a child who has been initiated into the responsibilities of adulthood before he/she is able to share in its pleasures. Such children are the daily fare of teachers. Teachers already know that children suffer. They suffer from divorce; family violence; alcohol problems; physical, sexual or psychological abuse; hunger; illness. Children are guileless and provide a window into the family. During a career, a teacher sees every type of family and many thefts of childhood.

Few people deny the critical importance of prevention and early intervention in child sexual abuse. Fewer people yet fail to recognize the vital and logical role of teachers in the prevention process. But schools cannot assume their role effectively without radical changes in community support and public funding. It is not enough to raise awareness regarding child sexual abuse and then rely on public pressure for schools to "do something about it." It is not enough to teach child sexual abuse prevention one year and replace it with something else the next. And it is not enough to mandate a new curriculum without allocating adequate time and funds to assure its success.

The clearest channel for reaching children who need help is through the schools. School professionals are ready to help but need their problems and concerns acknowledged.

Barriers to Program Implementation

The barriers to implementing prevention programs can only be overcome if they are first clearly identified. What are these barriers?

Time

Available time is by far the most critical issue for teachers. They have very little time for lesson planning, developing new material, attending training or searching through resource materials. Programs that demand a lot of preparation or teaching time are unrealistic for most teachers.

Fears

The subject of sexual exploitation is not one that most adults have been prepared to discuss. Most people have misgivings about their own ability to do an adequate job of explaining personal safety to children. In addition, teachers are often concerned about the reaction of parents to a sexual abuse prevention program in the classroom. Teachers fear the possible negative effects such discussions might have on children and some have irrational fears about their own immunity from suspicion.

Materials

Teachers want materials that are intended for educational purposes. They need spontaneous access to curriculum materials if they hope to capitalize upon "teachable moments." Prevention materials should be appropriate to the developmental level or age of the child.

Few teachers in the United States today have homogeneous classrooms. Prevention tools must be diverse enough to address the needs of an entire class, not a narrow cross-section of it.

Support

Teachers are seldom able to maintain enthusiasm for a program if it does not have the support of other teachers and the administration. Similarly, principals are seldom willing to support a program that is criticized by parents or receives no endorsement from the district. Thus, new curricula are usually set aside after a time if they are not a clear priority in a district or with school personnel and parents.

The barriers to the creation of school-based sexual abuse prevention programs can be overcome. Proper teacher training, adequate classroom materials, and good planning at the district level can engender support and assure success.

Training

Teacher training in sexual abuse prevention is important even if teachers will not be teaching a prevention program themselves. The best sexual abuse prevention programs give the clear message to children that, "Touching problems happen to some children and this school is a place to get help." All teachers need to know: (1) what indicators are typical of sexual abuse, (2) what reporting means and how a report is handled, (3) how to talk to a child who may need help, and (4) how to respond if a child asks for help. In addition, those actually teaching prevention lessons need to know how to talk to children about personal safety; how to answer their questions and address their concerns.

Training Environment

The foremost task of the trainer is to establish a climate of mutual respect and trust. Trainers should be too busy to lecture during the first 15 minutes of training. Instead they should find out what people's needs are, validate their concern for children and recognize the legitimacy of any fears. They need to meet the issue of discomfort head-on, acknowledge that men can feel "guilty by association" when child sexual abuse is discussed, and make it clear that men are needed in prevention efforts. Sexual abuse is a human problem. Women and men together must formulate the solution.

The creation of a comfortable training environment can occur only if individuals are treated with respect. Teachers have attended lots of training. They expect, and deserve, to skip the basics and get into the real issues of classroom management and skill enhancement. The experience of teachers in the group can be tapped as a major resource for learning. A trainer of teachers is, at best, a "guide on the side," not, as so often happens, a "sage on the stage."

Proper teacher training must influence four areas:

- information
- attitude
- behavior
- on-the-job action

In addition, training must be brief, relevant to the daily classroom environment of teachers and sympathetic to educators' constraints.

Aspects of Teacher Training

Information

The basic information that must be offered includes examples of what child sexual abuse means and does not mean, brief review of statistics and their relevance, discussion of behavioral, familial and physical indicators, and an explanation of state and district policy governing reporting.

Basic information regarding child sexual abuse can be communicated efficiently through lectures with question-and-answer format. A trainer can give "listening assignments" to encourage discussion after a brief presentation. This simple method involves asking a group to listen to a presenter with a particular question in mind. For instance, "What do treatment methods tell us about how to design a good prevention program?" Much factual information can be presented in written form, read and talked about in time-limited discussion or buzz groups. Films and prepared videotapes can be appropriate informational methods, but are often irrelevant, long or dull. Usually, people would rather talk.

Attitude

A more important area in training involves the fostering of positive attitudes regarding prevention and the role a teacher can play. A trainer can greatly influence attitude by modeling comfort with the subject and skill in speaking to children.

People often need an opportunity to talk in small groups about their confusion, anger, fear and reservations about child sexual abuse and its prevention. Task groups of three to five allow quiet individuals a chance to express themselves. Sustained interaction in a task group also provides an opportunity for people to hear differing opinions and can help them clarify their own thoughts and feelings.

Behavior

Influencing a teacher's ability to respond confidently and effectively to the needs of a child is the heart of teacher training. Information is not enough. People need a chance to translate information into new skills and behaviors. Case studies enhance a teacher's ability to analyze a situation and predict a response. This mental practice is encouraged by several methods including role play, tape recording or videotape with playback, demonstrations with practice sessions, simulation games, and "critical incident" training. If teachers will be teaching prevention, they need to observe excellent modeling of lessons and have an opportunity to practice the lessons until they are comfortable and ready to try them with their students.

On-the-Job Action

Finally, it is often necessary to provide time for the group to plan strategies for program implementation. For instance, questions usually arise about protocol for reporting, contacting parents if a report is made, access to materials, issues of parental consent. Who will substitute for teachers who aren't yet ready to teach personal safety lessons? Where will personal safety fit in the overall curriculum? These and other questions are best addressed in small planning sessions with reports back to the large group (if the group must be divided for discussion).

Materials

Good materials are another part of the solution for overcoming the barriers to school-based prevention programs. Many types of programs exist. Among them are:
- theater presentations
- curricula for daily classroom use
- audiovisual presentations
- guest speakers
- puppet shows

Guest speakers to a school need at least some background in educational issues. The author, in a recent discussion with a police officer who taught safety courses to elementary students, was told that his presentation consisted of a brief recital of police statistics on rape and sexual assault and a longer admonishment "not to go away with strangers." This type of information is neither age-appropriate nor consistent with educational principles. Similarly, in a telephone conversation several years earlier, the author was informed of a strategy an "educator" was using to discover cases of sexual abuse. She made a presentation on sexual abuse in a school assembly. At the conclusion, she asked everyone who had a sexual abuse problem to raise a hand. Teachers were supposed to note the children who did so and talk to them later. Not surprisingly, few children exposed themselves in this fashion.

On the other hand, many excellent community-based prevention programs visit classrooms. These programs engage children in age-appropriate dialogue and interaction, helping children understand and practice prevention skills through question-answer, theater and role play formats. It is often more acceptable to school staff for specialists to visit the classrooms than for the teacher to teach prevention him/herself. Community-based prevention programs also offer the teacher a support system if he/she is struggling with the question of reporting. They can help with the report itself or simply offer advice and moral support.

Materials for use by teachers should also be age appropriate. They should include a scope and sequence which suggests guidelines for implementation in each grade. Classroom lessons require clarity of purpose, learning objectives, guidance for structured discussion, and brevity to be realistic and useful to teachers. If possible, each teacher needs a set of materials, or, at the very least, ready access to them. Material durability is also an important quality. All classroom curricula should include the results of evaluation and field-testing. This information is useful for suggesting areas to be emphasized or supplemented by additional resources.

A combination of materials seems to work best for schools. For instance, several school districts in Washington state use one curriculum for kindergarten, another for grades one through four, a third curriculum for grades five and six, and a fourth for grades seven through twelve. These are accompanied by a self-defense course taught in physical education classes and a live theater presentation to all schools once a year.

Even strong school-based curricula benefit from interaction with complementary resources from the community. Video and film are popular program supplements. In 1985, Seattle's Committee for Children and the California affiliates of C.A.P. (Child Assault Prevention) Project cooperated on a training to demonstrate the compatibility of prevention methods. Schools can choose both models now, rather than choosing between them. The Committee for Children's *Talking About Touching* curriculum can be used by classroom teachers after the C.A.P. workshops for parents, staff and children. It is felt that a combination of models is the strongest option.

Criteria for appropriate materials are constant for all types of prevention programs. All programs should contain the following messages:

Personal safety means:

1. knowing it's okay to ask an adult for help if a child is touched on the breast, penis, vulva or vagina for no good reason (health or hygiene) by a bigger or older person;
2. knowing it's okay to say no to an older person who touches a child's bottom or other private parts or asks to be touched on their private parts for no good reason;
3. knowing that not *all* children have touching problems, but *some* children do and they need to know it's not their fault;
4. knowing children can try to say no, but even if they can't, or don't want to, or try unsuccessfully to say no, that the touching problem *still* isn't their fault;
5. knowing that children can have touching problems with anyone, even someone they know;
6. knowing that children should tell if they have a touching problem;
7. knowing it's never too late to tell;
8. knowing that most older people make good decisions about touching children;
9. knowing who to tell if they ever have a touching problem.

Planning

Good planning is the third solution to the school-based prevention education problem. Planning requires six steps:

1. review of existing prevention programs and local community resources by a team including teacher, administrators, parents and professionals from the community;
2. selection of one or more prevention programs;
3. a plan for parent support and education, teacher preparation, and analysis of the impact on community resources;
4. allocation of adequate funds to assure success;
5. a plan for field-testing, adoption of materials and incorporation into existing curriculum;
6. provision for parent and teacher training.

The chances for success of child sexual abuse prevention programs are diminished when steps in the process are missed. Teachers feel devalued if not invited to participate in decision making. A parent feels defensive if his/her role as an educator goes unacknowledged. Child sexual abuse professionals in the community feel resentful if their caseloads suddenly increase as a result of prevention efforts unless they have been informed in time to prepare for the change. School personnel fail to commit fully to a program that has been underbudgeted and underplanned. They may go along, even enthusiastically, with the program, but typically reprioritize when pressure is removed and time constraints resurface in the curriculum schedule. A district which does not plan carefully for teacher training and parent involvement is, in effect, giving the message, "If you really want to do this, go ahead, but don't look at us."

The Four R's

The real solution to preventing child sexual abuse is not, of course, the business of schools or parents alone. The solution lies in social and cultural perceptions about childhood, the uses of power, sex roles and sexuality. To accomplish social change on this scale, we must turn to social institutions for assistance. Our institutions are charged by society to maintain social norms.

Schools, foremost among our social institutions, are charged with the transfer of knowledge and norms to the children in the culture. What has been the predominant norm regarding child sexual abuse? For centuries, the norm has been to hide and minimize it. The norm has been to support the adult at the expense of the child. Schools have, until now, effectively maintained this norm at the direction of the culture. The rumblings we hear today as schools begin to change are the aches and pains of massive machinery left sitting too long in one spot.

Institutions are slow to change. They should not be confused with individuals, though, who are wonderfully flexible and adaptable and who care intensely about the well-being of children. Let us begin, as a culture, to change the norms surrounding incest and sexual exploitation—to speak out, to empower children, to prepare them for a complex, yet fascinating world. Let us insist that schools teach children *four* R's: reading, writing, arithmetic and reality.

Editor's Note: See "Committee for Children's Talking About Touching" in Part II, Prevention Programs at Work, *for a description of its program components.*

Chapter 10

The Role of the Teacher in Preventing Child Sexual Abuse

I. LORRAINE DAVIS

Although more and more teachers are realizing they have a vital role to play in the intervention and prevention of child sexual abuse, many express an understandable reluctance to bring education about a taboo subject into their classrooms. Teachers *are* interested, concerned, and in many instances, excited about the concepts being projected regarding the prevention of abuse, both physical and sexual. Part of their reluctance may result from the institutional foot-dragging by schools about any subject considered controversial. After all, anything that concerns "sex" must be controversial. This society has failed to come to terms with "normal sexuality," and now we are having to deal with sexual aberrations that can play havoc with a child's psychological and emotional future.

And what about prevention? At this very moment, interminable discussions about the concept of "prevention" are taking place throughout the country. The questions are endless. What is primary prevention? Where does primary prevention end and secondary prevention begin? How can we prove we're preventing abuse if we cannot precisely pin-point the causes? Questions and doubts abound. A better question might be, who's afraid of prevention? We must use our energies to discard "learned helplessness" (West, 1984) and substitute instead the courage and persistence it will take to stop child abuse.

We have in place prevention strategies that work. It's time to start using them. As Sol Gordon (1985) so aptly states:

"Are we so busy that we have lost our common sense which suggests we put most of our energies in trying to reduce the molestation in the first place and prevent it from occurring in the long run?"

If there is a question regarding the necessity of prevention, one need only have an extended conversation with a survivor of child sexual abuse to be convinced. Prevention programs can help to ensure that children are allowed to grow into adulthood rather than being thrown headlong into a morass of perverted adult behavior long before childhood is finished.

Sexual abuse is not an act of sex. It is an act of power, authority and degradation (Kreibich, 1985). The preventive key to sexual abuse, then, is building self-esteem, training for assertiveness and teaching protective behaviors. ". . . teaching . . . children about sexual abuse is as important as any other rule of health and safety . . . the best strategy for prevention is to prepare children so they won't be victims." (Spelman, 1985)

What more, might one ask, do we need to know in order to develop prevention programs that will have a sound base? Ones that are more than a mere mention of a prevention strategy? Ones that are not adapted quickly to meet the needs of the moment and then just as quickly lost or forgotten? Or, worse yet, ones that increase a child's jeopardy?

Each day some new audiovisual material, some new how-to booklet, some new strategy for dealing with sexual abuse is produced. We must, therefore, be careful of the resources we use in our classrooms. Inappropriate materials can only add to the damage and confusion already facing children. And some materials may actually increase the probability of their future victimization.

Teachers need to develop a network for evaluating materials. One suggestion is that a panel of teachers who have been previously involved in child sexual abuse prevention review curriculum materials and make independent evaluations to be shared with other teachers.

Aside from the usual requirements inherent in a good audiovisual presentation or educational curriculum, a resource must be reviewed for its potential to contribute to human growth and development. Does it begin at the children's level? Does it have strategies throughout for engaging the children's help to enhance and build on the curriculum?

The introduction to "Talking with Young Children about Sexual Abuse" includes this statement:

"This bibliography only includes materials that emphasize a positive, nonthreatening approach to sexual abuse education. This approach teaches children how to recognize appropriate and inappropriate touch coming from, or requested by, an older person and shows them that they have the right to control who touches their bodies. Rather than creating a sense of fear, this nonthreatening approach helps children learn to trust their own feelings and gain control over their bodies and lives." (Braune, 1984)

Judging from concerns expressed by a variety of people including teachers, rape crisis staff, college professors, parents, authors, student services personnel and others, it would be well to heed the cautions this bibliographer recommends.

Many sexual abuse materials designed for schools focus upon methods of helping students learn how to protect themselves in various situations and are targeted for use with preschool and K-4 students. Since elementary school children constitute half of all sexual assault victims, this is a vital place to start. However, there should be a continuum of health and safety strategies provided via a variety of approaches from kindergarten through twelfth grade (though it should be emphasized that preschool and K-6 are the crucial times for teaching these materials).

When working with younger children, the safety language and situations will be different from those used with pre-adolescents or adolescents. With young children we may be talking about uncomfortable touch from a babysitter. With an older child we may be talking about resisting an approach by an adult from the family she/he is babysitting for. Or we may be talking about situations that can lead to acquaintance rape.

Curriculum is not the only thing we need to be concerned about in prevention. Another important step is to put our own anxieties and misinformation about sex into perspective. We must learn about normal sexuality, deal with our own feelings, separate fact from myth, and come to grips with some of our confusion about the sexual mores of our culture. It is important to examine our own sexual experiences and values in order to put into proper perspective what is and what is not sexual abuse. The broad spectrum of human sexuality from self-awareness to building relationships should also be taken into account.

Appropriate training is vital if teachers are to become effective sexual abuse prevention educators. This training and awareness becomes more important in light of recent trends among teachers (and parents) who are reluctant to touch children at all because they fear they will be accused of abusing them. Jessie Potter, in *The Touch Film with Dr. Jessie Potter*, clearly points out the importance of touch in intellectual development, in physical and emotional well-being, in the healing process, and in fostering self-esteem. There are several classroom situations in Potter's film illustrating ways teachers impart caring touch to children. Teachers are aware of what constitutes problem touch, but after viewing this film, come away with a sense that it's still all right to pat a student on the back, put an arm around a shoulder, squeeze a hand.

"Sexual child abuse should not be confused with physical contacts between an adult and child that are fond or playful expressions of love. Responsible adults automatically limit their physical exchanges with a child, thereby respecting the child and at the same time maintaining a warm, healthy, affectionate relationship" (Basic Facts, 1978). Potter asserts that we talk a lot about touch in this country but do little of it. This may be one of the reasons we touch so inappropriately. Shayla Lever puts it well, "To deprive children of warm, nurturing touches is just as abusive as intrusive touching . . . An arm around the shoulder, holding hands—that is not intrusive touching." Fear of touching children works at cross purposes to our efforts to eliminate child sexual abuse and creates, for both adults and children alike, a greater probability of victimization.

Obviously, teachers must first be trained both at the preservice and inservice levels. It is a situation of trying to move forward and catch up simultaneously. Training in this instance means learning to sort out attitudes about safety, love and nurturing; about traditional roles of women and men; about violence; about cultural differences in the way boys and girls are raised; and about how we ourselves were raised.

We must also be prepared to educate school board members, superintendents, administrators, principals and other school personnel in the prevention of child sexual abuse. Administrative support is essential, and in order to have that support and understanding, those in decision-making positions must have the same knowledge-base as teachers.

Prevention education for children should cover the following areas:

- Right to safety
- Parenting skills (children as future parents—as nurturers)
- Early childhood development
- Awareness of factors that lead to child abuse
- Family and community living skills
- Awareness of one's potential as a human being
- Strategies for building self-esteem

To date, much of prevention has been victim-centered. But by teaching students the concepts of body safety, we are teaching them not to be abusers as well as not to be victims.

In addition, teachers know how to translate prevention concepts into teachable moments (West, 1984). By watching interactions between children in the classroom or on the school grounds and serving as a model, the teacher can point out behaviors that are acceptable and behaviors that are not. It is an opportunity for the teacher to seize the moment to impart gems of nonacademic wisdom that a child can carry through life. Students can be given a whole new system of vocabulary through this process. For instance, if a teacher observes one student pushing another, she/he might say, "It doesn't look like Jenny wants to be touched in that way!" instead of, "Cut out the horseplay in the hall!"

All this becomes part of the school environment. Students can then transfer this learning to other situations. If these concepts are taught well, there is no need to be fearful of touching. Students in the classroom will tell you when you're touching them in ways that make them feel uncomfortable. You can then reinforce such assertiveness by saying, "Good job. You've learned your lessons well!"

Research indicates that in 85 percent of child sexual abuse cases the victim knows the offender. In 95 percent of cases the offenders are male. In light of these statistics, it is essential for programs to include abuser prevention by teaching students:

- Not to confuse the desire for love and nurturing with the desire for sexual gratification.
- Being gentle, loving and kind is all right.
- Respect for themselves and others.
- Healthy ways to deal with stress, anger, anxiety, etc.

Teachers and parents must pool efforts to protect children from sexual abuse. Together they can learn from one another and share common concerns and positive approaches to prevention. In addition, schools must reach out to local community agencies. The role of the teacher must be performed in concert with the activities of the larger community. There are many prevention programs (perinatal bonding, early childhood, day care, parent education) being tried in communities across the nation and schools should be an integral part of these programs (Gray, 1984). More and more schools are beginning to initiate coalitions with community entities such as advocacy programs, parental stress centers, law enforcement, social services agencies, drug and alcohol rehabilitation centers, public health and mental health centers, rape crisis centers, and others.

Statistics show that five children out of a given classroom of 25, have been, or will be, sexually abused by the time they finish high school. Schools need to develop comprehensive sex education programs. Yet less than 10 percent of public school students are exposed to a meaningful, comprehensive sex education course (Gordon and Dickman, 1980).

There are 264 different magazines and countless films produced every month in the United States depicting children in sexual acts. Seventeen percent of these children are under the age of 13 (Kile, 1984). Teachers can help to counteract this through development of curricula to educate all school personnel about sexual exploitation of children in the media.

Workshops can be conducted within school districts to give teachers a forum for exploring avenues of incorporating safety and sexual abuse prevention techniques into the existing curriculum. For example, English teachers can explore concepts of self-esteem, parenting and feelings with their students either by using literature the class is already studying or selecting specific stories or books with these themes. Art teachers can utilize their skills to provide creative outlets for children. (Art is already being used to help identify troubled children.)

As a society we spend a great deal of time acquiring academic knowledge and too little time learning about our feelings, our wants, and most importantly, how to deal effectively with our common human needs. We are taught:

- If you express anger, you're too aggressive.
- If you cry when you're hurt, you're weak.
- If you reach out to someone, you're a soft touch.
- If you answer softly, you're a patsy.

Therefore, we downplay the affective side of ourselves and others.

The latest thrust in school curriculum is to be "concerned with the whole child." It must be assumed this means the affective as well as the cognitive needs of children. In order to come near the goal of shaping a better society for future generations, it is imperative that we teach future parents the coping skills so they can love and nurture children rather than mutilate their minds, bodies and spirits (Davis, 1977).

References

Anderson, Deborah. "Touching: When Is It Caring and Nurturing or When Is It Exploitative and Damaging?" Unpublished manuscript. Hennipen County Attorney's Office. Minneapolis, MN.

"Basic Facts About Sexual Child Abuse." Chicago: National Committee for the Prevention of Child Abuse, 1978.

Braune, Joan. "Talking with Young Children About Sexual Abuse: A Guide for Parents." An Annotated Bibliography. (December 1984) p. 2.

Broadhurst, Diane D. "The Educator's Role in the Prevention and Treatment of Child Abuse and Neglect." Washington, DC: DHEW Publication No. (OHDS) 79-30172, 1979.

"Child Abuse and Neglect." *Victimology: An International Journal* 2:2 (Summer 1977): 175-414.

Davis, I. Lorraine. "Child Abuse and Neglect: The Role of the School." *The Wisconsin Counselor* (September 1977): 6-7.

Education Commission of the States. "Education for Parenthood: A Primary Prevention Strategy for Child Abuse and Neglect." Report No. 93. Denver: ECS, 1976.

Gordon, Sol. "Any Messages for the Child Molester? . . . The Rapist?" *IMPACT '85* 8 (1985): 4.

Gordon, S. and I. Dickman. "Schools and Parents—Partners in Sex Education." New York: Public Affairs Pamphlets, 1980.

Gray, Ellen. "What Have We Learned About Preventing Child Abuse? An Overview of the Community and Minority Group Action to Prevent Child Abuse and Neglect." Unpublished manuscript. National Committee for Prevention of Child Abuse, 1984.

Halperin, Michael. *Helping Maltreated Children: School and Community Involvement.* St. Louis, MO: The C.V. Mosby Company, 1979.

Helfer, M. D. and E. Ray. *Child Abuse: A Plan for Prevention.* Chicago: National Committee for Prevention of Child Abuse, 1978.

Kile, Marilyn J. "What Would You Do If . . . ? A Guide to Teaching Young Children to Protect Themselves from Sexual Abuse and Exploitation." Ft. Atkinson, WI, 1984.

Kreibich, Nancy. Workshop Presentation on Child Sexual Abuse. La Crosse, WI, April 1985.

Lever, Shayla. "Spotlight on Child Abuse Alters Rela-tionships." *Kenosha Sunday News,* May 26, 1985.

Lofquist, William A. "Defining and Operationalizing 'Prevention'—A Major Human Service Task." Tucson, AZ: Associates for Youth Development, Inc. 1977.

Spelman, Cornelia. "Talking About Child Sexual Abuse." Chicago: National Committee for the Prevention of Child Abuse, 1985.

The Touch Film with Dr. Jessie Potter. Chicago: Sterling Productions, Inc., 1984.

Wasow, Mona. "Workshop on the Sexual Problems of the Retarded and the Adolescent." *Social Work in Education.* 1:4 (July 1979): 56.

West, Peg Flandeau. *Protective Behaviors: Anti-Victim Training for Children, Adolescents and Adults.* Madison, Wisconsin: Protective Behaviors, 1984.

Chapter 11

Parents as Primary Prevention Educators

CAREN ADAMS AND JENNIFER FAY

Parents Are Primary

The goal of insuring that all children have information to protect themselves from child sexual abuse might seem most easily met through school programs. Children are gathered there, teachers are trained professionals, and resources such as films and curricula are easily accessible. But as important as school programs are, their most important contribution may be to reach parents with information about child sexual abuse.

For several reasons, parents are crucial sexual abuse prevention educators. First, children vary greatly in their ability to understand and integrate the information presented in a prevention education program. No classroom teacher or guest lecturer currently has the luxury of a one-to-one approach. Informed parents, however, can adjust the information and approach to their child.

Most parents are glad to have the school initiate discussion and provide basic information. But it is an error to assume schools can do it all or that prevention programs "innoculate" children against sexual abuse. Studies of student retention levels following classroom

presentations indicate supplemental sessions are important. Parents who are informed can continue the education process and clarify any misconceptions the child may have.

Parents who are not involved in the school program may not know how to respond to their child's questions, may contradict accurate information, may not know how to correct any misconceptions the child may have, and may not recognize the signs that may indicate their child has been abused. Most prevention programs advise children to tell an adult if abused. Because parents are sometimes the offenders, they may not be as strongly emphasized as resources for children as they should be. Yet many children don't have anyone other than their parents to turn to for help. For that reason schools need to make every effort to be sure parents have the information to respond appropriately if a child reveals a sexual assault.

Sometimes prevention programs frighten children despite their best efforts not to do so. Children may become anxious, sleepless or nontalkative. They may develop new worries. (One child was unable to go anywhere with his mother without asking, "Is that the man who would abuse kids?" anytime he saw an adult male.) Usually parents are the ones who must understand and comfort the child. With information about sexual abuse they can do that and continue the education process.

Educators know that simply telling children something is not enough to change their behavior. To become a part of children's responses, desired behavior must be repeated, modeled and rewarded. School programs rarely have the time to do all that. Parents can. In addition, parents are usually the ones who hear about it if a child has resisted an approach. Children need to be rewarded when they yell no at a stranger or tell someone they don't keep secrets. (It is particularly important for parents to reward their child. The natural response if a child has been approached is to add new restrictions but this causes the child to feel punished, not rewarded.)

Another reason parents must be intrinsically involved is that talking about sexual abuse prevention means talking about values. For example, the idea that children have the right to say no, or as some programs promote, the obligation to say no, is a value many parents do not necessarily agree with. It is parents who are in the position to teach children when it is safe or correct to say no and when no is not acceptable. And if children do not have parental permission to say no under some circumstances, even the most adept teacher is unlikely to convince a child that she or he has the right to question adult authority. (Some experts question whether children, especially children under eight, are capable of saying no to adults and suggest it may be asking the impossible at their developmental stage.)

Talking about touching also involves family values. Families have different comfort levels with touching. Thus, the idea of good touch and bad touch can leave children whose families are not physically affectionate feeling left out. Other children may misunderstand and decide nobody should touch them. Educators must recognize the high potential for misunderstanding about this seldom-talked-about subject and provide concrete information to parents that emphasizes nurturing touch. Parents can reassure children that affection is expressed in a variety of ways, but that it is never acceptable for an adult to sexually use a child.

Parents who are not involved and informed may react with hostility to a school prevention program that *seems* to promote children's rebellion, lessen parental authority and discourage affectionate touch between family members. Parents who participate in a program are less likely to be upset by differences between what is being said in the classroom and their family values when they know they will have an opportunity to clarify the approach with their children and have been given suggestions about what to say.

Prevention cannot continue to be based solely on informing children who may become victims. Genuine prevention, not just self-protection, means changing factors that allow sexual abuse to occur. This means changing some of the ways we raise children. Parents then become a critical instrument for change in long term prevention.

Parents Are Involved

Parents are currently involved in school

prevention programs in a variety of ways. Examples from three major prevention programs are given below. (See Part II, *Prevention Programs at Work*, for comprehensive descriptions.)

The Child Assault Prevention (CAP) Project based in Columbus, Ohio provides a sample letter for schools to modify and send to all parents informing them of the upcoming program. Parental permission slips are included. Before the school program begins, an informational meeting for parents is scheduled. Attendance at the meetings varies. Sally Cooper, director of the national office, believes that attendance is dependent on income level more than any other factor. That is, the lower the income of the parents, the less likely they are to attend. CAP encourages attendance by urging the school to provide child care during the meeting and/or send additional notices home.

Many CAPs (there are about 150 across the country) attempt to reach specific populations. They use bilingual print materials (Spanish, Cambodian, Vietnamese, French, Japanese, Cantonese) and cultural adaptations for Native Americans, Hispanics and Blacks. Since many of these groups have community or neighborhood centers, CAP may offer to hold a parent meeting there. CAPs are required to have a multi-cultural staff. They also offer signing at parent meetings as one of the ways they serve hearing-impaired parents. Their outreach also includes going to parent groups not associated with schools (day care centers, Girl Scouts, churches, etc.)

The Committee for Children (CFC), a Seattle-based prevention program, is increasing efforts to reach parents. The CFC will not provide training to a school staff unless a parent meeting is planned by the school. As they train teachers, they emphasize reaching parents and provide suggestions for doing so. CFC has noticed a decrease in attendance at parent meetings. Ann Downer, CFC's Training Director, attributes it to parents feeling more informed about sexual abuse. Ms. Downer considers parents to be sophisticated in their understanding of the problem and looking for the best available program.

The CFC is developing a parent/child workbook to accompany their school curriculum. Parents and children can do the activities together at home on an optional basis. They are also developing a series of pamphlets for parents in different family forms. (For example, a pamphlet for single parents will include suggestions for screening potential dates.)

The Illusion Theater, based in Minneapolis, reaches a large number of families with their live performances after school. During the teacher training phase of their program, the school is encouraged to include parents in as many ways as possible. At least half of the time they reach parents through workshops about how to talk to children of all ages about sex abuse. They also reach parents with their statewide media campaigns.

The Illusion Theater has developed a new play, *For Adults Only*. It looks at the confusion between sex and violence; what is healthy and what is not. The intent is to help parents sort out the difficult issues that arise during discussions with children and teens about sexual abuse.

Barriers to Parent Participation

Programs are taking creative steps to involve

parents. But too many parents are not receiving information when schools implement prevention education. If parents are so important why aren't they involved more? Some of the problem seems to rest with parents. Schools often have difficulty getting their participation. This may be due, in part, to the fact that many programs do not attempt to involve parents beyond a superficial level. It may also be due to the extensive media coverage of child sexual abuse. Parents believe they have done all they can, or conversely, feel there is nothing they can do. David Finkelhor's finding that parents are aware of sexual abuse but believe that it won't happen in their neighborhood or to their children is a factor as well.

Participation by parents of teenagers is even more difficult to achieve than participation by parents of younger children. Parents of adolescents are tired. Their children don't seem to listen to them. They have often begun new work outside the home or are busy with volunteer activities. They are concerned about drugs, alcohol, suicide and pregnancy. (To the extent that a relationship between these problems and sexual abuse can be shown, parents may be more likely to respond.) In addition, talking about sexual abuse with teens means talking about sex. There is no longer any way around it. Perhaps because adults find it difficult to deal with adolescent sexuality, they tend to be more blaming of teen victims than they are of younger children. This, in turn, makes prevention efforts more difficult.

Still another factor is the professionals' focus on incest. Unfortunately this focus has tended to cast parents in general in the role of bad guy, and as a consequence their positive contribution to prevention is overlooked. Prevention educators need to remember that over half of sexual assaults are not committed by parents, but by other relatives or friends about whom the parents have no suspicion. The relative involvement of the mother in incest is being debated, but it is obvious that many mothers act to protect their children. They need support and help from prevention educators.

Another factor may be the lack of status given to parents in this society. The importance, the necessity, the difficulty of the parenting role is rarely acknowledged or supported. It is sometimes easier to go directly to the schools where children can be reached with greater certainty.

Ways to Involve Parents

Make the approach to parents concrete, with suggestions about exactly what words they can use when talking to their children. Provide suggestions about how to reward children for self-protective behavior and how to respond if the child does come to them with a problem.

Recognize the valuable contribution parents have to make in preventing sexual abuse. Most prevention programs are experimental. The best are based on what a particular group of people have concluded children need to know. As yet there is little substantive research to indicate how children respond to these programs in terms of skill development, although there are anecdotal success stories to support programs. Parents are useful collaborators to prevention programs based in the schools. They can provide feedback to prevention educators as to how their children responded. And they may have other ideas about how to reach children.

Acknowledge parental expertise. Parents know their own children better than anyone else can. Recognize that parents are the primary educators of young children and continue to be influential all through children's lives. Most of the time they will be the ones to respond to children's concerns and have the most opportunity to detect abuse or potentially abusive situations. (The numerous day care cases that have come to light emphasize the importance of parents having access to information about recognizing and responding to sexual abuse.)

Once prevention programs recognize the primary role of parents, other avenues suggest themselves. Prevention programs for parents could incorporate more information about positive, nurturing touch within the family; ideas for promoting bonding; and help with sorting out complex issues such as what to do with natural feelings of attraction toward a child. High risk families (those with alcoholism, battering, chronic unemployment, prior sexual abuse victimization, divorce and remarriage and other chronic stressors) could be targeted for special emphasis.

To promote a more active role for parents in a school-based prevention program:

- Seek parent involvement in the development of the program as well as their ongoing participation in its implementation.
- Incorporate homework activities for parents and children to do together on an optional basis.

- Send home specific follow-up discussion ideas relating to the classroom presentation.
- Send home, or provide to parents, information on how to talk about sexual abuse with children, how to recognize signals of victim and victimizer and what to do.
- Encourage fathers specifically to participate in sex abuse discussions. Most parent meetings currently are composed primarily of mothers. When couples are in attendance provide specific information for fathers.
- Hold family night presentations on such topics as sexual abuse, family violence, normal sexuality and encourage families to participate. This is especially appropriate for the secondary level.
- Incorporate information about offenders into programs for parents. Parents need information about what factors might contribute to their children becoming victimizers, and how to recognize and respond if that is suspected. While teaching children to resist approaches is a worthwhile goal, genuine prevention means children are not approached in the first place.

The most important role schools can play in preventing sexual abuse is to be sure all parents (1) have information about how to talk to children about sexual abuse, (2) understand the indicators of sexual abuse, and (3) know how to respond and where to find help if their children are abused.

Chapter 12

Guidelines for Selecting Prevention Education Resources

JENNIFER FAY

In recent years a significant number of films, filmstrips, books, booklets and curricula have been developed for educating children from preschool through high school about sexual abuse and how to avoid it. Prevention programs were first developed in the late 1970s when sexual abuse was identified as the "last frontier of child abuse." Treatment specialists were disseminating new information about victimization and offenders. Rape crisis centers (who were primarily involved in self-defense instruction for adults) began to receive more and more calls from parents of child victims. Many adults were speaking up about sexual abuse in their childhoods. Prevention concepts grew directly from what was being learned about the realities of child sexual abuse: strangers were not the primary danger, and such abuse was neither rare nor harmless.

Before the current volume of materials was available, prevention educators were often asked, "Is there anything available for preschoolers?" "Are there any booklets directed at the elementary age group?" "Do you know of any films appropriate for adolescents?" A more common question today is, "Which of the ma-

terials available would you recommend? The question for many school personnel, parents and other adults has become, "How do I choose among all these resources?"

The criteria for choosing among films, curricula and other written materials has been based on intuition, time limitations, cost and/or ease of implementation. By far the overriding factor, however, has been availability. Now that so many resources are obtainable, educators can enjoy the luxury of choosing among a variety of prevention approaches and materials. Prevention approaches differ greatly, and each one's particular messages to students must be carefully considered.

The following guidelines discuss several aspects of films, curricula, books and booklets, and provide criteria for assessing them. Based on this assessment, educators can choose components of a resource, see where the deficiencies are and supplement it with additional materials or information. Each item is an important element in meeting the objective of helping children and adolescents recognize and avoid sexual abuse in a way that minimizes their fear or mistrust and increases their sense of security and competence in the world. While not a complete list, many important factors are covered. The questions are designed to be used as a checklist.

Definition and Information

1. *How is sexual abuse defined?* There is a wide range of definitions from "being touched in an unacceptable way" to "touching you any place or way that makes you feel uncomfortable and feel like not sharing your body" to "adults touching your private parts" to "secret touching" to "being touched under your jeans." Does the material contain specific examples (stories, role plays) of "secret touching" etc.? If directed to teens, does it provide a more sophisticated definition?

2. *Does the definition give enough information for the child to understand? Is it too general or abstract?* Preschool and elementary age children seem to have difficulty learning in the abstract. They need specifics. One young boy, after hearing that sexual abuse is anyone touching your private parts, decided he could never touch his own private parts again.

3. *Are sexual abuse and related concepts defined appropriately for the age of the students?* Certain concepts and/or vocabulary may not be comprehended by younger students. For instance, terms such as incest, support system or offender may be used without adequate definition. A resource may be recommended for grades K-6, but may be understood only by children in grades 4-6.

4. *If sexual abuse is defined in terms of touching, is adequate time allotted to positive touching and its importance?* Some children are learning that touching is the problem. Adults are expressing fears about touching children affectionately; they are afraid children may misinterpret it and falsely accuse them of sexual abuse. This confusion stems partially from definitions of sexual abuse in terms of touching, rather than in specifically sexual terms. (It also stems from the notion that children lie about being sexually abused, fantasize about it or randomly accuse adults.)

5. *Does the definition include a range of forms of sexual offenses and provide examples?* For example, does it discuss both touching and nontouching offenses including indecent exposure, obscene phone calls, voyeurism, pornography?

6. *Are "people they know" (acquaintances, friends and family members) emphasized as the most likely offenders?* Only 10-15 percent of offenders are strangers, so only a portion of the program should be devoted to strangers. Even fewer children with developmental disabilities are approached by strangers. Neither are most abductors strangers to the child. In addition, it is also important to include peers as potential offenders when teaching teens.

7. *Is it emphasized that sexual abuse of children usually involves bribes, threats, manipulation and authority, not physical force?* Most children are involved in sexual abuse by nonviolent, coercive methods. Some prevention programs teach self-defense techniques. While they are useful skills, does teaching them mislead students? Are they learning to expect physical attacks? Are children capable of using these methods in an actual abusive situation with an adult she/he cares about? With a stranger? Whether or not the skills are ever used, are

they useful as confidence-builders, or is their primary effect to frighten the child?

8. *Are students taught the necessary vocabulary, including names of body parts, to enable them to talk about sexual abuse?* If adults are embarrassed or afraid to use the words, students will be too. One of the reasons children do not report sexual abuse is because they do not have the necessary vocabulary or have never heard anyone else talk about it. (After seeing a public service announcement of Bill Russell talking about sexual abuse, a boy in Seattle called the police to report. The boy said if Bill Russell could talk about it, he could too.)

9. *Is it clearly emphasized that the offender is responsible for sexual abuse; the child is not to blame?* This must be repeated often. It isn't enough to say "it's not your fault," and then say "You should say no," or imply the child is obligated to say no. (There is a big difference between the message, "It's okay to say no" and "You should say no.") Prevention information is not meant to be the new "shoulds," which place the responsibility for stopping sexual abuse with the children where it does not belong.

10. *Are stereotypes used for offenders? Are offenders depicted as strangers, ugly, poor, minority, mentally ill, scary-looking, elderly?* Certain offenders may fit a stereotype, but it is misleading if a resource reinforces the idea that offenders are different from ourselves.

Skills

11. *Are the student's skills in recognizing potentially abusive situations ranging from nontouching to touching offenses increased?* Children need to know what abusive behavior is before they can protect themselves from it.

12. *Are the student's skills in avoiding abusive situations increased?* New skills may include questioning confusing behavior, seeking help from others, saying no and other assertive responses, and/or self-defense. So far this information has been directed primarily at the cognitive level. Programs often spend too much time lecturing and not enough time demonstrating. Most programs need to incorporate more guided rehearsal.

13. *Does the self-protection approach address the developmental level of the student?* For example, no more assertiveness should be expected from an adolescent than we expect from an adult. Preschoolers may not be capable of learning to fight back.

14. *Are the student's skills in identifying people at home and in their community who can help increased?* Are children taught to identify person(s) who will believe and support him/her, know what to do, and/or answer questions about confusing behavior? Younger children have difficulty understanding generalizations such as "someone you trust" or "someone at church." They need to name specific people in their lives. (This is an ideal activity for children to take home to complete with parents.)

15. *Are students given practice such as role plays or sample phrases of how to tell if they are abused or are confused or afraid?* Children often cannot formulate the words to tell on their own.

16. *Are students encouraged to tell even if the abuse has stopped?* It is never too late to tell.

Style of Presentation

17. *Is the tone frightening?* Programs should decrease rather than increase fear about sexual abuse. Children are already scared. They don't need more "watch outs" or "bewares." The "dangerous stranger" portions of the program should not be threatening.

18. *Is the material culturally appropriate to the intended audience?* For example, it is not useful to teach direct eye contact (one aspect of assertiveness training) to children whose cultural values dictate that direct eye contact with adults is rude. Some ethnic minority children (Asian, Hispanic) have difficulty initially understanding the concept that everyone has the "right" to be safe, according to one prevention program.

19. *Are stereotypes of race, ethnicity, age or sex used or implied?*

20. *Is time allotted for questions and discussion?* Hesitant students may be encouraged to bring up concerns by the use of anonymous question cards. Is there also practice time, worksheets, activities, role plays?

21. *Is the material sensitive to the probability that some students in the class have been sexually abused?*

22. *Is the material directed at both boys and girls, both as potential victims and potential victimizers?* This message is particularly important for an adolescent audience, who may include some sex offenders among their numbers. Currently, no prevention program addresses adolescent offenders directly, or attempts in any organized way to prevent children from becoming offenders. Prevention programs sometimes are criticized for being anti-male. It helps to recognize the exploitative behavior of girls as well as boys, although the majority of sex offenders are male.

23. *Is there recognition of the social factors that contribute to sexual abuse?* This is important for teenagers since they are in the process of developing values about sexual and violent behavior. The long term goal of sexual abuse prevention is to end sexual abuse, not just teach children to be less vulnerable.

Organization

In order for a sexual abuse education program to have maximum effectiveness in a school setting, the following elements are essential.

24. *Will teachers receive training in sexual abuse recognition and prevention? Will they learn how to help an abused child in the classroom?* Even teachers who are not teaching a prevention program need this basic information.

25. *Will the school counselors, nurses and consulting physicians also receive specialized training?* These people are an integral part of the prevention team. They need training in identification, reporting and treatment of sexually abused children and adolescents. They also play a role in prevention, particularly since the children who have been abused once may be abused again. There is opportunity to provide self-protection information in both the counseling and the medical setting.

26. *Will all school personnel be included in the training?* A child or adolescent may decide to talk to anyone they trust in the school setting.

27. *Will the information be presented as a*

routine part of the general educational curriculum in all twelve grade levels and preschool? Although this is not immediately possible in many schools, it is the goal to work toward. Children do not learn well from one-time presentations. They need to hear this information continuously throughout their development. A booster session six months or so after the yearly classroom time may help retention. Current programs vary between from one class period to fifteen class periods. Although the optimum amount of time is not clear, it seems obvious that one class period is not enough.

28. *Does the program involve parents?* It is crucial that parents be aware of and support the information and concepts their children are learning. Conversations and reinforcement at home are important aspects of the learning process. Parents must not be given the impression that the school program will innoculate the child against sexual abuse. Parents need encouragement to talk further with their children of all ages about abuse. Schools play an important role in disseminating information all parents should have including indicators that a child has been abused and how to respond and help with the child's recovery. Parents are also important supplements to the school program, clearing up any misconceptions or fears their children may have.

29. *Does the program encourage the school to review its own process for responding to an abused child?* Each school should have a working policy for implementing the mandatory child abuse reporting laws of its state. Does it help the school identify the state and community resources available to provide assistance?

30. *Does the program have a built-in means of evaluating the effectiveness of its approach?* It is important to know what individual children learn from a prevention program and how long they retain it. For instance, does it include a pretest and posttest, a suggested method for keeping statistical records of children who report abuse incidents, and/or success stories?

Prevention programs are in the process of learning what will help children and adolescents be less vulnerable to sexual abuse, and what will not. Knowledge about sexual abuse is also growing at a rapid rate. We do not currently have all the answers, but we are now in a position to choose resources that appear to be most effective in teaching children to avoid victimization.

Acknowledgements: *This paper grew out of work originating with the Washington State Coalition for Child Sexual Abuse Prevention Education subcommittee on evaluating curricula. Thanks to Nancy Kerr, Diane Robbins and Paul Gregorio.*

Chapter 13

Considering Children's Developmental Stages in Prevention Education

CAREN ADAMS

Sexual abuse prevention education began in response to requests for adult rape prevention information. Parents wanted to know what to say to their children that could help protect them. By looking at how sexual abuse often begins and who the offenders are, some general statements were developed to guide parents in talking with their children. It was assumed parents would tailor what they said to their particular children, depending on their developmental stage and readiness.

With increasing concern about sexual abuse and the desire to reach all children came the expansion of these general premises into curriculum, often for presentation in schools. When the information is designed with consideration for the developmental stage of children, it is usually done by giving younger children less information about the sexual nature of abuse, and sometimes with the use of age-appropriate materials such as coloring books, dolls or puppets.

Despite such program adjustments, children may be exposed to information that is not developmentally appropriate. Thus it is time to reexamine prevention premises in light of child development and reconsider what children are being taught in school programs. What works for parents because they can monitor their child and help her or him understand through repetition and modeling, may not be as appropriate in a school setting.

The four basic concepts of sexual abuse prevention education are discussed below.

1. Children need to know enough about what sexual abuse is to recognize it if it happens or begins to happen. Children may need information about who an offender might be, what force (such as trickery, secrets or bribery) might be used, some description of specific abusive behaviors, and perhaps a possible answer as to why some people abuse children. The definition of sexual abuse has often been reduced to "someone touching your private parts," or "when children get forced or tricked into touch/sexual contact." The concept of good, bad and confusing touch has been used as a way to explain abuse without always having to use sexual vocabulary.

2. Children need to know they have the right to say no or resist in some other way. The levels of resistance suggested include getting away,

saying no, and resisting physically.

3. Children need to tell someone if they are uncomfortable or unsure of a situation.

4. Children need to know it isn't their fault if abuse happens.

These concepts are logical and are based on what is known about how sexual abuse occurs. They are not necessarily based adequately on knowledge of what makes sense to children at different ages. When parents are the educators, they can be the judge of what is appropriate. Although parents often underestimate their child's ability to understand and cope if the subject is explained honestly, they can avoid some of the mistakes of the more general classroom presentation.

Programs often spend a great deal of time teaching children how to react, say no and/or use physical self-defense. But they may spend little time identifying what sexual abuse actually is. The definition is usually vague and/or describes only one form of sexual abuse. Because of the fear of prevention education being perceived as sex education, most programs have avoided defining abuse in sexual terms, and have preferred instead to talk about touch or private parts. The unfortunate consequence is that touch appears to be the problem. It is also misleading in that abuse may begin with requests to undress or look at an adult who is undressed, rather than with touching.

Children often make assumptions when they are given simple generalizations, such as no one has the right to touch your private parts. Some children have decided a beloved caretaker shouldn't wash them. Others have concluded they should not touch themselves. Thus, the issue of touching needs much more attention

in developmental terms. What generalizations can children make about sexual abuse? How specific is it necessary to be? The more specific the information, the more time must be spent and resources developed covering each aspect.

Although prevention programs make efforts to include the benefits of good touch, the emphasis is on refusing bad or confusing touch. Cordelia Anderson's original concept encouraged children to talk about different kinds of touch, and in so doing, encouraged children to accept good touch. But the message is sometimes so diluted when it is shortened and retranslated in the process of curriculum development, that sexual abuse prevention appears to be antitouch.

Most programs sidestep the specific identification of possible offenders because they don't want to be accused of making children suspicious or of betraying family trust. Educators usually deal with the issue by saying "if someone you know touches you . . ." Unfortunately most children, even older children, do not have the ability to translate this generalization to mean father, grandfather, Uncle John, cousin Carol or the babysitter. Furthermore, including avoidance of abduction within the safety curriculum leads children to consider anyone a stranger.

Prevention programs present different strategies to help children avoid victimization. Children should tell, say no, get away, follow the rules, have a safety plan, and/or learn a self-defense yell. Although these are good ideas, the ability of children of different ages to understand and use these strategies needs to be examined. Above all, the idea that children *should* respond in a certain way must be avoided. Children have the right to grow up free of unwanted sexual contact. That they don't does not mean they are obligated to know how to respond. Children may be getting the message that sexual abuse is their fault if they don't know how to stop it. This is exactly the opposite of what is intended. Prevention educators want children to know that it is not their fault no matter what they did or didn't do. But they are working against the moral development of children who believe if an adult does something, it must be right. So if it was wrong, the child must be at fault.

Simply telling children otherwise is not sufficient if other prevention activities carry the message that children are responsible for protecting themselves. Self-protection strategies should be viewed as optional skills for children to have. Adults should be protecting children by not preying on them and by being alert for signs that others are.

Developmental Issues and Conflicts

For preschoolers, no one is a stranger after the first hello. Thus, some programs attempt to teach the difference between acquaintances and strangers. Given the fact that 85 percent of children are abused by someone they know, the need to help children make this distinction may not be a high priority.

Children under the age of six are especially afraid of monsters, ghosts and other imaginary figures. They may frighten easily at the idea that yet another danger is out there somewhere. Their fear may be compounded by the fact that young children use small details and examples to try to make sense of generalizations. If the man in the film is wearing a red shirt, they may decide that all men wearing red shirts are bad.

Asking young children to say no to adult authority seems unfair. Children need to be able to trust adults and feel secure in their care. The notion that adults can be untrustworthy and may hurt children is disturbing and potentially frightening. Children will either ignore the message or blame themselves. Prevention programs need to balance their approach with more statements that the majority of adults would not hurt them in any way.

The message that no one has the right to touch your private parts should be reevaluated for preschoolers. While preschoolers can be taught self-care as part of their move toward independence, many circumstances—including hygiene, medical care and first aid—legitimately require a caretaker's touch.

Prevention programs need to carefully evaluate the messages they are conveying about parents and other caretakers. Sexual abuse is serious and many more children are vulnerable than the public believes. However, when considering the balance between making children aware and undermining their trust in adults, it is important to remember that many children will not be sexually abused, and many more children will not be sexually abused by a parent or parent figure. There are many who doubt that abuse by trusted authority figures can be prevented by programs for young children because they simply don't have the power to resist.

Children in kindergarten through second grade are still likely to view adults as godlike. Although this age group is in the process of changing, they still believe adults are right, and continue to believe if something bad happens to them, it must have been their fault. They may also focus on wrongdoing they understand (such as telling lies or breaking rules) rather than the sexual abuse. They also may be concerned about being a tattletale. Boys of this age and older are convinced of their ability to use super heroic force to get out of any situation. Their need to be tough and strong may not allow them to see any of the sexual abuse prevention information as relevant to them.

Children in third through sixth grades are moving toward making independent judgments about people's behavior and the consequences of breaking rules. By fifth and sixth grades, children display great diversity in development. Some children, mostly girls, are maturing physically and encountering pressure for sexual contact from older boys. Children of this age will readily agree that adults make mistakes and can be wrong. Unfortunately they may not see adults as helpful with the problems they face. They may resent being treated like little children or they may be embarrassed.

For children in junior high, an important developmental shift is occurring. They are beginning or continuing an interest in opposite sex relationships. They may begin dating. Some are already involved in sexual intercourse. Assault by peers or older teens becomes part of the gamut of sexual abuse. But talk about touching private parts or confusing touch isn't necessarily helpful in identifying an abusive situation. Most touch at this age is confusing and ambiguous in its meaning. Adolescents beginning to experiment with kissing, hugging and other sexual interactions are unlikely to tell an adult about puzzling or confusing touch. Often they are most interested in knowing:

Does this mean he likes me? How far can I get her to go? And even abusive, exploitative touch or sexual interaction may seem preferable to a teen than nothing.

By junior high, young teens are under enormous pressure. They are uncertain of who they are and what values they hold. They are trying to break free of parental restrictions. It is a time of extreme vulnerability; a time when they need information about relationships and sexuality. But their overriding need to be cool, sophisticated and appear knowledgeable about sex often prevents them from asking the questions about confusing or abusive touch they might like to. They must be given specific permission to ask those questions. They are rarely reached by prevention programs, which too often are simply an extension of younger children's programs. Besides, sexual abuse prevention for teens means addressing sexual issues, and prevention programs have been reluctant to do so.

The transition in ability to reason abstractly begins as teens enter high school, but junior high students still need concrete examples and suggestions.

Young people in high school consider themselves to be independent and competent. This belief may be so strong teenagers won't ask for protection even when they realize they may need it. They want to be able to handle situations on their own and not feel like babies who need their parents' help. They are ready for information about how an offender might behave.

Teens, unlike younger children, are less likely to make black and white distinctions between people. They react negatively to anything that feels like an attack on peers and to anything that sounds antimale. Teens are at a developmental stage in which they are taking risks rather than being careful. They may be more concerned about being liked than in resisting abuse.

Recommendations and Modifications

1. Prevention programs for preschoolers should recognize the potential for frightening children and/or overgeneralizing. Preschoolers should only be taught to tell an adult if they don't understand why someone is touching them. Programs to help them gain the vocabulary to tell if they are abused and to label their feelings are probably most consistent with other learning going on at this time.

The major prevention effort for this age child should be directed toward their parents. Parents need to know the indicators of abuse and how to respond. And preschoolers must be told

they can tell their parents if they need help. Even though some parents are offenders, most will help their children if they have adequate information and resources.

2. The original goal of prevention was to give children enough information to be able to respond to a sexual abuse situation before it became serious, not to make them responsible for protecting themselves. That distinction needs to be reaffirmed and strengthened. We want children to know enough to react, not to feel responsible if they are unable to respond.

3. The importance of parents, especially to elementary age children, needs to be incorporated more fully into prevention programs.

4. Programs for teens should address more adequately the complex issues of relationship interactions, abusive behavior in general and values about coercive behavior. Educators should recognize the adolescents' need to be competent and independent.

Chapter 14

The Role of Theater in Child Sexual Abuse Prevention

DON YOST and ELAINE SCHERTZ

During the last ten years, a great many people have become aware of the problem of child sexual abuse. Large numbers of parents, educators and social workers are seeing the importance of programs to warn children about the dangers of sexual abuse. Prevention programs developed in the late 1970s and early 1980s are being replicated in many communities across the United States. Programs are being developed to meet the needs of special audiences.

While the number and variety of programs have increased, the differences in approach have more to do with the method of transferring information than with content. Some programs use a teacher or social worker to speak to children; some use films, puppet shows and other media. Many programs use a combination.

Ever since the earliest efforts at prevention education, theater has played a major role in the movement to warn and educate children. Cordelia Anderson and the Illusion Theater of Minneapolis were pioneers. Bridgework Theater in Indiana and Bubbleonia in Kansas built on Illusion Theater's work. Theaters in Virginia and Colorado have also written plays.

The Little Bear *cast*

It is not a fluke that so many prevention programs use theater arts. This article will list some of the problems inherent in educating children about sexual abuse and the important role theater plays in solving these problems.

Background

Information for this article comes from six years of experience with Bridgework Theater, Inc. Bridgework is a nonprofit, educational theater company located in Goshen (north central), Indiana. Bridgework performs its original plays for audiences in the Great Lakes region. Most of the plays are for children. The company has written plays about peer pressure, self-esteem, conflict resolution, families of prisoners, and victimization. The most well known of Bridgework's plays, however, help children recognize and avoid sexual abuse.

Bridgework Theater began its work in child sexual abuse prevention in 1980. Early efforts were soon recognized with a grant from the National Center on Child Abuse and Neglect (Department of Health and Human Services). Bridgework was one of six sites chosen from across the nation to devise and test prevention strategies. As part of this federal project, the theater wrote and tested two plays for children. *Little Bear* is Bridgework's play for elementary school children. *Out of the Trap* is for secondary students.

Since 1980, Bridgework has performed the plays for over 80,000 children. Other groups use scripts to the plays, thus more than a half million children see the plays every year.

Prevention Education — The Challenges

A program that hopes to educate children about sexual abuse must address the needs of two distinct groups. The first group is, of course, the children themselves. The second group consists of those adults who have the power to control access to children. Because most children spend a great deal of time in school or in day care centers, the people who control access to children are teachers, principals, school board members, social workers, school nurses, school counselors and parents.

Some of the greatest challenges for a prevention program arise because the needs of these two groups (adults and children) are not the same. Many of their needs are, in fact, contradictory.

What do children need from a sexual abuse prevention program?

1. Children need a program that is specific. Children need to know exactly what is meant by sexual abuse. If a prevention program uses vague generalities, children get the idea that the adults involved don't really want to talk about sexual abuse. Children get the message that adults are embarrassed; that the subject is too painful or "dirty."

If children have the impression that adults don't really want to talk or hear about sexual abuse, they will be less likely to report abuse. A prevention program that is specific is easier to understand, easier for children to trust.

2. Children need a program with "rules" that can be applied to many kinds of situations. They need a program that will, indeed, assist them in the application of these prevention rules or principles. Testing shows that young children especially have trouble applying general principles to specific situations.

3. Children need a program that is simple. Too many prevention programs become complicated in response to the needs of adults to deal with intricacies, subtleties and exceptions to the prevention principles. Children need a program that uses language and thought processes that are easily understood and easily remembered.

4. Children need a program that involves the nonrational, the intuitive and the sensorial. Children understand, recognize and categorize their experience by feelings, by intuition and by their senses. A child may be able to recite a definition of sexual abuse, but that definition may have little meaning in real life experiences. A child who knows some of the feelings, the sights and sounds of sexual abuse is much more likely to recognize a dangerous situation.

5. Children need to be entertained. Children need a prevention program that will hold their attention. Some of the children most vulnerable to sexual abuse are the least able to sit through long sessions that rely on reasoning, deduction or memorization. These same children respond well to liberal doses of humor, imagination and action.

What are the needs of the adults who control access to children?

1. Adults need a program that is in good taste; a program that is safe. Adults need a program that inspires confidence and will inspire the participation of other adults.

2. Adults need a program that is cost effective. They need a program that can be easily replicated; a program that is efficient and "self-contained."

So this is the dilemma. What means of prevention education can be specific without offending adults? What kind of program is both inexpensive and effective? What program will inspire the confidence of adults and, at the same time, entertain children? How can a method of education be easily replicated, yet deal with the nonrational—with emotions and with senses?

The Art of Theater—A Tool for Child Sexual Abuse Prevention

The use of performers on a stage in a live presentation for children solves many of the problems of sexual abuse prevention education for children.

Specific Yet Acceptable

A play can be specific without offending adults. How is this possible? Theater by its very nature allows both specificity and safety. In *Little Bear*, for instance, children can see and sense and experience a very specific instance of sexual abuse. But the abuse is not real. It is an imitation.

Because we use a carefully crafted imitation, we insure safety. The costumes, for example, are bulky and furry. The animals have no specific genitalia. The audience's experience is vicarious, not direct, and because it is vicarious, it is without trauma.

The stage gives us immediacy and distance. At one level, the audience (especially children) believes and cares about what happens on the stage. At another level, however, the audience (especially adults) is aware that the presentation is planned, tested and carefully controlled. The audience knows these are actors who have rehearsed the scene. They know the actors are pretending; that the actor playing Big Bear does not want to harm the actor playing Little Bear. The audience benefits from seeing an *imitation* of sexual abuse but is spared the disturbance that would result from experiencing a real instance.

The use of theater works so well that no adult who has actually seen a live performance of *Little Bear* has complained or expressed opposition to the play. No child has ever become ill or disturbed. Bridgework consistently receives expressions of appreciation for the sensitivity and propriety of the plays.

Cost Efficient Yet Effective

Plays such as *Little Bear* and *Out of the Trap* effectively teach prevention skills to large numbers of children at a reasonable cost. In a nine-month period from September, 1984 to June, 1985, Bridgework Theater reached 33,000 children at the cost of $20,000. Many of the organizations using scripts to the plays rely on volunteer help and reach 10,000 to 15,000 children on budgets of $1,000-$3,000.

How effective are the plays? In a written post-test given to 92 third and fourth grade students two years after they had seen a performance of *Little Bear*, 77 students (84%) correctly identified instances of sexual abuse and could list acceptable strategies for avoiding abuse (say no, tell a trusted adult and refuse to keep harmful secrets).

Over the centuries, theater artists have perfected ways of effectively communicating with large numbers of people. Techniques have been developed to help actors speak and move so as to be seen and heard from a distance. Using trained actors, Bridgework Theater regularly performs for 300 to 400 children at a time, yet each child feels as if they are a part of the program.

In the play *Little Bear*, the actors ask children for suggestions. The opportunities for participation draw children into the action and give them the sense that the play is being performed especially for them. Because theater uses the language of the senses and can demonstrate as well as verbalize, the entire program becomes less complex. Just as a picture may be worth many words, one action by an actor in the context of an interesting story can communicate so much more than words in a classroom.

It is not uncommon to hear children repeat verbatim line after line of dialogue from the play after having seen it only once.

Engages the Attention of Children

"Spellbound." "Riveted." "You had them every minute." These are words adults have used to describe the reactions of children to live performances. While some adults may not value the ability of a prevention program to entertain children, most adults will admit that unless a program invites participation and interest, unless children pay attention to what is being said or shown, there is little value in attempting to educate them.

A play is, first of all, a story. Children listen and watch to see what will happen next. In the first few minutes of the play, they identify with Little Bear. They care about what happens to Little Bear and cheer for the character's success and safety. A play engages the imagination. Children are fascinated by new sights and sounds. They are surprised by the unexpected and delighted by the humor.

A live play has an advantage over television or film. The audience sees actors who are real human beings, not images produced by a machine. The actors respond to the audience. No two performances are ever the same. Each is tailor-made to suit the needs of the audience. If, for example, the children are tired or tend toward impatience, the actors can exaggerate. They can pick up the pace of a performance. If, during a specific moment in the play the children are especially entranced, the actors can slow the pace and capitalize on the magic of the moment to realize the full potential for communication.

Involves the Nonrational Yet Can Be Replicated

A live play evokes our emotions. Actors can communicate even the most subtle shifts and shades of emotion. In a classroom, we can tell children that offenders may trick them. In the play *Little Bear*, children see and hear Big Bear tell Little Bear, "You're too young to understand that the reason I give you these gushy hugs is because I love you." Children sense the lie. The actor communicates through many slight changes in voice and movement that, in fact, there is a no real love, only a selfish desire for self-gratification. Children can easily compare their feelings during the play with their feelings about experiences in real life.

On the other hand, these emotions can be replicated via the script and the role of a play's director. Theater artists are skilled at finding the subliminal, emotional messages inherent in the script. The scripts to *Little Bear* and *Out of the Trap* insure accurate replication by dividing the play into sections and listing the prevention goals for each, including goals concerned with emotions and subliminal messages.

The Limitations of Theater

While theater is a valuable and proven prevention tool, persons who use theater should be aware of its limitations and be prepared to make several adjustments.

1. Actors and audience have a transient relationship. In live theater, the actors appear for a few brief minutes in the lives of the children in the audience. It is critical, then, that a play refers children to their ongoing support system. At the end of *Little Bear*, for instance, Big Moose asks the children to make a mental list of all the adults in their lives who can help them. The list includes teachers, parents, school nurse, grandparents, neighbors and clergy.

Prior to performances, Bridgework helps a community make sure that its support system (parents, the schools, the child protection team, the prosecuting attorney's office and therapists) is in place and working well.

2. Theater cannot address specific questions. With up to 400 children in an audience, the actors cannot answer the questions of individual children. Bridgework Theater requires that all the children who see the plays be given the opportunity to discuss it with a trained adult in a classroom-size group. In addition to answering any questions, the teacher helps children apply the concepts they have learned from the play to a number of different hypothetical situations.

3. A "quick fix" is not enough. Parents and educators may hope that sexual abuse prevention education can be "taken care of" by a thirty-minute play and follow-up discussion. Effective prevention requires repetition and must involve adults in the community as well as children.

4. Adults must trust a prevention program. Actors and other theater artists are often seen as irresponsible. Theater groups must work to counteract this stereotype and make sure that only responsible people with sound reputations

are used for prevention plays.

Even with its limitations, theater has a great deal to offer society's efforts to prevent sexual abuse. We can easily predict that theater will continue to play a major role in sexual abuse prevention education and look forward to the new ways in which the art of theater will be applied to improve the quality of our lives in the years to come.

Editor's Note: See "Bridgework Theater" in Part II, Prevention Programs at Work, *for a description of its program components.*

Chapter 15

Child Sexual Abuse Prevention Project in an Hispanic Community

GERALDINE A. CRISCI and MARIA IDALI TORRES

The project described below originated as one of six model demonstration projects funded by the National Center on Child Abuse and Neglect in October, 1980. (See Chapter 1, "Prevention Education in Perspective" by Carol Plummer for background information.) This project entitled Child Sexual Abuse: Education and Prevention Among Rural and Hispanic Children, focused on a rural, Anglo site and an urban, Hispanic site. Both sites are situated in western Massachusetts. The rationale for site selection was a concern for making prevention information accessible to populations having the least access to services.

The project used a train-the-trainer model. Staff trained teachers at both sites to work directly with children. The target populations were children from preschool through sixth grade. In addition to a classroom curriculum guide, resources included the puppet production, *What Should I Do?* and the film, *Who Do You Tell?* This project reached the largest number of non-Anglo children and was the only one attempting extensive work with preschoolers.

The purpose of all six projects was to increase knowledge and awareness of child sexual abuse through the development and implementation of educational strategies. Questions initially posed included the following. Can child sexual abuse be prevented? If so, can educational materials be developed for use with children and families? Can such materials be evaluated as having an impact on the problem? Can programs gain access to schools and communities? This last question was perhaps the most critical. The finest educational materials have limited value if they do not reach children and their families.

Gaining access to the target population is primary. The approach used by this project was based on a public health model of prevention and a mental health model of community needs assessment.

Site Description

The Massachusetts Migrant Education Program (MMEP) was the formal site for our work with the Hispanic community. MMEP is a federally funded supplemental education program for the children of migrant farm workers. The MMEP provides an eight-week summer program, operating five days a week, 8:30-3:00, for children preschool through grade 12. Children participating in the summer program attend public school during the academic year and live, for the most part, with their families in the urban areas of Springfield, Holyoke and Chicopee. The MMEP provides supplemental education in reading, math and language skills as well as offering physical education, art and theater. Paid staff include bilingual and bicultural teachers, teacher aides and parent aides who work in teams in the classroom.

Parent involvement is achieved through large parent meetings held at the beginning and end of the summer, various special parents training workshops and events held throughout the summer, and the unique classroom parent-aide program. The parent aides work daily with the children. Their involvement enriches the classroom environment culturally and provides skill training and part-time jobs for participating parents.

The population served is 97 percent Puerto Rican, 1 percent Black, 1 percent Portuguese, and 1 percent Anglo. This project was given a unique opportunity to work with Puerto Rican children and their families in a formal educational setting. The structure of the MMEP and its many services (including transportation for children and parents) provided an almost ideal environment in which to develop the Hispanic component of a prevention program.

Prevention and Community Assessment Model

This project followed a public health model of prevention and used both formal and informal assessment methods in each stage of the work. This point cannot be emphasized enough. Project descriptions and conceptualizations often look great on paper, yet fail in their attempt at implementation. A clear assessment process that follows the three stages of project development and completion—planning, implementation and evaluation—is a critical factor in the success of a prevention program.

This process becomes especially important when working with a community whose culture is not Anglo. Additionally, the sensitive (and often confusing) issue of child sexual abuse prevention heightens the necessity of careful planning and community preparation that allows for direct input and feedback from representative members of the community. In this project, parents, children, community spokespeople and teaching staff were defined as representative members.

Public Health Model of Prevention

Prevention is defined as efforts made to reduce the incidence and prevalence of the problem. There are three levels of prevention in this model: primary, secondary and tertiary. Primary prevention efforts are aimed at the general population and geared toward providing education and training in health and skill enhancement. At this level it is sometimes possible to identify high risk groups or detect the initial stage of a problem. There are secondary gains; however, the focus remains general and educative.

At the secondary level of prevention, efforts are aimed at those persons who are already in a problem situation and who may have a short history of abuse, or who live in abusive families. All efforts are geared to a group already identified as having a problem and requiring specific clinical intervention.

At the tertiary level of prevention, the effort is clinical intervention with a population having a long history or chronic problems. Again, the population and intervention are specific.

This project is a primary prevention effort based on the belief that education is the most effective method of prevention. Through the development of creative problem-solving skills and understanding and use of social support systems, children can attain the life skills needed to prevent sexual abuse and to insure safety in their lives. The best educational strategies develop skills transferable to other life situations, especially in the identification of potentially dangerous situations.

Needs Assessment

During the planning stage, meetings with parents, teachers, social service providers and community liaisons provided an informal needs assessment. At these meetings staff explained the project and conducted an awareness training on child sexual abuse. This awareness training has proven to be one of the most successful components. It provides a way to inform participants about the extent of the problem, its definition and dynamics, and most of all, to engender empathy for sexually victimized children. The goal is to facilitate an understanding of the necessity for prevention programs and to form an alliance with participants in working toward implementation. Awareness is essential. People cannot support prevention unless they

understand the need. Most parents are not aware of the risks to their children and many think that "stranger danger" is the greatest risk. Therefore they only provide their children with warnings about kidnapping.

At the conclusion of the meeting participants were asked to voice their concerns, identify potential problems, make suggestions for teaching, and define their individual roles in prevention efforts. Participants were also asked to work with project staff, preferably taking a leadership role in helping us learn community norms and understand priorities, problems (for instance with the formal support system) and concerns. Community leaders and groups were informed about the project and included in the assessment as well.

Curriculum Concepts and Goals

The classroom curriculum is built on four major concepts believed to be the building blocks of sexual abuse prevention education: support systems (formal and informal), privacy, the touch continuum (developed by Cordelia Anderson) and assertiveness. The goals are to help children: (1) learn and understand the touch continuum, (2) be able to use their instincts in differentiating between exploitative and nurturant touch, (3) know that support systems exist for them (families, friends, neighbors, schools and community), (4) be able to identify the support systems that will be most useful to them in any given situation, (5) learn to use various community resources, (6) know ways to avoid and resist unsafe situations, (7) learn to use problem-solving skills to generate alternatives in potentially dangerous situations and (8) learn assertiveness skills.

Clearly these concepts are value-laden; families differ in their beliefs about privacy and touch. Further, teaching children to use support systems and assertiveness in their relationships with adults may be potentially threatening to a family's authority figures. The curriculum, titled the *Personal Safety Curriculum*, is taught within the context of body safety and protection from potentially dangerous situations through early identification. It is important for parents to have the opportunity to understand this context and use the concepts at home. Thus parent involvement is a key component and understanding cultural values is critical to successful implementation. We will share our findings through a discussion of the four concepts looking at cultural implications with a focus on the Hispanic community.

Support Systems

Who can you tell if you are in a potentially dangerous situation? The concept of family is a strong value within Puerto Rican culture. It has been our experience, however, that a typical Puerto Rican family is a myth. Great diversity exists among Puerto Rican families.

Nonetheless, the family is seen as the main source of support. The concept of extended family is a belief that is held to be true whether or not, in practice, an extended family exists. Parents tried to teach this concept, but their children did not easily relate to it, given few role models and the emphasis on the nuclear family in school. Many of the families who participated in the project, in fact, fell into the transitional family structure between extended and nuclear.

Two other sets of information proved helpful in understanding how to teach the concept of support systems. The first is an awareness of the cultural differences between Anglo and Puerto Rican families. (See Figure 1.)

Differences vary according to level of acculturation. The second is an understanding of help-seeking preferences. Our observations that

Cultural Differences Between Anglo and Puerto Rican Families		
Concepts	**Anglo**	**Puerto Rican**
Language	Monolingual	Bilingual
Culture	Monocultural	Bicultural
Age	Segregation	Integration
	Children have their own activities	Children must spend time with the family
	Adolescents geared toward peers	Adolescents geared toward elders
Attitudes	Assertiveness	Nonassertiveness
	Egocentric: own needs first	Other-oriented: other's needs first

Figure 1

Puerto Rican families follow a 3-step process, are similar to those of Sonia Badillo-Ghali and Melvin Belgado. (See Figure 2)

Human service agencies are often perceived by the Hispanic community as being inaccessible. Often they use the services only for economic reasons.

The concept of family is emphasized in the curriculum. But children are also taught that sometimes their family may not be available, or may not understand the problem and how to solve it. This necessitates the need for children to know what is offered in the community.

In assessing cultural factors in teaching this concept we looked at the language, beliefs, attitudes, practices and values of the community. Information about each of these factors was gained through our informal assessment process. Other factors considered in our assessment were: age of parents, number of years child and family had lived in the United States (this may differ among siblings and between parents and children), family structure, bilingualness, generational picture and demographics. All of these factors were further assessed within the context of the American culture (given that children were being socialized within the public school systems) with two major influences requiring special consideration: traditional culture and socioeconomic class.

Failure to understand and integrate this information about Puerto Rican families considerably limits intervention efforts. The major questions are: Who are the families in the community? Do they need prevention education?

Some considerations we found helpful in assessing the Puerto Rican family included: number of years in the United States, level of acculturation, rural vs. urban background, age of parents and age of children.

Privacy

Two factors required consideration in teaching the concepts of the right to privacy in general and the right to body privacy as well. First, Puerto Ricans are family oriented and believe personal problems are family problems. The positive aspect of their belief is that the family

---

Help-Seeking Preferences of Puerto Rican Families

1	2	3
family	teachers	community agencies
relatives	clergy	
friends	educated people	
neighbors	(within social	
acquaintances	service network)	
shopkeepers	bilingual/bicultural	
	people working in	
	social services	

Figure 2

is willing to be supportive with personal problems. The negative aspect is that if the problem is caused by a family member, the child may not want the rest of the family to know.

Secondly, Puerto Rican family members express a willingness to accommodate the needs of others, which are considered more important than one's own needs. This can mean individuals have no private space or private conversations. We approached the privacy concept directly through a discussion of private body parts. This direct educational effort was more comfortable for parents who reported teaching children body privacy from an early age. (Note: This was in direct contrast with our work in the rural, Anglo site where parents felt the abstract concepts should be taught prior to body privacy concepts.)

Touch Continuum

Physical affection and expressed warmth for children was a cultural value and norm in the communities in which we worked. Teaching the touch continuum to children was viewed as positive and helpful. There is a very clear understanding of the differences between nurturance and exploitation on the part of Puerto Rican parents. (Note: This seemed a more complex issue at other sites.)

Assertiveness

The goal of this concept is to teach the right to say no to an unwanted touch. This was a foreign concept within the Puerto Rican culture and required considerable discussion between staff, parents and teachers to find acceptable ways of teaching this skill. (This concept has required the most work with parents across sites.) In the Puerto Rican families the major concern was that children not lose respect for parents. Clearly, teaching assertiveness conflicts with their cultural norms. Puerto Rican children are taught not to look directly at adults when speaking to them; direct eye contact is an assertive body language posture. Cultural expectations of children are that they be obedient and meet other people's needs. Saying no and meeting one's own needs (for safety) may be in conflict with meeting someone else's needs.

Even though the concept was in conflict with cultural norms, mothers supported the idea of teaching assertiveness skills and participated in assertiveness workshops arranged by project staff. We found that responding to requests for more adult training assisted in the problem-solving process around cultural-norm conflicts. Initiative for the problem solving was taken by the parents.

Implementation

A formal process for assessing the implementation of the program was conducted in the following manner:

1. Project staff and teaching staff draft curriculum activities
2. Activities presented to parents
3. Parent feedback incorporated into activities
4. Activity presented in the classroom by teacher, teacher aide and parent aide
5. Results and observations of the presented activity shared with parents
6. Activity again presented in classroom (with revision if necessary)

7. Activity again presented to parents

Parents reviewing the curriculum activities met weekly for 90 minutes. Through this process the cultural appropriateness of activities was evaluated. Our goal was to produce bicultural as well as bilingual curriculum materials.

Evaluation

Young children (ages 3 to 7) who participated in the preschool and elementary school program were interviewed to determine their comprehension of the topics covered. The critical question was whether children of these ages have the cognitive ability to understand the concepts. One colloquial assumption about child sexual abuse prevention is that the information is too complex or too scary to be presented to younger children. Our results indicate that even young children were able to grasp the basic information of a personal safety program.

The *Personal Safety Curriculum* was taught during the eight-week summer program of the MMEP to children from preschool through grade five. However, only preschool through second grades were included in this study. The children received weekly lessons from the *Personal Safety Curriculum*, each lesson ranging from 15 to 50 minutes in length. Posters and coloring sheets from the lessons were posted in the classrooms throughout the summer sessions. Children in the first and second grades also say the film, *Who Do You Tell?* Children in preschool through second grade saw the puppet show, *What Should I Do?*

Since children ages 3 to 7 have no or limited reading and writing ability, the testing was conducted by interview. Children were shown pictures from the book *Red Flag/Green Flag People* and from the *Touch* educational materials developed by Illusion Theater. All children were shown two good touch pictures and two bad touch pictures, and asked questions concerning the concepts illustrated.

The study was conducted during the last 10 to 14 days of the summer program. All interviews were conducted at the MMEP site by the Project Educator who was bilingual. Children were asked the questions in both Spanish and English, and responded in whichever language they wished. Younger children tended to use Spanish and older children English.

The most striking result was that even young children were able to comprehend the curriculum, which concentrated on the concepts of good and bad touch and telling someone. Only first and second grade children were asked the question about privacy, but seven of the eight groups indicated an understanding of the concept. The overall percentage correct was 70 percent for preschool, 75 percent for kindergarten, 80 percent for first grade, and 85 percent for second grade. The statistics are even more impressive for the preschool and kindergarten children who were interviewed individually. The first and second grade children were interviewed in groups, which would tend for them to have higher scores.

The children's verbal responses to all questions were recorded during the interviews for a purpose other than evaluation. The words and phrases the children used to convey their ideas served as a resource list for the final translation of the *Personal Safety Curriculum* into Spanish.

References

Badillo-Ghali, Sonia. "Cultural Sensitivity in the Puerto Rican Client." *Social Casework* (October 1977).

Badillo-Ghali, Sonia. "Understanding Puerto Rican Traditions." *Social Work* 27:1 (1982).

Belgado, Melvin and Denise Humm-Belgado. "Natural Support Systems as a Source of Strength in the Puerto Rican Community." *Social Work* 27:1 (1982).

Chapter 16

Prevention Programs for Children with Disabilities

ELLEN J. SHAMAN

Since 1978 the Disabilities Project at Seattle Rape Relief has provided services and staff training, and has developed educational resources in sexual assault prevention for persons with physical, developmental and sensory disabilities. The purpose of this article is to share our experiences and recommendations for building a sexual assault prevention program for children with disabilities.

Talking About the Problem

The definition of sexual assault shapes the strategies and priorities of any prevention program. Defining sexual assault as a continuum of violent behaviors is effective. At one end of the continuum is verbal harassment, the sexist joke, advertisements that portray women and children as sexual objects or commodities. At the other end of the continuum are more violent attacks such as rape, incest, child molestation and rape-murder. If the goals of prevention education are to provide information and skills to reduce and ultimately eliminate sexual assault, it is necessary to understand and incorporate prevention skills that address all points along the continuum.

The availability of educational resources for the prevention of sexual assault has dramatically increased and addresses the concerns of the toddler, adolescent, parent and service provider. It is not an oversight that few materials and training resources are available to speak to the needs of persons with disabilities. It is important to ask why. To do this we must look historically at how our society perceives people with disabilities.

Our society continues to perpetuate, both institutionally and individually, the myths that people with disabilities are asexual, pathetic, dependent burdens on society. These myths, coupled with the myths of child molestation and rape, keep people from taking sexual assault of disabled persons seriously. Making sexual assault prevention education accessible to people with disabilities contradicts those myths. People with disabilities are sexual, capable and have a right to sexual assault prevention skills as a tool to maximize their independent living.

We know several of the factors that make all children vulnerable to sexual assault. These include dependency on adults, the value society places on obeying an adult's authority regardless of his/her behavior, and the belief that children make up stories and tell lies. For the child with a disability, these same factors exist but with a greater intensity and frequency. Often the child with a disability has to be prepared to take greater risks to break the silence and get help.

For example, consider the factor of dependency. The child who has severe cerebral palsy is dependent on a variety of caretakers and therapists for day-to-day survival. The dependent relationships are ongoing and long term. A disability does not inherently mean dependency on others. It does require specialized care and services. Data indicate that victims of sexual assault who have a disability have known the offender 99 percent of the time (as compared to 65-85 percent for the nondisabled population). The offender might be a parent, stepfather, boyfriend, bus driver, home attendant, etc. A prevention program must emphasize development of positive and nurturing relationships with a variety of caretakers. It must also include self-protection skills for situations involving strangers as well as caretakers and family members.

Children in our society are taught to obey authority. Children with disabilities receive the same message. In addition, they often have a greater need to be accepted and to receive approval from adults. The child with mental retardation might only have experienced attention from adults that is exploitative. The abusive adult takes advantage of this child's lack of vocabulary and communication skills. A prevention program must teach the child ways of identifying and telling about the problem.

The fact that adults often assume children fabricate stories and tell lies can continue the patterns of abuse. The offender manipulates and coerces the child to expect that no one will believe her or him. Adults who listen to the child's disclosure and deny it impede the process of the child's getting help. Prevention programs must emphasize that no matter what the abusive behaviors have been, the child is not at fault and her or his disclosures must be believed.

Specific to children with disabilities is the factor of isolation. Often they are denied access to normal, day-to-day rhythms and activities that teach children about their world. The child with a disability misses much of the informal exchanges that teach about relationships, communication and choices. Peer interaction may also be limited. For example, the deaf student may use an interpreter in his or her classroom but misses the important communication in the hallways, on the bus or in the cafeteria.

Solving the problem of helping children with disabilities be safe by restricting their activities is not the answer. Restricting their experiences only continues the patterns of isolation, dependency and discrimination. The solution is accessible sexual assault prevention education for children, parents and staff. Children with disabilities are capable and entitled to self-protection education adapted to their specific strengths and needs. It is with this philosophy that prevention training must be approached.

Training Model

The Disabilities Project has developed an original training model that effectively teaches teams of educators, parents and service providers from all parts of the country to plan and implement prevention programs for children with disabilities. The educators who have participated in this training work with children with disabilities in a variety of ways. They may be teachers, nurses, psychologists, advocates, parents, administrators, inservice trainers, therapists, group home staff, physicians or law enforcement workers. The common thread linking the participants is that first they learn for themselves and then they teach others the skills and knowledge necessary to ensure effective sexual assault prevention for persons with disabilities. Some of the highlights of the training model are discussed below.

1. *Value and Attitude Clarification.* In order to effectively teach and support sexual assault prevention one needs to look honestly at one's own values and attitudes. For example, a parent may ask, "If my child learns about private body parts, won't she get pregnant?" An educator's response will be most helpful if she/he is able to share accurate information while separating out personal values. The training helps educators look at the issues of sexuality, disability, violence, and cultural differences so that they can give accurate information. The training also provides participants with an opportunity to explore personal experiences and understand how attitudes can affect an educator's ability to help students.

2. *A Team Approach.* Agency teams receive the training together. This maximizes collaboration and builds an emotional support system. As a result, successful networking in the community can develop. A train-the-trainer approach is a cost effective method to have staff return to their agencies equipped with knowledge and skills and an awareness of local resources to teach coworkers, parents and admin-

istrators about the possibilities of prevention education.

3. *Awareness of Differences.* Making the program accessible to specific groups means being aware of and sensitive to cultural diversities and different lifestyles. For example, in the Asian culture it is often not acceptable to discuss sexual behavior in public. This fact will influence the organization and content of a parent meeting. Accessibility also means respecting the range of differences in religious beliefs and lifestyles. The training model encourages adaptation of the curriculum to address the differences in abilities that children with disabilities have. It also incorporates the diversity of living situations. Thus materials and activities speak to children living at home with parent(s), in group homes, institutions or independently.

4. *Parents/Caregivers as Allies.* Experience demonstrates that parents are more likely to support sexual assault prevention programs if they participate in the planning process, preview the curriculum and have an opportunity to voice their concerns. The training model emphasizes strategies for successfully working with parents and caretakers. It is often possible to teach parents how the child with a disability can learn prevention strategies while she/he continues to operate within a specific family value system.

A Curriculum for Developing an Awareness of Sexual Abuse and Self-Protection Techniques was developed by the Disabilities Project as a tool for special educators to teach self-protection to their disabled clients/students ages six to adult. It was originally designed for persons with developmental disabilities, however the training now offers ways to adapt the curriculum to meet the needs of persons with varied disabilities. Ways to effectively use this curriculum and other educational materials are a priority in the training. The curriculum has been effectively used in the classroom with parent groups, and at inservice trainings.

Making sexual assault prevention education available to children with disabilities has the potential to positively impact their lives and change society in many ways. Prevention education can:

- Increase children's self-esteem and positive self-image
- Provide children with the vocabulary and experience to talk about the assault and understand they are not to blame
- Decrease children's isolation and increase support from peers
- Provide education in appropriate sexual behavior
- Increase response from legal, medical and social service systems to the needs of children with disabilities.

Editor's Note: *See "Disabilities Project, Seattle Rape Relief" in Part II,* Prevention Programs at Work, *for a description of its program components.*

Chapter 17

Evaluating Prevention Education Programs

JON R. CONTE

The last five years have witnessed a dramatic explosion of programs to prevent the sexual victimization of children. Although it is not known how many children have received such programming, it is likely that the number is well into the hundreds of thousands. Programs have been offered through day care centers, schools, church and civic groups, as well as on television and through print and audiovisual media.

Preventing the sexual victimization of children is an admirable motive that most parents and professionals support. However, a number of concerns about these programs have been voiced. Will children become more fearful or distrustful of adults? Can programs be effective in preventing sexual abuse? This brief essay will review what is known about the effects of prevention education and suggest some preliminary guidelines that may be useful in assuring the quality of prevention education programming. (For more extensive information about educational materials see "Child Sexual Abuse Prevention Resources"; Finkelhor and Aragi, 1983; Conte et al, in press.)

What Is Sexual Abuse Prevention Education?

Prevention education programs may differ in several ways. The terms used to describe prevention concepts, the number of hours the program requires, the training and occupation of the person delivering the program, and the ages of the children the program is designed to teach may all be different.

Nevertheless, most prevention programs are designed to enable children to do three things:

- Programs help children discriminate among often subtle and confusing situations, experiences or behaviors that are thought to be partly responsible for sexual abuse. These include helping children understand the differences between a secret and a surprise, and the difference between different types of touching (good vs. bad vs. confusing touch).
- Programs teach children safety concepts such as the following. Your body is your own, you don't have to share it with anyone. If someone touches you in a way that isn't ok, say no! Then run and tell! You don't have to keep a

secret about touching.

- Most programs want to teach children assertiveness and other behavioral skills that may be useful in preventing or escaping from potentially abusive situations.

Do We Teach What We Should Be Teaching?

One of the important things to keep in mind about preventing sexual abuse is that the content of most programs is based upon our best guesses about what children will find useful in preventing their own sexual abuse. In fact, there has never been a systematic investigation of the processes through which adults select, develop a relationship with, manipulate, coerce and subsequently maintain the silence of children they abuse.

The more we learn about sexual abuse, the more it appears that we may not be teaching children all the concepts and skills really necessary to prevent at least some forms of sexual abuse. For example, nothing that we currently teach is likely to be useful to a child who has watched the head of a living animal torn off and been told that this would happen to her/his parents if she/he tells anyone about the abuse (*Newsweek*, 1984).

It seems very clear that professionals who deliver prevention education to children must keep constantly abreast of new findings about the nature of sexual abuse and the processes through which abusers groom and coerce children. Only then will they be effective in incorporating new prevention content that is being developed as new knowledge is gained.

What Effects Are Programs Having?

Increasingly, professionals are conducting evaluations to determine how effective their programs are. These evaluations have tended to focus on children's knowledge gains. For example, Carol Plummer used a likert scale in a twenty-four item questionnaire (e.g. "Is it ok to say no to adults? always, often, sometimes, never") and found that a prevention program was successful in increasing children's knowledge (Plummer, n.d.). However, at two and eight month follow-up contacts, children exhibited significant losses in knowledge.

JoAnn Ray used a twelve-item questionnaire and found that a booster session sometime after the last education session was useful in maintaining children's knowledge gains (Ray, n.d.). In a study using a prevention education group and a wait-list control group, Jon Conte and colleagues found that children exposed to education learned significantly more than did control group children (Conte et al, 1985). However, on the whole, children in the education group only learned about 50 percent of the knowledge the program intended. This latter study also found that children had greater difficulty learning prevention content that was of an abstract rather than concrete nature.

Although most programs indicate they seek to increase children's skill acquisition, few programs have demonstrated that they successfully are able to actually teach children prevention skills. For example, Ann Downer found that 90 percent of children in her study were correctly able to define assertiveness, but only 47 percent could give an example (Downer, n.d.).

These results, preliminary as they are, suggest

that many children are able to learn at least some of the information prevention programs try to teach. Some children appear to learn most of what programs try to teach. But children are going to forget over time, thus some kind of periodic booster or reminder of what they have learned appears important. There is little evidence currently available to suggest that programs are successful in actually teaching children the behaviors (skills) thought to be useful in preventing or escaping sexual abuse.

Unanticipated Consequences

Some adults are concerned that sexual abuse prevention programs will make children fearful or distrustful of adults. There is currently no research shedding any light on this concern. Anecdotal information does raise some concern, however. For example, a Midwest program has reported that after one of its education sessions, some preschoolers were afraid to ride home with anyone but their parents. In the Chicago study Jon Conte and colleagues conducted, review of audiotapes of the programs indicated that some educators were using frightening stories to get children's attention (e.g., "There are people out there who want to take you away from your Mommies"). These stories produced an unknown effect in the children and were not prescribed by the education program.

It is not known how often particular educators vary from the prescribed prevention program. Such variation does raise concern

about the effects of material they may introject. More to the point here, it is not clear what unanticipated effects prevention education may have.

Therefore it seems prudent to recognize that *prevention programs are experimental and should be approached with the care and attention to evaluation that any potentially powerful intervention deserves.* This does not suggest that prevention education should cease. The negative risks of sexual abuse are clear and programs that may be helpful to children in preventing or escaping sexual abuse are well worth the effort. There are, however, a number of guidelines that may be helpful in reducing the risk of unanticipated consequences. These follow.

Guidelines for Program Evaluation

Prevention professionals should consider the following.

Evaluation is part of prevention education.

Evaluating what children learn through knowledge questionnaires or interviews is an essential aspect of prevention education. Children who fail to learn up to the program's criteria should be given additional education. Failure to actually confirm that children have learned what the program intends may give children, and those who care about them, a false sense of security.

Systematically look for unanticipated consequences.

Programs should systematically look for unanticipated consequences that may result. Children should be interviewed by program staff or informally by adults indigenous to their environment (e.g. parents or teachers) after the prevention program. Such interviewing should probe for children's misunderstanding of prevention content, fears resulting from the program and other unanticipated consequences.

Programs should be monitored.

Variation from prescribed program content by individual educators seems inevitable. Such variation may involve material more likely to produce unanticipated consequences or simply result in important material not being presented. To help keep educators within the prevention model, their delivery of the program should be monitored by audio or videotape recordings or in vivo. Checklists could also be developed to help the educators stay within the prescribed model.

Maintain current knowledge.

It is clear that knowledge about the nature of sexual abuse is changing radically and swiftly. Prevention educators should recognize the great flux surrounding sexual abuse generally and prevention specifically. Efforts to obtain the latest knowledge or new findings about sexual abuse and sexual abuse prevention are inherent necessities of those who assume the responsibility of trying to help children prevent their own abuse.

References

Child Sexual Abuse Prevention Resources. Chicago: The National Committee for the Prevention of Child Abuse (NCPCA, 332 S. Michigan, Suite 1250, Chicago, IL 60604).

Conte, Jon R. "Research on the Prevention of Sexual Abuse of Children." Unpublished manuscript. (The University of Chicago, 969 East 60th St., Chicago, IL 60637.)

Conte, Jon R., Carole Rosen and Leslee Saperstein. "An Analysis of Programs to Prevent Sexual Victimization of Children." *The Journal of Primary Prevention,* in press.

Conte, John R., Carole Rosen, Leslee Saperstein and Roberta Shermack. "An Evaluation of a Program to Prevent the Sexual Victimization of Young Children." *Child Abuse and Neglect: The International Journal* (1985).

Downer, Ann. "Evaluation of *Talking About Touching.*" Unpublished manuscript. (Author, P.O. Box 15190, Seattle, WA 98115.)

Finkelhor, David and Sharon Aragi. "The Prevention of Sexual Abuse: A Review of Current Approaches." Unpublished manuscript, 1983. (Family Violence Research Program, University of New Hampshire, Durham, NH 03824.)

Plummer, Carol. "Research on Prevention: What In School Programs Teach Children." Unpublished manuscript. (Author, P.O. Box 421, Kalamazoo, MI 49005.)

Ray, JoAnn. "Evaluation of the Child Sexual Abuse Prevention Project." Unpublished manuscript. (Author, 1226 N. Howard, Spokane, WA 98201.)

"A Sordid Preschool 'Game'." *Newsweek,* April 9, 1984, p. 38.

Chapter 18

New Myths About Child Sexual Abuse

MARY ELLEN STONE

Individuals who are concerned about child sexual abuse are familiar with the myths and stereotypes associated with the problem. The following chart summarizes common misconceptions on the left, the reality on the right.

Myths	Realities
A dangerous stranger	• A known person, often a relative or friend of the family, is most often the offender (85% of the cases)
Isolated incident	• Over and over again
Out-of-the-blue	• A situation that develops gradually over a period of time
Rare and extreme	• Frequent incidents; many forms of sexual assault
A violent attack	• Subtle coercion rather than extreme force

(Lois Loontjens in Fay, 1979).

Educators in schools, rape crisis centers, theatre groups, parent organizations and synagogue and church associations, have caused a significant shift in public thinking about child sexual abuse. Curricula, books, pamphlets, theatre presentations and film and video productions have been developed for both parents and children. The premise is that accurate information is a key to prevention.

Education for prevention is just beginning. But along with exciting new developments in teaching approaches and program evaluation also has come a whole new set of myths. These new myths fall into three categories.

1. Child sexual abuse prevention education causes additional problems.
   - Children will fabricate stories about sexual abuse.
   - Children will fear closeness and touch.
   - Children will become suspicious and paranoid.
2. Children who recant about a sexual assault were lying about the initial report.
3. There are only a few "demented" sex offenders.

The emergence of these new myths illustrates once again that sexual abuse remains very much a part of our culutre. Yet, great effort is being spent to deny its existence. It is still easier to assume some fault in our children, such as lying, than it is to believe what study after study indicates: one out of every four to one out of every two girls and one out of every nine boys are sexually assaulted by the age of 18 (Kinsey et al, 1953; Landis, 1956; Gagnor, 1965; Russell, 1984). We would rather teach our children the dangerous stranger myth than have them question the actions of a trusted adult, questioning that is interpreted as being suspicious or fearful of closeness.

Children are not the ones who are questioning reality. Adults are. Sigmund Freud, well known for his pioneering work in the field of psychoanalysis (as well as many other contributions), was also responsible for some of the early documentation of child sexual abuse. In the course of developing his theories on the origins of hysteria, he noted that without exception, all women exhibiting such symptoms reported having been sexually abused by their fathers. Freud concluded these assaults did not occur. Instead he decided they were fantasies. As he wrote to his colleague Fleiss in 1897, "it was hardly credible that perverted acts against children were so general" (Freud, 1954).

The words may be different but the message is the same today. Children are being sexually abused but many adults refuse to believe them. The findings of hundreds of rape crisis centers and treatment programs across the country consistently demonstrate:

1. Children rarely fabricate stories of sexual abuse. In the instances where this happens, falsely reporting sexual abuse is an indication of another problem the child is unable to express.

2. When prevention programs are appropriate to the child's age and development, and presented in a safety-oriented and calm manner, children are not frightened. They are relieved. Most children live with the unexplained fear of strangers. So having specific information about what an adult they know might do and what action they can take gives them more control.

3. Children may recant when the offender, their parents or law enforcement officials pressure them to do so. They recant not because they were not abused but because the need for family acceptance and security is crucial to their survival.

As educators our task is twofold. First, we must encourage new research and inquiries into more effective means of presenting information to children. Evaluation of our presentations should be ongoing. How long do children retain this information? What is useful and what isn't? How can prevention information truly be an integral part of a child's development? Second, we must stay current on new myths about child sexual abuse. They reflect community concerns and must be addressed and demystified if prevention education is to be effective.

References

Fay, Jennifer. *He Told Me Not To Tell*. Renton, WA: King County Rape Relief, 1979.

Freud, S. *The Origins of Psychoanalysis: Letters to William Fleiss, Drafts & Notes 1887-1902*. New York: Basic Books, 1954.

Gagnon, J. "Female Child Victims of Sex Offenses." *Social Problems* 13 (1965).

Kinsey, A. C., W. B. Pomeroy, C. E. Martin and P. H. Gebhard. *Sexual Behavior in the Human Female*. Philadelphia: W. B. Saunders, 1953.

Landis, J. T. "Experience of 500 Children with Adult's Sexual Relations." *Psychiatric Quarterly* 30 (1956).

Russell, D. *Sexual Exploitation: Rape, Child Sexual Abuse and Workplace Harassment*. Beverly Hills, CA: Sage, 1984.

Chapter 19

Implications for Theory, Research and Practice

DAVID FINKELHOR

Research about child sexual abuse is critical to the prevention effort. David Finkelhor is a research scientist who has worked in the area of child sexual abuse since 1979. His surveys and studies have provided educators and other professionals, parents and public officials with the theoretical perspectives necessary to develop, implement and improve prevention and intervention techniques.

This excerpt from his latest book, Child Sexual Abuse: New Theory and Research, *discusses future directions for theory, research and practice in child sexual abuse prevention. It, therefore, is a fitting conclusion to this book as well.*

Interest in the problem of child sexual abuse is not merely a fad. As this book (*Child Sexual Abuse*) has shown, the problem is substantial, not just in terms of its scope and its impact on victims and their families, but also in terms of the issues it raises for scholars, practitioners and policy makers. Interest in the problem is destined to grow because it poses many challenges to people engaged in a variety of endeavors. Challenges that they will want to confront rather than avoid. Although these challenges will not appeal to everyone, they will draw in committed and idealistic people looking for new solutions to old dilemmas.

As new people are drawn, we will undoubtedly see the field develop rapidly in new directions. Older ideas and approaches may become obsolete. While it is impossible to predict all the new directions the field may take, I think certain directions will prove more fruitful than others. I would like to conclude this book (*Child Sexual Abuse*) by outlining some of the developments that I think will be most important to the field. They fall into three areas: theory, research and practice. I will address each one in turn.

Theory Development

Theories about child sexual abuse have been slow to emerge, and this slowness has in turn hampered research as well as practice. New theories have a way of generating a sense of

133

intellectual excitement as well as practical activity—two developments the field could desperately use.

One way to foster new theory is to attract people with a theoretical bent into the field. Such people are often from academic backgrounds and have been in short supply in the field partly because sexual abuse treatment and research have grown up outside academic institutions. Instead, interest in sexual abuse has developed in social service agencies, prosecutors' offices and rape crisis centers. The major medical and mental health centers, which sponsor a great deal of new thinking and research (and which have been active in the field of physical child abuse), have been slow to become involved.

However, more theoretically oriented people will increasingly get involved, either on their own or with some major institutions. As such people become more interested in sexual abuse, they will apply new theoretical approaches to the problem. We can speculate on what some of those new theoretical approaches might be.

Borrowing Theory from Other Fields

A variety of theoretical perspectives in the field of social psychology might be applied usefully to the problem of sexual abuse, as they have been applied to some other social and psychological problems. One example is attribution theory. Attribution theory concerns itself with the interpretations and assumptions that people as "naive psychologists" make about their own and other people's behavior (Bem, 1972). Attribution theorists have taken an interest in such questions as what prompts people to hold rape victims responsible for their own rapes (Cann et al, 1979) or what prompts battered women to see themselves at fault for being beaten (Frieze, 1978). There are many parallel questions in the field of child sexual abuse: What factors contribute to abused children's seeing themselves as to blame for their victimization? What factors contribute to professionals' or the public's feeling unsympathetic toward child sexual abuse victims? Another question is, What contributes to sexual abusers' and others' seeing many children's normal affectionate behavior as sexually provocative and sexually motivated? These questions are ripe for theoretical work.

Another theoretical framework that might be well-borrowed is from the field of moral development. The literature on moral development, which was originally conceived to explain how children acquire the capacity to solve ethical dilemmas, has recently been applied to adults, who may also display different levels of complexity in their moral thinking. Newberger (1980; Newberger and Cook, 1983) has recently developed theory suggesting that physical abusers are characterized by a more primitive level of moral development than nonabusers. Sexual abusers appear unable to identify with the potential harm their actions may cause their child victims (Summit and Kryso, 1978).

This suggests that deficits in moral development may exist in sexual abusers as well. Writers on moral development also have theorized about the different patterns of moral development that are displayed by men versus women (Gilligan, 1982). These different patterns may be part of what explains the low incidence of women engaging in sexual abuse. If we can identify the sources of some of the deficits or differences in moral development, we may be able to better identify the individuals at high risk to become abusers.

These are but two examples of theory-borrowing that might prove fruitful. Unfortunately, theory-borrowing is sometimes more difficult than it might seem at first glance. Some of the difficulties can be seen by looking at two other fields from which theory-borrowing would seem to have been natural, but which have been quite problematic.

It would seem natural to look for new insights about sexual abuse by borrowing theories concerning sexual behavior in general. Yet of all the branches of behavioral sciences, this is one of the least developed (Gagnon, 1977). Imagine how useful it would be to have a general understanding of how sexual proclivities develop and thus why some individuals come to be sexually interested in children. Instead we have only some very sketchy, ad hoc clinical theories of why some men become pedophiles and practically no understanding of how people in general come to choose certain sexual objects.

For another example, imagine how useful it would be to have an understanding of how sexual dynamics are managed in healthy, nonabusive families so we could see clearly what is different about incestuously abusive ones. Imagine how useful it would be to know how ordinary, nonabused children develop conceptions of their own sexuality, so we could restore a normal process to those who had been abused. Instead we know practically nothing about either of these matters.

The field of sexual abuse will be greatly enriched by theoretical developments in the general field of human sexual behavior. We need to keep this in mind and try to encourage the development of knowledge and theory in that field.

Another field from which theory-borrowing has been problematic is anthropology. At one time, writers in the field of sexual abuse regularly tried to draw from anthropology (Bagley, 1969). Articles from anthropology journals regularly cascaded out in literature searches giving "incest" as a key word. But in retrospect this literature has turned out to be of fairly limited usefulness.

The main problem concerns the fact that although anthropologists share the term incest with sexual abuse researchers, in reality, the two groups are concerned with very different and rather unrelated problems. Anthropologists are primarily interested in explaining the development and existence of a social institution—the incest taboo—whereas sexual abuse researchers are interested in explaining a certain form of deviant behavior among specific individuals and families.

Moreover, the term incest itself means something very different for each group. For anthropologists, in addition to sexual behavior, it also covers violation of rules of marriage and applies to relationships between blood relatives, whatever their age and relationship. Sexual abuse researchers, however, are not very interested in 26-year-old cousins who marry each other. Incest for them means sexual contacts between adults and dependent children, and matters of consensual sex among adults, marriage, blood relations, or even whether actual intercourse occurred are of little importance.

In the end, I think the sharing of the term incest between these two fields has been more confusing than helpful. Sex abuse researchers are continually thrown off base when they find people using the anthropological definition of incest to make some point that seems offensive to their perspective (Cohen, 1978); for example, "such and such a culture practices incest [e.g., cousin marriages] with no bad effects."

In the past, I have tried to encourage people in the field of sexual abuse to relinquish the word incest and talk about family or intrafamilial sexual abuse (which is what they mean). But this advice has made little headway, especially given the evocative character of the word incest, which makes it attractive to everyone from journalists to graduate students.

While I believe that researchers in the field of sexual abuse need to recognize the irrelevance of much of the anthropological literature of the past, they may still look to anthropology to offer some extremely valuable insights in the future. But these insights will require new anthropological research.

What is curious about the field of anthropology is that it has dwelt so extensively on the question of incest (meaning marriage and sexual intercourse among blood kin) and so briefly on the question of sexual contacts between adults and children. How society regulates sexual behavior between the mature and the immature is of substantial theoretical interest, as much as how it regulates sexual behavior among blood kin. Anthropologists have debated whether all societies have some form of incest taboo. Do they also all have some form of taboo or regulation on sex between adults and children? My guess is that this latter is as widespread

as the former. Anthropology could obviously be of great assistance to the field of sexual abuse if it were to investigate and theorize about this question.

There are many other potential questions to answer as well. For example, if in some societies sexual contact does occur, as it seems to, between the mature and the immature, how is it controlled, what effects does it have, and how is it regarded? Does some violation of the norms against adults having sex with children occur in all societies? What factors may account for such violations being more or less widespread? For example, anthropologist Peggy Sanday (1981) analyzed 95 societies according to their prevalence of rape and found that rape was part of a cultural configuration of societies that had high levels of interpersonal violence, male dominance and sexual separation. Is there a cultural configuration that produces high levels of child sexual abuse in addition to rape? It will be an exciting development when anthropologists turn attention to questions such as these.

Some of the most active transfer of theory into the field of sexual abuse has come from feminism. In fact, it was in part the feminist postulate that sexual assault was endemic to American society that prompted attention to sexual abuse in the first place. Indeed, feminism has proposed a variety of theoretical speculations about sexual abuse, many of which are waiting to be refined and investigated.

For example, feminists have argued that the large disparities of power between men and women in American society contribute to the occurrence of sexual abuse (Herman, 1981; Rush, 1980). There is some evidence that this is true. Part of what is still needed, though, is detailed articulation of the various ways in which these power inequities create offenders, make children vulnerable, increase the trauma, and inhibit reporting.

Feminists have also suggested the notion that the different ways in which men and women are socialized contribute to the problem (Herman, 1981). Differences in male and female socialization are still being actively explored in theory and in research (Gilligan, 1982). As new insights develop concerning sexual socialization, they should be tested as quickly as possible for their applicability to the problem of sexual abuse.

Feminists have recently turned a substantial amount of attention to pornography and have suggested that it may play a role in the promotion of sexual exploitation of children (Rush, 1980). Most detailed analysis of pornography, however, has concentrated on its contribution to rape. The connection between pornography and child victimization deserves a similar kind of serious scholarly investigation. It seems likely that such attention is simply a matter of time and that many of the new directions in feminism, such as its interest in pornography, will provide intriguing potential for theory in the field of sexual abuse.

Theory Building Within the Field

Borrowing theory from outside the field is not the only route to developing new theory. Theories can be developed from within the field by combining, expanding and adding on to what already exists. There are some obvious ways for this to proceed.

Currently, there are two virtually separate and unconnected bodies of theory: theories developed from work with offenders and theories developed from work with victims and their families. These two fields need to be reconciled. The reconciliation has been hampered for several reasons. First, the theorists work with very different populations. Most of the offender theory has been developed through work with incarcerated pedophiles—men who have sexually abused outside the family. Most of the victim-related work has been done with incestuous families or with families where the offenders were no longer present. Second, the theorists have little professional contact with one another. They attend different professional meetings and write for different journals.

Two things need to happen. These groups have to begin collaborating on clinical work and on research. Offender researchers need to look at offenders together with their victims and the victims' families. They need to study incest offenders as well as pedophiles. Victim researchers need to pay much closer attention to understanding the offenders and begin to delve into the offenders' backgrounds. Moreover, a dialogue needs to be encouraged professionally among these researchers. Conferences need to be organized to bring the two groups together.

One factor in particular that has hampered the pooling of offender and victim research is family-systems theory. Family-systems theory has been one of the most eagerly welcomed theoretical developments in the field of mental health in generations. It has proven useful for clinicians working with families where sexual abuse has occurred and has been widely adopted throughout the field.

But the family-systems perspective has also introduced two unhealthy biases into the field.

First, it has created strong theoretical interest in one form of sexual abuse, father-daughter incest, to the exclusion of all other forms. Second, it has discouraged interest in studies of offenders.

Family-systems theory concentrates on one form of sexual abuse because that is the form of sexual abuse that its theory best explains. In father-daughter incest, according to the theory, the marital relationship has broken down, the mother is alienated from the roles of wife and mother, and the father makes an alliance with the oldest daughter that substitutes for the marital relationship and becomes sexual. This theory encompasses some of the most cherished principles of the family-systems perspective, including the danger of cross-generational alliances and the collusion of all family members in family pathology.

Many criticisms have been made of the theory, including raising the question of whether it unfairly makes the mother and the daughter responsible for the incest. But one additional criticism is that the theory tends to focus all attention on one form of sexual abuse. Father-daughter incest is a common form of sexual abuse but it probably accounts for less than a third of all abuse. Other forms of sexual abuse, by older brothers, uncles, grandparents—not to mention abuse by nonfamily members such as neighbors, teachers, and friends, all of which is also common—are not so easily explained. Theoretical attention needs to be devoted to these types of abuse too.

One reason why some of these other forms of abuse have not received attention is that family-systems theory also makes an implicit theoretical distinction between family sexual abuse and nonfamily abuse. Family abuse can utilize family dynamics and family-systems theory to explain it; nonfamily abuse has to look elsewhere. Because family-systems is the dominant paradigm, theorists have not tackled nonfamily abuse.

But is this theoretical division warranted? No, not at least in light of theoretical and empirical work done to date. Abuse by a grandfather who lives across town may not be so different from abuse by a neighbor who lives next door or down the street. More attention needs to be paid to developing theory that can apply to broader categories of abuse than simply father-daughter or intrafamily contacts.

The popularity of family-systems theory has also led to a relative neglect of theorizing about offenders. For the most part, family-systems theory has treated sexual abuse as a problem of family dynamics. Questions about the history, attitudes, and motivations of offenders have been considered matters for traditional individual psychology, which family-systems theory avoids. This has been another reason for the lack of communication between offender researchers, who are individual-oriented forensic psychologists, and victim researchers, who are more often of the family-systems persuasion.

However, focus on family dynamics alone is not adequate. Clinicians are finding that offenders need individual work as well as family treatment to stop their abusing. Some research has found that incest offenders are less different from other pedophiles than was once thought (Abel et al, 1981). Family-systems theory has many insights about how family dynamics may contribute to the abuse situation, but this theory needs to be melded with other theoretical insights about offenders.

New Directions in Research

Research on child sexual abuse is so badly needed that it is hard to think of any kind of study that would not be welcome. Yet some particular undertakings should be given priority.

Prevalence and Incidence Studies

As more people have become aware of the problem of sexual abuse, the demand for accurate statistics about its scope has intensified. A few studies do make a start at meeting this demand. But there are still important shortcomings to all of these studies and any future efforts should be directed toward trying to remedy these shortcomings.

The studies reported in *Child Sexual Abuse*, as well as Russell's San Francisco study (1983), establish that adults in the community can be surveyed about their own childhood sexual abuse experiences. In both these surveys, the majority of cases uncovered had never been reported to any professional. This type of study clearly gives a more accurate picture of sexual abuse than studies based entirely on reported cases.

However, this adult survey design has the disadvantage of not being current. We have no way of knowing whether the present cohort of children is experiencing the same level of sexual abuse as a cohort who are now adults. One improvement on the adult survey design which would make it more current would be to concentrate on the youngest cohort of adults available. Thus, for example, a survey of 18-year-olds would give a more accurate picture of the sexual abuse experience of children for the last decade. It is even conceivable that children, particularly older children, could be surveyed. If the interviewees were children, certain ethical problems would have to be confronted, such as protecting them from possible retaliation by abusers and providing them with services when cases were uncovered.

Another design alternative is to interview parents about the victimization of their own children, as we did in the Boston survey. The results of this survey suggest, however, that parents either do not know about or are reluctant to volunteer information about the abuse of their children by intimates. But by refining and experimenting with interview techniques (such as allowing parents to fill out self-administered forms or giving them a great deal of specific encouragement to be candid), it may be possible to improve reporting of intrafamilial abuse. Certainly the success of the National Survey of Family Violence (Straus et al, 1980) in getting parents to reveal that they had used serious force against their children (3 percent said they had threatened to use a knife or gun on their child sometime in the child's life) suggests that it is possible to get parents to confide embarrassing, serious normative violations. We should not yet discount the possibility that we might be able to coax parents to reveal sexual abuse incidents that they, their partners, or other close relatives have committed.

Even if we find we cannot get sufficient candor from perpetrators, we can certainly gather much more information about sexual abuse from other individuals in the community besides the perpetrator or victim. In our Boston survey, 20 percent of the adult respondents knew of a child of a friend or a neighbor who had been sexually abused. We did not gather enough information to allow us to judge the quality or the source of these respondents' knowledge, but clearly much information about cases unknown to professionals can be obtained from the general public. Some statistical problems naturally exist in going from such third-party reports to a true incidence rate (Light, 1974), but the large number of cases uncovered from these sources would, undoubtedly, provide a completely different perspective on the sexual abuse problem, as well as on the possibilities for increasing levels of official reporting.

Ultimately, of coure, some restraint needs to be put on the demand for more and better incidence and prevalence figures. Although they do alert people to the size of the problem, such figures are of limited usefulness to social scientists, clinicians and policy makers. They do not necessarily add to our understanding of how to identify or prevent abuse. Since precise figures on prevalence may be difficult and expensive to obtain, they should not be emphasized in research to the exclusion of other important issues. Once we have figures making an unambiguous and persuasive case that the problem is widespread, then they will be accurate enough.

Risk Factors

The line of research that would be most productive for both theory and practice would focus on identifying what characteristics put children at high risk for abuse. The identification of such characteristics would give practitioners some markets that could direct their efforts toward prevention and detection and would push researchers to develop theories to account for why these characteristics are associated with abuse. Think, for example, of how important to the field of child abuse it has been to discover that teenage mothers and mothers whose bonding with their children is interrupted are at particularly high risk to abuse. Whole programs of research and intervention have developed as a result of such a finding. No similar risk factors are, as yet, so clearly identified in the case of sexual abuse.

A broad range of risk factors need to be explored, including class and ethnic variables, demographic variables, and family constellation variables. We also need to look at characteristics of adults that make them high-risk to offend and characteristics of children that make them highly vulnerable targets. At present, we have only rough hypotheses about a small number of risk factors and very little evidence.

Explorations of risk factors can occur in many ways. Nonclinical populations—students, organization members, professionals, whole communities—can be sampled and the victims of sexual abuse compared with nonvictims on a wide range of suspected or possible risk factors. Random sampling of populations, as in Russell's (1983) study, makes for much better designs, but it is not necessary for the kinds of exploratory studies that are needed at this stage.

Risk factors can be done also with clinical samples if a plausible comparison or control group can be found within the same setting. This type of design has the obvious problem that all the sexual abuse cases are reported cases, but such studies still are eminently worth doing given the current level of knowledge.

Given what hunches we already have about sexual abuse through clinical work and preliminary studies, certain types of risk factors should be looked at particularly carefully.

1. Any type of physical or emotional challenge to a child—illness, handicap, learning disability, stigma, psychological disturbance—that may compromise a child's ability to avoid molestation.
2. Any type of impairment in parenting capacities, particularly ways in which mothers may be incapacitated, that may reduce the supervision and support that would protect against sexual abuse.
3. Characteristics of potential offenders that may allow them to be identified from the general population: a history of other forms of sexual deviance, alcohol problems, social isolation, having been the victim of sexual abuse, hypersexuality.

The identification of risk factors within these broad categories will be a major advance on the road to identifying where sexual abuse occurs.

Topics in Need of Research

Several additional questions are in need of research. One is the sexual abuse of boys. Probably the most serious question in regard to boys is how their response to victimization differs from that of girls and how clinicians can take this difference into account. Even purely descriptive accounts of work with sexually abused boys would be an important resource given the current state of ignorance on the subject.

Questions surrounding the long-term effects of abuse also need much greater elaboration. What is desperately needed is a study which follows a cohort of victimized children through-out their development and charts the ongoing effects at different stages of development. One of the most important points made by recent research on the long-term effects of divorce on children (Wallerstein, 1983) is that traumatic childhood experiences have different effects at different stages of the life cycle. While these effects are somewhat predictable from what we know of the demands of different developmental stages, how a particular child will respond to those demands cannot be specified. A child who seems relatively free from effects at one stage may develop symptoms in response to the demands of another, depending on the nature of the abuse, personality, and other stresses posed by the developmental process. Researchers need to follow children throughout their development and document the impact of abuse at each point.

The nature and diversity of research on offenders also needs to be expanded. Almost all research to date on offenders has been on incarcerated populations, who are clearly not representative of all offenders. To study a more diverse group of offenders, researchers need to broaden the subject pool to include those who are just entering the criminal justice system, those who plea bargain out of jail sentences, offenders in diversion programs, offenders in voluntary treatment, and those who have been detected by child protection workers but are not the subject of criminal justice action. It is also possible to try to study undetected offenders. Studies have been conducted on undetected rapists (Kanin, 1957), and at least one qualitative study interviewed a large number of undetected pederasts (Rossman, 1976). Work needs to be done on the possibility of studying adults who have had sexual contact with children, but who are not the subject of child welfare or criminal investigation.

Finally, there is a pressing need to evaluate the effects of various intervention strategies. Communities around the country are currently struggling to set up programs to respond to the challenge of sexual abuse. A variety of long-standing programs offer themselves as models, but policy makers have little objective evidence to guide them in decisions about what are the relative advantages and disadvantages of different models. Such outcome research will greatly advance the welfare of sexual abuse victims.

New Directions in Practice

I would like to draw out in greater detail a few implications of the current work for the practitioner.

Unreported Cases

Any research such as that reported here, which attempts to assess how widespread abuse really is, cannot help underline the fact that a great deal more sexual abuse occurs than ever gets reported. A little arithmetic demonstrates this fact clearly. Suppose 10 percent of all girls were victims of sexual abuse and one boy was victimized for every five girls. (These are conservative figures since the figures from our Boston survey were actually 15 percent for girls and one boy for every three girls. Russell's (1983) figures for girls are even higher—38 percent.) Such a prevalence rate in a population of about 60 million children under 18 should result in over 210,000 new cases of sexual abuse every year. The National Incidence Study (NCCAN, 1981) estimated that approximately

44,700 cases of sexual abuse are uncovered by professionals in a year. This would mean that *only one out of every five cases* is coming to the attention of professionals.

However, such mathematics are not needed to convince us of the extent of the problem; nearly everyone is in agreement that sexual abuse is terribly underreported. Moreover, nearly everyone is engaged in some form of activity designed directly or indirectly to increase the level of reporting. The problem is that we know relatively little about which of these efforts pay off and which do not.

There are three distinct levels at which efforts can be directed: (1) Children themselves need to be encouraged to reveal sexual abuse. (2) Other adults, such as parents and relatives, who know of sexual abuse, need to be encouraged to take their suspicions to professionals. (3) Finally, professionals who know of or suspect cases must be encouraged to pass such information on to official reporting agencies.

There is reason to think that the biggest bottleneck is at the first level: children who do not reveal abuse. Retrospective surveys of adults have never shown that any more than half of them told about the abuse that was occurring. Our surveys of parents' knowledge about their own children also provided evidence that parents do not seem to be hearing from their children about abuse of the same type and in the same quantity that they themselves experienced in their own childhoods. This evidence points toward giving a high priority to reaching children themselves and urging them to tell someone.

Such a message has been one of the main objectives of a variety of sexual abuse prevention programs that have tried to educate school children. These programs have had a great deal of success in Minneapolis, Washington State, the Bay Area in California, and Columbus, Ohio, but they need to receive wider distribution. In another innovative development, sex abuse educators in Seattle, Washington, have recently made a television spot featuring basketball star Bill Russell, who tells children to report anyone who tries to molest them. Efforts are under way to gain national exposure for these messages, and this is a very encouraging development. Efforts that try to reach children through school, television, and other media appear to have the greatest potential to whittle away at the most serious obstacle to greater reporting.

Underreported Groups

Efforts to increase reporting must pay attention to certain groups in which nonreporting is particularly severe. For example, a variety of evidence suggests strongly that the abuse of boys is less likely to come to public attention. This stems from a greater reluctance on the part of boys and their guardians to reveal abuse and a greater reluctance on the part of professionals to suspect it. To increase the reporting of such abuse, special efforts will undoubtedly have to be made. Such efforts should broadcast explicitly the fact that abuse of boys is common. Boys and their families need public reassurance that boys are not at fault for such abuse and that such abuse does not mean that the boys will become homosexuals. However, the under-reporting of abuse of boys has deep roots in sex-role stereotypes and homophobia that will not be easily changed short of a direct assault on these attitudes. Boys will be less likely to report abuse as long as it is considered unmanly

to ask for help or suffer a hurt and as long as being the victim of a sexual assault is a threat to masculinity. So those who would work to increase reporting must help change these attitudes as well.

Young children are another group whose victimization is less likely to be reported. This tendency shows up in the generally younger age of victimization revealed in nonclinical than clinical samples. It also is manifested by the trend for average age of victims to drop as treatment programs become more widespread and better trusted. As trust and awareness build, less easily reported cases of young children being abused slowly get revealed.

Cases involving young children do not get reported for a variety of familiar reasons. Younger children are more intimidated and don't tell. Parents are fearful of the effects of disclosure on the child. Finally, parents and professionals do not entertain suspicions of abuse with such young children.

The methods for combatting these tendencies are also familiar. The fact that younger children are victims needs to be widely publicized, as do some of the symptoms that can be used to diagnose sexual abuse. Parents and children need to hear reassurances about reporting. Perhaps most important, programs need to develop expertise in dealing with cases involving young children so that parents and professionals in the community have a sense of trust that such cases will be skillfully handled. Such trust will foster greater reporting.

Focus on Prevention

The realization that most sexual abuse goes unreported leads to other implications besides the idea that reporting effort needs to be increased. One of these implications is that we need to put more effort into prevention to forestall abuse before it occurs.

The argument for prevention is bolstered by other facts we have uncovered about sexual abuse. Enough children in all segments of society are at-risk that general prevention certainly is worth the effort. Moreover, our Boston survey reinforces the general impression that educators have: most children are currently receiving little accurate or useful information. Parents, according to our results, are eager for their children to receive more education about sexual abuse.

It is an encouraging sign that the challenge of sexual abuse prevention is being taken up. Since 1980, a raft of curricula, children's books, school programs, films, puppet shows and theater performances have appeared. These efforts demonstrate a great deal of creativity and diversity, which has resulted in their adoption and dissemination.

As of the end of 1983, however, there were some obvious gaps in prevention. First, prevention efforts were still highly localized, with areas like Minnesota, California and Washington State out in front, while in many other areas little or nothing was being done. Second, prevention efforts have yet to receive much in the way of national endorsement or promotion. Virtually no federal funding had been directed to sexual abuse prevention and no national organization is actively coordinating or promoting the field.

A key question of prevention waiting to be addressed is whether such efforts can be targeted at particularly high-risk groups. In the case of physical abuse, for example, prevention strategies have focused on educating and monitoring teenage, unmarried and economically stressed parents. What would be parallel strategies for the field of sexual abuse?

One possible parallel direction might come from the fact that children who live with stepparents are at apparently higher risk of abuse. If information could be targeted at families where parents were remarrying, to alert them to some of the foreseeable strains that contribute to vulnerability, some sexual abuse in these families might be avoided. Another group of possibly high-risk children, the developmentally disabled, have been the focus of a well-designed prevention program put together by officials in Minnesota (O'Day, 1983). Still other high-risk groups who might be specially targeted include foster children, adopted children, and those who live in rural or isolated circumstances.

Offender Treatment

Some of the most glaring deficits in the field of sexual abuse currently concern work with offenders. While programs that treat victims and families have proliferated rapidly (Giarretto, 1981), there have been many fewer advances in work with offenders.

The reasons for the difficulty are readily recognized. Offenders generally deny their offense; they are hard to bring to justice or to treatment; and therapists and criminal justice officials do not relish working with them. Unfortunately, techniques for working with offenders have not received widespread dissemination, and many communities lack any concerted approach. However, expertise in working with offenders is improving, and the conclusions from experience around the country need to be made available. Some of the most important conclusions from such work include the following.

1. *Success for both prosecutors and therapists seems to be enhanced by mutual cooperation.* This notion has received increasing endorsement in jurisdictions throughout the country, and new models are being developed and implemented, although entrenched institutional patterns have slowed their adoption.

2. *It is not true that effective treatment can occur only with offenders who are "motivated" to get help, even though this attitude is widespread.* Programs have been successful in treating offenders who were pressured into treatment through threats of prison or parole revocation.

3. *Many incestuous abusers require more than family therapy to insure against re-occurrence of abuse.* Some of the important issues that lead to incestuous abuse, such as a history of childhood trauma, may not be adequately dealt with in family therapy and require individual treatment of offenders as well.

4. *There now exists a wide variety of treatment technologies for dealing with child sex offenders, many of which have proven successful* (Kelley, 1982). These include such techniques as masturbatory reconditioning (Laws and O'Neil, 1979), desensitization (Abel, 1978), heterosocial skills training (Marshall and McKnight, 1975; Whitman and Quinsey, 1981), insight therapy (Kelley, 1982), and antiandrogen drug therapy (Berlin and Meinecke, 1981). While there are controversies about the effectiveness of various approaches, the issue for many experts is not whether any effective approach exists, but rather how to mix and match approaches to types of offenders.

5. *The treatment of child sex offenders is a highly specialized field, and most clinicians, including many who treat other types of offenders, are not skilled enough to treat them.* In spite of this, many child sex offenders are routinely remanded by courts and attorneys to therapists with limited experience in this kind of treatment. This misplacement needs to be monitored and changed.

In summary, in all regions, there is a desperate need for development of specialized child sex offender treatment programs and training of clinicians with expertise in this area. Along with that, research needs to focus on evaluating the effectiveness of various programs and treatment strategies.

Obviously, a great deal needs to be done, and not everything can be done at once. Sexual abuse is a field which in terms of social problems is just being discovered. But its newness can be an asset. In a new field, thinking and practices are not yet set in concrete. We owe it to the children who suffer from this abuse, and who will suffer in the future, to apply our best thinking and our best effort, making sure that what we do has the greatest potential for relieving the present and future toll of sexual abuse.

References

Abel, G. "Treatment of Sexual Aggressives." *Criminal Justice and Behavior* 5 (1978): 291-293.

Abel, G., J. Becker, W. D. Murphy and B. Flanagan. "Identifying Dangerous Child Molesters." In R. B. Stuart (Ed.), *Violent Behavior.* New York: Brunner/Mazel, 1981.

Bagley, C. "Incest Behavior and Incest Taboo." *Social Problems* 16 (1969): 1186-1210.

Berlin, F. and C. F. Meinecke. "Treatment of Sex Offenders with Antiandrogenic Medication: Conceptualization, Review of Treatment Modalities and Preliminary Findings." *American Journal of Psychiatry* 138 (1981): 601-607.

Bern, D. "Self-Perception." In Leonard Berkowitz (Ed.), *Experimental Advances in Social Psychology,* Vol. 7. New York: Academic Press, 1972.

Cann, A., L. Calhoun and J. Selby. "Attributing Responsibility to the Victim of Rape: Influence of Information Regarding Past Sexual Experiences." *Human Relations* 32 (1979): 57-67.

Cohen, Y. "The Disappearance of the Incest Taboo." *Human Nature* (July 1978): 72-78.

Frieze, I. "Self-Perceptions of the Battered Woman." Paper presented at the Annual Meeting of the Association for Women in Psychology, Pittsburgh, PA, 1978.

Gagnon, J. *Human Sexualities.* Glenview, IL: Scott, Foresman, 1977.

Giarretto, H. "A Comprehensive Child Sexual Abuse Treatment Program." *Child Abuse and Neglect* 6 (1981): 263-278.

Gilligan, C. *In a Different Voice.* Cambridge, MA: Harvard University Press, 1982.

Herman, J. *Father-Daughter Incest.* Cambridge, MA: Harvard University Press, 1981.

Kanin, E. "Male Aggression in Dating-Courtship Relations." *American Journal of Sociology* 63 (1957): 197-204.

Kelley, R. J. "Behavioral Re-Orientation of Pedophiliacs: Can It Be Done?" *Clinical Psychology Review* 2 (1982): 387-408.

Laws, D. R. and J. A. O'Neil. "Variations on Masturbatory Conditioning." Paper presented at the 2nd National Conference on Evaluation and Treatment of Sexual Aggressives. New York, 1979.

Light, R. "Abused and Neglected Children in America: A Study of Alternative Policies." *Harvard Educational Review* 43 (1974): 556-598.

Marshall, W. I. and R. D. McKnight. "An Integrated Program for Sexual Offenders." *Canadian Psychiatric Association Journal* 20 (1975): 133-138.

National Center for Child Abuse and Neglect (NCCAN). *Study Findings: National Study of Incidence and Severity of Child Abuse and Neglect.* Washington, DC: DHEW, 1981.

Newberger, C. "Cognitive Structure of Parenthood." In R. Selman and R. Yando (Eds.), *New Directions in Child Development,* Vol. 7, 1980.

Newberger, C. and S. J. Cook. "Parental Awareness and Child Abuse and Neglect: A Cognitive Analysis of Urban and Rural Parents." *American Journal of Orthopsychiatry* 53 (1983): 512-524.

O'Day, B. *Preventing Sexual Abuse of Persons with Disabilities.* St. Paul, MN: Minnesota Department of Corrections, 1983.

Rossman, P. *Sexual Experience Between Men and Boys.* New York: Association Press, 1976.

Rush, F. *The Best Kept Secret.* New York: Prentice-Hall, 1980.

Russell, D. "Incidence and Prevalence of Intrafamily and Extrafamily Sexual Abuse of Female Children." *Child Abuse and Neglect* 7 (1983): 133-146.

Sanday, P. "The Socio-Cultural Context of Rape: A Cross Cultural Study." *Journal of Social Issues* 37 (1981): 5-27.

Straus, M. A., R. Gelles and S. Steinmetz. *Behind Closed Doors: Violence in the American Family.* New York: Doubleday, 1980.

Summit, R. and J. Kryso. "Sexual Abuse of Children: A Clinical Spectrum." *American Journal of Orthopsychiatry* 48 (1978): 237-251.

Wallerstein, J. "Children of Divorce: Preliminary Report of a 10-year Follow-Up." Paper presented at the American Academy of Law and Psychiatry. Portland, OR, 1983.

Whitman, W. and V. Quinsey. "Heterosocial Skill Training for Institutionalized Rapists and Child Molesters." *Canadian Journal of Behavioral Science* 13 (1981): 105-114.

PART II

Prevention Programs at Work

Bridgework Theater
Goshen, Indiana
Audience: Children ages 4 - 16, teachers

Bridgework Theater was formed in 1979 as a touring theater company dedicated to creating original plays about current issues. In 1980 Bridgework received a grant from the National Center on Child Abuse and Neglect to create sexual abuse prevention resources for children.

Bridgework's prevention program centers on two plays. *Little Bear* is for children ages 4 to 11 and *Out of the Trap* for ages 12 to 16. The productions are used in schools to teach children to recognize sexual abuse and increase prevention information and skills. The plays are available in three forms: live performances, video recordings and scripts.

A classroom discussion led by a trained teacher accompanies each presentation. In addition to helping children apply prevention concepts to a wide variety of possible situations, the discussions establish that the teacher is a person who is willing and able to help.

Teachers are trained in one 30-minute session that includes information on reporting suspected abuse, indicators of sexual abuse, prevention concepts and guides to leading the group discussion. This training is available both on a person-to-person basis and as a video program.

Bridgework's prevention concepts are the same as those used by many other programs; the form of communication is unique. Bridgework's plays capture the attention of young audiences with story forms and the theater arts. The plays employ language children understand and remember—the language of sights, sounds and emotions.

Bridgework's resources were developed to meet the needs of small, rural, conservative communities. While the resources are also used in cities, including Chicago and Detroit, more than 75 percent of the groups using Bridgework's programs are in counties with populations under 100,000. Over a half-million children see performances by Bridgework or groups using Bridgework's scripts each year.

The live plays have been successful because they elicit enthusiastic participation from children. School administrators find them to be in good taste. Bridgework's program is cost efficient ($.75 per child) and trained and dedicated staff people are readily available.

A six-page coloring book containing prevention suggestions for parents is sent home with children in grades K-2. Community performances of the plays are scheduled in the evenings for parents and include a discussion period.

Performance sites are encouraged to establish an inter-agency task force. The task force assists with funding and insures that a viable referral, treatment and prosecution network is in place. Media packets including news releases and an audio public service announcement tape are provided to each performance site. In preparation for the performances, the task force often establishes a speaker's bureau and a committee to advocate for the inclusion of sexual abuse prevention as a part of the established school curriculum.

Bridgework Theater, Inc., 113½ East Lincoln Ave., Goshen, IN 46526, (219) 534-1085.

The Child Assault Prevention Project
Columbus, Ohio
Audience: Preschool-grade 12, teachers, parents

The Child Assault Prevention (CAP) Project of Columbus, Ohio was the collective brainchild of a small group of Women Against Rape members who met in January of 1978 to respond to a Catholic elementary school's request for a speaker. A second grade student had been raped and the child's teacher sought to offer both emotional support and prevention information to her class.

This group of women, all trained in rape crisis and prevention, brought a variety of backgrounds and educational disciplines to the program, including experience in teaching, creative arts, social work, psychology, child development and parenting.

After months of intensive research and development, the CAP program was piloted in the small parochial school in Columbus. The program was so well-received that organizers began to investigate the possibility of funding an ongoing project to continue the development and piloting of the program. In 1979 the program was piloted in elementary schools in the greater Columbus area. In 1982 CAP created a leader's guide, *Strategies for Free Children: A Leader's Guide to Assault Prevention.* In 1984, the first national CAP training conference was held in Columbus, Ohio. Currently, there are approximately 100 CAP projects in 18 states, Canada and Great Britain.

The three components of the CAP Project are a teacher in-service training, a parent program and a children's workshop.

Teacher In-Service Training: The teacher in-service training requires approximately two hours and is held during the month prior to the children's workshops. All school staff are encouraged to attend this training since any of them might be approached by a child for help. The training includes an overview of child sexual assault; a detailed explanation of the children's workshop; information on the identification of sexually abused children; crisis intervention guidelines; community resources for reporting abuse; legal rights and responsibilities of reporting; and evaluation.

Parent Program: The parent workshop was developed as an extension of the teacher/staff in-service. While much of the material presented is similar, the emphasis is on prevention and communication with children, rather than reporting procedures, identification and crisis skills. The parent program demonstrates a community commitment to a working network for children and is an integral part of the CAP project.

The program begins with an acknowledgment of parents' fears about sexual abuse and how these fears influence the messages passed on to children. CAP's prevention approach and a detailed account of the classroom workshop, which includes a demonstration of one of the role plays, is presented.

Discussion in the parent workshop includes the role of parents in the prevention of child sexual abuse, and the need for communication between parents and children about sexual assault. The children's workshop teaches children they have a right to say no to an adult. This raises questions for parents and teachers who fear losing their authority if children gain these rights. Adults are encouraged to examine their attitudes and fears about the issue of children's rights and explore the ramifications with their children. Finally, the workshop focuses on the information parents need to effectively respond to a child who has been abused.

Children's Workshop: One-hour classroom workshops are facilitated by three CAP leaders. All leaders are trained both as facilitators and as crisis intervention counselors. Using role plays and guided group discussion the classroom workshop trains children to recognize potentially dangerous situations and to make effective use of the options available to them. CAP emphasizes self-assertion, peer support, communication and reporting skills as potential prevention strategies.

CAP approaches the question of assault within the framework of basic human rights. Assault is defined as a violation of one or more rights (for instance, the right to be safe, say no or not be touched).

The opening discussion of rights is followed by three role plays. These role plays represent the most common abuse experiences a child might encounter: child against child (the playground bully), adult stranger against child, and abuse involving an adult the child knows. The role plays provide situations from which the children can brainstorm successful strategies. Each role play is enacted twice. The first time, the CAP leader plays the role of a child who is confused, frightened and passive. The second time, the child uses strategies such as self-assertion, self-defense, peer support, adult support and reporting to an authority. Role plays are then reenacted as "success stories" incorporating positive prevention techniques. Children

are given an opportunity to participate in supportive roles to practice new behavior.

In a final role play, the classroom teacher plays her/himself as a supportive adult responding to a child's request for help. This role play gives children an opportunity to visualize what would happen if they needed to talk to someone about a similar problem.

Following a summary discussion, children are told that the CAP leaders will be available for individual conversations. Many children seek out workshop leaders to discuss a variety of problems, ranging from sibling arguments to neighborhood bullies to incest.

CAP is easy to replicate and can be adapted to the specific needs of a community. CAP offers a 3-day workshop series to train communities in prevention. The workshops include the following topics.

- Understanding child sexual assault: an overview of the problem, myths and statistics, available community resources
- The why and how of prevention: an evaluation of traditional approaches to rape prevention as applied to children
- Getting started: including school and agency negotiations, strategies for fund-raising, budgeting and project administration
- The worker as child advocate: an overview of the project's role in sexual assault cases, crisis intervention, identification of possible victims, legal rights, responsibilities to the child and the school, and social service referrals.
- Working in culturally diverse communities: a commitment to bringing every child culturally sensitive prevention information in their primary language

- Classroom philosophy: specifics of working with children, alternative methods of interaction between adults and children as applied to different classroom situations
- The adult workshops: training for both parents and teachers programs
- The classroom workshop: training to present a children's workshop including grade-specific issues

---

The Child Assault Prevention Project, CAP Project National Office, P.O. Box 02084, Columbus, OH 43202, (614) 291-2540.

Child Assault Prevention Project
Junior High Boys' Program
West Contra Costa Rape Crisis Center
San Pablo, California
Audience: Junior high boys

Adolescent boys are at high risk to be involved in sexual abuse for three reasons. They can become victims. They can become offenders. And they can become the husband, partner, friend or father of a sexual abuse victim. Prevention workshops for boys in this age group must address them not only as potential victims, but also as potential offenders.

The goals of the Contra Costa CAP Junior High Boys' Program are to prevent victimization of the boys, prevent them from becoming offenders in the future, and teach them to respond to female victims outside the framework of repressive rape myths. The program operates on the assumption that if men are more aware of the truths about rape, they will be less likely to act in a sexually aggressive and violent manner toward women.

Further, studies indicate that violent treatment often begets violent or aggressive behavior. The program tries to identify boys who have been victims of physical or sexual abuse and disrupt the cycle of violence.

The program consists of two one-hour workshops using role plays and discussions to disseminate information about sexual abuse. The workshops are conducted by two male staff members who have extensive experience working with adolescents.

The first hour focuses on the victimization of boys both physically and sexually. Leaders open the workshop by introducing themselves and sharing their own experiences of victimization. In the first role play, the rights of a teenage boy are taken away by his father through physical abuse. After the role play, the class discusses what they saw. Using the class's suggestions, the role play is then reenacted so that the boy is not abused. Points that come up in the discussion include the idea that the father is passing on to his son abuse he may have suffered from his father, that the boy doesn't have to take away his father's rights in order to keep his own, and the possibility of telling a trusted adult about the abuse.

The second role play portrays an adolescent boy who is sexually abused by his uncle. Discussion focuses on dispelling myths about sexual abuse: it is not the victim's fault, will not make the victim gay, and happens to many people. Possible solutions include assertively standing up to the uncle and asking a trusted adult, friend or rape crisis center for help. The role play is repeated to incorporate these suggestions.

On the second day, activities focus on ways men and boys pass on the violence that has been done to them. It begins with a role play in which a teenage boy is trying to force another boy to harass a girl with whom the second boy is friends. The boy is unable to say no to the goader and harasses the girl against his will. Discussion focuses on how both boy and girl are victims in this situation and includes ways in which males fight with one another by using females; how to say no; and how to ask for help. The scene is replayed with the boy acting assertively.

The final role play involves a teenage boy and his girlfriend. The girl has been raped and is telling the boy about it. He responds in an angry, abusive manner. Discussion focuses on dispelling rape myths. The boys learn that rape is an act of violence, not sex; that women don't ask for it, enjoy it or lie about it; and that anyone, including boys and men, can be raped. It is pointed out that the response of family and friends after an assault is very important to a victim's adjustment. The role play is repeated with the boy responding in a supportive and empathetic manner.

Pre- and posttest questionnaires were administered to 127 participants. Boys who participated in the program: (1) demonstrated less adherence to rape myths, (2) demonstrated less acceptance of interpersonal violence, and (3) demonstrated a greater awareness of personal rights than they did at the beginning of the program. In addition, one out of six boys reported being a victim of sexual abuse on the posttest.

The program has been revised many times based on evaluation results and input from teachers, principals and workshop staff members. It has been a challenge to discover ways to talk with adolescent boys about sexual abuse so they can listen and not feel threatened. Perhaps most difficult has been helping them to take a look at their own feelings of victimization.

Child Assault Prevention Project, Junior High Boys' Program, West Contra Costa Rape Crisis Center, 2000 Vale Road, San Pablo, CA 94513, (415) 236-7273.

Child Assault Prevention Project
Casa de Esperanza
Yuba City, California
Audience: Preschool-grade 12, parents, teachers, other professionals

Casa de Esperanza is a rape crisis center and shelter for abused women and children. A high percentage of women seeking services at the Center revealed they were victims of sexual abuse as children. The staff suspected this was a contributing factor to their present abusive situation, and determined to develop and implement a prevention program for children.

The Center examined over 18 different child sexual abuse programs before selecting The Child Assault Prevention Project (CAP) in 1982.

Despite public resistance and a limited budget, the staff of Casa de Esperanza and dedicated volunteers completed the first elementary school program in January of 1984. By June 1985 the project had expanded to reach children in preschool through high school in every classroom in 32 schools. Projects for the developmentally disabled, senior citizens and minority peoples are being developed.

The CAP Project addresses the vulnerability of children and teaches them three strategies to combat it. CAP empowers children to (1) be assertive and say no to anyone if they feel uncomfortable or scared; (2) band together to help and assist each other; and (3) have a trusted adult in their lives; someone who listens, believes and acts on what the child tells him or her.

CAP is unique in its presentation of these principles. Children learn they have three special rights: to be safe, strong and free.

For preschool and kindergarten classes, "friends" (two male child dolls, two female child dolls, and one male adult doll) act out successful situations. Colorful posters depicting the "friends" being safe, strong and free; saying no and giving the CAP yell (a low yell, not a scream) to alert others to help the child immediately are also used. It is very effective and the children learn it easily. Basic self-defense is also demonstrated. The preschool/kindergarten program is conducted in three-day increments. At the end of the third day, the children are given a coloring book to take home. Two workers can handle a preschool class with ease.

The elementary program is different from the preschool project in that unsuccessful role plays are shown first. After class discussion of CAP strategies, the role plays are reenacted. Three role plays with group discussion are completed in one hour and fifteen minutes. The junior/senior high program is similar, but the situations are upgraded to their age level.

In keeping with the CAP model, parent and school staff workshops are held prior to the children's program.

Child Assault Prevention Project, Casa de Esperanza, P.O. Box 56, Yuba City, CA 95992, (916) 674-5400.

Child Sexual Abuse Prevention and Treatment Program
Council on Child Sexual Abuse
Tacoma, Washington
Audience: Preschool–grade 12, parents, teachers, professionals, community groups

In 1976, Dr. Marlys Olson developed a program to address the problems of abused children and their families. She began with a few students at Edison Elementary School in Tacoma and involved many community resource people including Child Protective Services, law enforcement, rape relief, Parents Anonymous, hospitals and treatment therapists. The program soon expanded to workshops for educators and the community, and the development of a comprehensive curriculum for teaching child abuse prevention called *Personal Safety*.

As the program evolved, support from the business community developed. The Council on Child Sexual Abuse represents a merging of expertise from the school district program with the resources of the business community to provide a high level of effective community involvement.

The Tacoma Child Sexual Abuse Prevention

and Treatment program promotes the child abuse prevention curriculum; provides workshops for teachers, professionals and general community groups involved in child abuse prevention; organizes networks within the community to coordinate and improve sexual abuse services; provides a school-sponsored counseling and support group for children who have been sexually abused and their families. The program is unique in this comprehensive scope of its activities and its incorporation into the school district with the support of the business community. Twenty-seven thousand students in Tacoma Public Schools are being taught the *Personal Safety* lessons.

Parents have been involved in the prevention program from the early development and piloting of the curriculum. Community awareness meetings are held when prevention lessons are being taught in the schools, and brochures about the personal safety program are sent home. A parent support group for child sexual abuse victims meets in conjunction with the children's groups. "Sunshine Girls" is for girls ages 5-12 and "Super Kids" is for boys ages 5-12.

Personal Safety, the curriculum developed by the Council on Child Sexual Abuse, is centered around the student learning objectives for health education programs for the State of Washington as recommended by the Office of the Superintendent of Public Instruction.

The curriculum is divided into five levels: preschool, kindergarten through grade 2; grades 3 and 4; grades 5 and 6; junior high; and high school. There are four units in each level: (1) personal safety, (2) appropriate and inap-

propriate touching, (3) assertiveness, and (4) support systems.

Council on Child Sexual Abuse, P.O. Box 1357, Tacoma, WA 98401, (206) 593-6624.

Children Need To Know Personal Safety Program
Health Education Systems, Inc.
New York, New York
Audience: Children ages 3-12, parents, teachers, other professionals

In 1980-81, Health Education Systems, Inc. (HES), under the direction of Sherryll Kerns Kraizer, developed a comprehensive training program for children, parents and professionals in the areas of sexual abuse, prevention of ab-

Youngsters listen to Children Need To Know Program

duction and safety for children staying alone. Over 50,000 children ages 3-12 have participated in the Children Need To Know program, which is presented to schools, professional associations and community groups throughout the United States. HES has offices in Colorado, California, Missouri, Virginia and New York. Each part of the program is standardized and taught by a trained professional. The program is available anywhere in the United States and Canada by arrangement.

The need that parents, teachers and other professionals express for specific training and information for their children is high. Beyond the specific and limited issue of sexual abuse, there is a broader desire of parents to feel their children can competently handle a variety of life situations. These include such skills as thinking independently, making decisions, exercising judgment, communicating effectively, and handling embarrassment and peer pressure. HES programs are based on these broader issues and a belief that prevention education can be accomplished without fear, anxiety or diminishing the child's basic trust in his/her family and community.

The Children Need To Know program consists of three parts. The first step is professional training. The program recommends not only teachers, administrators and psychologists, but also school nurses, cooks and secretaries be trained in the concepts of prevention, the signs of abuse and their obligation to report. Training is also available to police officers, pediatricians, attorneys and social workers.

The second part of the Children Need To Know program is parent education. To maximize the effectiveness of the program, parents need to understand and support the prevention techniques taught to children. The parent seminar is usually sponsored by the parent/teacher organization and is conducted on a school night. The program includes discussion of the problem, offenders and how they operate, and what makes children vulnerable. A review of the children's workshops includes ways in which parents can support prevention education at home.

The actual workshop for children is a 90-minute program for groups of 12-18 children. The children's workshops are paid for by individual parents, by the parent-teacher organization or by the school district. Children are taught the prevention techniques and given numerous opportunities to practice the new skills by role play. This allows the teacher to correct, coach and assure that each child has mastered the techniques.

The Children Need To Know program is based on the belief that children do not need explicit information about sexual abuse and abduction to be safe. Prevention occurs before abuse begins and children can learn to think for themselves, speak up for themselves and get help when they need it without being told that the people they love most in the world might abuse them. This program is designed to foster positive mental health and trust in the world while teaching effective, usable prevention skills.

The concepts of the Children Need To Know program are the foundation for *The Safe Child Program,* a school curriculum that uses videotapes for initial presentation of concepts. Activities and follow-up materials are highly structured and classroom teachers are trained in their use. Teachers' manuals, parent materials, posters, games, children's worksheets and other planned activities complete the program and provide extensive reinforcement and application.

Children Need To Know Personal Safety Program, Health Education Systems, Inc., P.O. Box 1235, New York, NY 10116, (914) 365-1121.

Children's Creative Safety Programs
Safety and Fitness Exchange
New York, New York
Audience: Children ages 5 - 12

In 1981, Tamar Hosansky and Pam McDonnell, founders of the Safety and Fitness Exchange (SAFE) in New York City, teamed up with social worker Flora Colao to develop a practical, upbeat approach to the prevention and treatment of child abuse. They established a pilot program with a group of children ages 5 - 12. The instructors worked with the children to create appropriate teaching tools including role plays, songs, games and exercises.

They were particularly concerned with incorporating children's words and ideas into their approach. This vocabulary insures that children are comfortable discussing the problems and can therefore understand and benefit from the instruction. It also provides adults with models for introducing the subject of personal safety to children.

The programs developed by SAFE are unique. They integrate a variety of techniques to teach personal safety, including psychological reinforcement, physical fitness, self-defense strategies, post-assault recovery techniques and immediate and effective easy-to-implement safety strategies. The end result is educated, empowered children and adults more sensitive and supportive to children's needs.

In SAFE's classes and seminars, children ask many questions and are actively involved in the discussions. Children say that the restrictions and regulations placed on them by adults do not work for them. Problems that arise often call for action directly contrary to parents' restrictions. For instance, children are repeatedly told never to lie. Yet in certain situations a lie would be a sound safety strategy. When a child is home alone, it is best when answering the phone or the door not to appear to be unsupervised. Therefore, the safest response is a lie: "My mother's busy and can't talk to you right now."

SAFE programs have been sponsored by over 200 private and public schools and over 300 parents' associations in the New York-New

A SAFE class works out

Jersey-Connecticut area alone. Hundreds of teacher-training sessions and programs have been held throughout the country. SAFE's workshops and seminars are offered nationwide in schools, youth groups, community organizations, hospitals and social service agencies.

Children's Creative Safety Program, Safety and Fitness Exchange, 541 Avenue of the Americas, New York, NY 10011, (212) 242-4874.

Children's Self-Help Project
San Francisco, CA
Audience: Children ages 2½ - 15, parents, teachers and other professionals

The Children's Self-Help Project is a community-based abuse prevention program. Its major goal is to teach children ages 2½ - 15 skills to protect themselves against abuse by strangers or people they know. In addition, the program aims to facilitate reporting and crisis intervention for children who have already been victimized. The uniqueness of this project is its focus on incest. The nonthreatening information prepares children for potentially confusing encounters and gives them support to stop an already developing situation.

The CSHP provides two basic services: a direct service program for parents, teachers and children, and a training program for professionals interested in starting their own CSHP. There are three components of the CSHP direct service program.

1. School Personnel Workshop. This one-hour training workshop for teachers, principals and school nurses presents child sexual abuse prevention techniques and discusses signs of abuse in children.

2. Parents' Workshop. This two-hour session suggests prevention exercises for parents to use with children, and do's and don'ts when a child reports sexual abuse.

3. Children's Workshop. Two one-hour sessions at preschool, elementary, middle and high school levels are given. Using skits, songs, discussion and puppets, professionals present the material in a sensitive easy-to-understand manner. The program is upbeat and positive. At the same time it is serious. Extra time is allowed

The Children's Self-Help Project in action

for children to speak privately with one of the presenters.

The program began in 1981 as a committee of concerned child sexual abuse professionals and educators. Their hope was to reach children before they became victims. Since then, the CSHP has served over 13,000 children, 5,000 parents and 3,500 teachers in San Francisco's schools and day care centers. Five California chapters are currently using the CSHP model in their communities. The nationwide training program provides trainer trainings for professionals interested in using the CSHP model.

CSHP believes in providing information about abuse to correct myths that make children vulnerable. Posters show a variety of people who might abuse children, most of whom are ordinary looking people of all ages and ethnic groups. Children are encouraged to focus on and trust their intuition. They practice making instant decisions regarding uncomfortable touches. Songs, skits, interaction, visuals, puppets and role plays involve children in the teaching process. Throughout the two-session workshop they learn and practice new safety skills.

Prevention programs must work closely with local child protective service agencies. Children in CSHP programs are provided with community resources to help them with a variety of problems. If a child discloses abuse, he or she is referred to the appropriate child protection or law enforcement organization. CSHP's success in linking abused children with the system has been due in part to coordination with these agencies.

Children's Self-Help Project, 170 Fell Street, Room 34, San Francisco, CA 94102, (415) 552-8304.

Community Education Program
King County Rape Relief
Renton, Washington
Audience: K-12, parents, teachers, other professionals

Community education has always been an important component of King County Rape Relief's (KCRR) overall approach to sexual assault. In the past few years, KCRR has focused significant energy and expertise in the area of child sexual assault prevention education. KCRR's publications *He Told Me Not To Tell, Top Secret* and *Talking to Children/Talking to Parents About Sexual Assault* have become national bestsellers.

Locally, KCRR volunteer speakers reached over 6,000 people in 1984. Sixty percent were children and teens. Volunteers, who complete advocacy training and a speaker's training before they appear before community groups, are the key to reaching this number of people.

One of KCRR's goals has been to insure that all county school districts have a sexual abuse prevention curriculum. This goal has been accomplished and the demand for both parent presentations and professional trainings has increased significantly. KCRR has collaborated with Pierce County Rape Relief and Alternatives to Fear to develop the Teenage Acquaintance Rape Package. This program offers communities a tool to address the issue of teen acquaintance rape.

Nationally, the PBS series "Child Sexual Abuse: What Your Children Should Know," featured KCRR's prevention programs. Over six million people in 250 cities saw the series and more than 30,000 wrote to KCRR requesting more information. The series was favorably reviewed in over 300 newspapers, from small town weeklies to *The New York Times*. The PBS series received endorsements from the National PTA, National Education Association and the Academy of Pediatrics. It also received an Emmy and the Corporate Public Broadcasting Award for the Best Show for a Target Audience.

As a direct result of this series, KCRR has become a significant resource for educators and rape crisis centers interested in implement-

ing educational programs. KCRR staff consulted with the producers of ABC's "Webster" (The "Uh-Oh Feeling," aired January 25, 1985) and James Stanfield & Company in the production of a filmstrip, "Child Sexual Abuse: A Solution."

Community Education Program, King County Rape Relief, 305 South 43rd, Renton, WA 98055, (206) 325-5531.

Disabilities Project
Seattle Rape Relief
Seattle, Washington
Audience: Special education personnel, persons with developmental disabilities ages 6-adult

Seattle Rape Relief's Disabilities Project has been in existence since 1977. It is one of the only programs nationwide to offer training and consultation in sexual assault prevention for persons with disabilities. The training for special education personnel on how to plan and implement a self-protection program for students with disabilities uses a training-teams-of-trainers approach. After completing this training, teams return to their agencies with the knowledge, skills and support necessary to train administrators, parents and coworkers in sexual assault prevention. Seattle Rape Relief accepts applications from agencies nationwide to co-sponsor workshops.

There is a critical need for accessible self-protection education for children with disabilities. Making these skills available challenges

A KCRR volunteer addresses a classroom

the myth of dependency and offers skills to maximize independent living.

Educational materials have been developed to teach about disabilities, sexual assault, staff training, prevention, counseling and advocacy. *CHOICES: Self-Protection Workbooks for Persons with Physical Disabilities, Visual Impairment and Deafness/Hearing Impairments* addresses multi-cultural diversity and supports the empowerment of persons with disabilities.

A Curriculum for Developing an Awareness of Sexual Abuse and Self-Protection Techniques is designed for use with students with developmental disabilities ages 6-adult. The curriculum includes a variety of goal-oriented lesson plans, filmstrips and group activities. Self-protection skills in the areas of travel, social and home situations are presented, and students are taught how to report sexual assault.

Disabilities Project, Seattle Rape Relief, 1825 So. Jackson, Suite 102, Seattle, WA 98144, (206) 325-5531.

Project PAAR-Plus
Greene County Prosecutor's Office
Xenia, Ohio
Audience: Preschool-grade 12, parents, professionals

Project PAAR-Plus (Prevent Abuse, Assist Recovery) is a child sexual abuse prevention and intervention program developed by the Victim/Witness Division of the Greene County Prosecutor's Office in Xenia, Ohio. The program consists of three major components: advocacy for child victims of sexual abuse at the time of intervention by other social service agencies or police; a school education program; and seminars for professionals who work with child sexual abuse victims.

The school education program is available to all schools in Greene County, as well as to day-care centers and other children's groups. In 1983, the programs were presented to 1,750 children. In 1984, 3,216 children participated.

Project PAAR-Plus began in December, 1982 with a grant from the Ohio Department of Public Welfare (now the Ohio Department of Human Services). Until that time, no agencies or organizations in the county were presenting child sexual abuse prevention material to school children. The increasing sexual abuse caseload of the Victim/Witness Division indicated a clear need for such a program.

Each fall, the principal in every elementary school in the county is contacted by the Victim/Witness Division to schedule presentations. Age-appropriate programs have been developed for the first, fourth and sixth grade levels.

An original slide show, *Tickles and Touches,* is for first graders. *Tickles and Touches* depicts three children on a playground discussing touching problems. The children talk about what they need to do to solve the problems. A discussion session follows the slide show. The children are instructed on two points: (1) they have the right to say no to unwanted touch, and (2) if someone touches them in an inappropriate way, they need to tell an adult. Children receive a coloring book, also entitled *Tickles and Touches,* at the conclusion of the program.

MTI's film *Who Do You Tell?* is used in the

fourth-grade program. The film introduces the idea of support systems. It covers several problems children of this age may encounter, including the dilemma of unwanted touch. It illustrates how support systems can help. A discussion session follows the film. Each child is given an original comic book called *A Touching Situation,* the story of a girl who solves a touching problem through the use of support systems.

The Worrisomes, an original videotape play, is used with sixth graders. In the play, an adolescent boy is visited in the night by characters who represent situations that worry him in the daytime. "Worrisomes" are Unfinished Homework, Unfriendly Kids and Unwanted Touch. Each one forces the boy to confront his worries and helps him find a solution. A bookmark listing referral sources is given to the children after a discussion session. Junior high and high school students receive sexual abuse prevention information in conjunction with rape awareness and prevention information and also through the Victim/Witness Division.

In addition to the school programs, presentations are available to parents, church groups and civic organizations. *A Touching Problem,* a film produced by MTI, is available for these programs. A brochure entitled "Something Awful Happened: Prevention, Intervention, and Investigation of Child Sexual Abuse" is distributed. The brochure includes information on the scope of the problem, symptoms, discovery and identification, intervention, mental health questions and solutions to the problems of child sexual abuse.

Four seminars are presented annually for professionals. There are seminars for police and law enforcement personnel, medical personnel, social service agencies and educators. Each seminar is individually designed to meet the needs of the audience. Expert speakers and the Victim/Witness Division staff provide pertinent information and participants receive a textbook that includes comprehensive information about intervention in child sexual abuse.

Project PAAR-Plus is the only program in Greene County to provide both prevention information and advocacy at the time of intervention. The prevention information has clearly increased the possibility of prosecution. To date, children as young as five have been found competent to testify and all cases prosecuted have resulted in guilty pleas or verdicts.

Project PAAR-Plus, Greene County Prosecutor's Office, Xenia, OH 45385, (513) 376-5087.

Project S.A.A.F.E.
Jackson Mental Health Center
Jackson, Mississippi
Audience: Children ages 4-10, parents, administrators, educators

The original impetus for Project S.A.A.F.E. (Sexual Abuse Awareness for Everyone) was an increase in reports of child sexual abuse to the local child abuse hotline and the department of public welfare. In the fall of 1983, the Jackson Mental Health Center and the Mississippi State Department of Public Welfare met to discuss possible funding for a pilot project in Hinds County. Project S.A.A.F.E. was piloted in the spring of 1984 with 356 third grade children, their parents and teachers.

The program begins with a presentation to parent/teacher groups in each school. Parent/teacher sessions include: general information about child sexual abuse, the prevalence of abuse (local and national statistics), sexual abuse indicators, how to respond to a situation of abuse, how to communicate with a child about the topic, a viewing of Project S.A.A.F.E. materials, a description of the classroom program, local resources, and finally, a question/answer/evaluation session.

Following the parent/teacher meeting, separate meetings are held with appropriate school staff. A teacher training videotape (demonstrating a classroom program); a detailed description of the classroom program, including teacher roles and responsibilities; and reporting procedures for the school and the state are included in this session. Comfort with the material is discussed and the importance of the teacher as a potential resource for children is emphasized. Teachers can then opt for a model classroom presentation by the Project S.A.A.F.E. educator or decide to implement their own program, using the manual as a guide and the Project S.A.A.F.E. educator as a consultant.

The preschool program includes a discussion about good, bad, and confusing or secret touching, using the workbook *My Feelings* by Marcia Morgan. The Project S.A.A.F.E. educator reads the book to the children and a filmstrip is shown, followed by a discussion/summary. Total time for the program is 40 minutes.

The classroom program for grades 1-4 also includes a discussion about touch. *My Very Own Book About Me,* an interactive workbook, is read with the children. A filmstrip is shown,

followed by a discussion and role play activities. Total time for the elementary program is approximately 90 minutes.

The Project S.A.A.F.E. educator contacts the school two weeks after program implementation to discuss progress, concerns and future needs or resources. A cooperative working liaison is accomplished through periodic phone contact and by letter.

Project S.A.A.F.E. has had great success involving the media in efforts to educate the public. This has established the program's credibility in the community. Newspapers have featured extensive articles on the project and local television stations have broadcast a sexual abuse prevention message. Word-of-mouth has also been useful in program expansion.

This program is multilevel, involving parents, administrators, teachers, and children as essential factors. The emphasis is on adult/child communication as the primary prevention ingredient. As much as possible, the significant adults in the child's life are involved.

Another unique component is the self-help structure of Project S.A.A.F.E. Trainers teach school personnel how to duplicate the program, thereby insuring its inclusion in succeeding years. Consultation with school boards is often undertaken to encourage inclusion of Project S.A.A.F.E. into the curriculum.

Evaluation and feedback procedures are used to determine the extent to which Project S.A.A.F.E. goals and objectives are met. Overall, teachers, parents and children have expressed significant growth in their understanding of child sexual abuse and could clearly articulate safety steps. Adults have supported continuation of prevention efforts. The program has reached more than 5,000 people in Hinds County, Mississippi.

Project S.A.A.F.E., Jackson Mental Health Center, 969 Lakeland Drive, Jackson, MS 39216-4699, (601) 982-8811.

Rape Crisis Network Children's Program
Lutheran Social Services
Spokane, Washington
Audience: Children ages 5-16, community groups, professionals, teachers

Rape Crisis Network, a program of Lutheran Social Services of Washington, was established in 1974 to meet the needs of sexual assault victims. A special program for children was begun in 1979 when it was noted that more than half the clients were under the age of 18. Since the establishment of the Children's Program there has been a 240 percent increase in the numbers of child clients (infant to 16 years).

The Children's Program has two purposes: (1) to establish direct service, including crisis intervention and therapy, and (2) to deliver prevention information. The prevention program has been particularly impactful. It involves training, consultation and curriculum development in thirty-five elementary schools. In addition, consultation with schools in seven adjoining counties for workshops and training for professionals is provided. The child sexual abuse prevention program trains volunteers, teachers and administrators, who in turn work with children and parents to expand the program's impact.

An important component has been the development of *My Very Own Book About Me*, a workbook for children and parents. It is distributed nationally to individuals and school districts. Another important element has been the development of the Spokane County Sexual Abuse Team (SCSAT). SCSAT is a network of professionals who deal with child sexual abuse (law enforcement, child protective services, victim advocacy, etc.) SCSAT also networks with a broad segment of the community to maintain the support and credibility needed to work effectively.

The Children's Program involves the community by being involved in the community. Community support is exemplified by the cooperation of diverse groups such as the Junior League, church groups, educators and preschool cooperatives, which aid in the development of volunteer trainers, speakers' bureaus and fund development.

Rape Crisis Network Children's Program, Lutheran Social Services, North 1226 Howard Street, Spokane, WA 99201, (501) 327-7761.

Red Flag Green Flag Program
Rape and Abuse Crisis Center
Fargo, North Dakota
Audience: Third graders, parents, teachers

The Red Flag Green Flag program was developed in 1979 to provide nonthreatening sexual abuse prevention information to children. The program is presented annually in public and parochial schools to approximately 2,000 third grade students in a two-county area.

The three major components of the Red Flag Green Flag program are the teacher's in-service training, the parents' meeting and the children's program. Teacher and parent meetings are informational. The children's program is reviewed with each group and specific questions or concerns are addressed.

The children's program is presented in the classroom for one hour on two consecutive days. Day one deals with problems, support systems and types of touches. Day two deals with prevention and the importance of telling an adult about a "red flag" (bad) touch.

All information is presented through the *Red Flag Green Flag People Coloring Book,* which provides pictures and activities to help the children learn the basic goals of the program: (1) their bodies are their own, (2) they have a right to say no, (3) if a child has been touched in a way that is confusing or frightening, he or she should tell someone. In addition, the movies *Who Do You Tell, No More Secrets* and *Child Molestation: When to Say No* are shown.

One major factor in the local success of the Red Flag Green Flag program is its broad-based community support, especially from teachers and parents. Another is the popular coloring book each child takes home to be used again in talking with parents.

A manual for program facilitators and a videotape have been developed so that the Red Flag Green Flag program can be distributed outside the local area. The program is currently implemented in all fifty states and several foreign countries. The coloring book and facilitator's manual are available for Spanish-speaking audiences.

Red Flag Green Flag Program, Rape and Abuse Crisis Center, P.O. Box 2984, Fargo, ND 58108, (701) 293-7298.

Safety, Awareness, Prevention Program
DC Rape Crisis Center
Washington, DC
Audience: Preschool-grade 6, parents, professionals

Since 1976, the DC Rape Crisis Center's Safety, Awareness, Prevention Program has been an established part of the Washington, DC public school curriculum. Programs reach approximately 2,000 students per year.

The goals of the Center's prevention programs are to teach children: (1) how to communicate, (2) that they have autonomy over their bodies, (3) that they have control over who touches them, (4) that they have the right to say no, (5) to follow their instincts, (6) to take care of themselves. The program uses an interactive approach to teaching. Children answer questions, respond to films and take part in role plays.

Through the utilization of the school system and the community, the DC Rape Crisis Center is attempting to implement a holistic approach to educate children and prepare teachers and service providers to participate in the process.

The DC Rape Crisis Center offers two programs for elementary school children. Four 30-minute sessions are conducted in preschool through second grade. For third through sixth grades, there are three sessions over a three-day period. The first day is a half-hour orientation and the second and third day presentations each last one hour.

The sessions (1) cover safety and prevention rules, (2) examine safety and prevention in various potentially dangerous situations, (3) make children aware of child sexual assault, (4) examine safety and prevention for children in family situations, (5) make children aware of community support systems, (6) clarify children's rights.

In 1984, the Center's Community Education Department reached more than 20,000 men, women and children in the Washington Metropolitan area. A 24-hour hotline and short term counseling and crisis intervention for adults are well known to the community, so many presentations are by request. In addition, the Center's staff appear on numerous local television and radio shows, and on national programs such as National Public Radio and Cable News Network.

Seminars for adults discuss (1) general information and statistics, (2) risk factors and preconditions, (3) prevention, (4) examples of prevention techniques, (5) changes in behavior that may indicate sexual abuse, (6) what to do if a child has been assaulted.

The Center also conducts programs for school counselors. These sessions enable counselors to detect signs of child sexual abuse and be more aware of available resources for addressing the problem should a student need help. Another component of the adult program is a parent awareness session conducted just before each classroom program.

The workbook *Staying Safe: How To Protect Yourself Against Sexual Assault* serves as a tool for adults in teaching children about prevention. It includes field-tested stories, questions and games. *Staying Safe* has an introduction for adults; the balance is for children.

Safety, Awareness, Prevention Program, DC Rape Crisis Center, P.O. Box 21005, Washington, DC 20009, (202) 333-7273.

Sexual Abuse Prevention Project
Illusion Theater
Minneapolis, Minnesota
Audience: K-12, parents, teachers, other professionals

One of the oldest prevention programs in the nation, Illusion Theater's Sexual Abuse Prevention Program (SAPP) was the first to use theater to educate children and adults about sexual abuse prevention. The Illusion Theater of Minneapolis, Minnesota, was founded in 1974 as a company of performing artists creating new works through the collaborative process.

Michael Robins and Bonnie Morris, producing directors of Illusion Theater, were interested in using educational theater for children. In 1977, they began a collaboration with the Sexual Assault Services division of the Hennepin County Attorney's Office, which was conducting a child sexual abuse program formerly coordinated by Cordelia Anderson. This collaboration led to the development of an elementary curriculum and a unique fusion of social services and theater.

Combining content from Anderson and other human service and theater professionals, the Illusion Theater created the theatrical presentation entitled *Touch*. Using the concepts of the *Touch Continuum*, they pioneered a vocabulary and prevention program for children. Their concepts have been widely adapted and are now incorporated into most prevention programs.

The prevention program outgrew the prosecution focus of the county attorney's office and was moved to the Illusion Theater in 1980 as the Sexual Abuse Prevention Program with Cordelia Anderson as director.

The focus of SAPP has now shifted from being primarily a resource in the Minneapolis public schools to providing technical assistance and consultation to communities nationwide interested in implementing prevention programs with or without the use of educational theater. The training and theatrical program is constantly expanding and changing as the Theater assimilates new information about prevention education.

Illusion Theater's presentation entitled *Touch* is geared to elementary age children and examines touch that is nurturing, confusing and exploitative. *Touch* provides children with the vocabulary to discuss sexual abuse and protection and prevention skills.

No Easy Answers is for adolescents and explores sexual development, sexual abuse, and protection and prevention skills. Their latest play, *For Adults Only* is designed to help adults examine some of the ways in which sex and violence are confused and how these attitudes perpetuate sexual abuse.

Since the Program's inception, over 2000 performances and training sessions have been presented throughout the nation to more than 512,000 people. In addition, Illusion Theater's plays have been licensed by other agencies for use in their own communities. *Project Trust* is a specialized licensing model that incorporates high school students as actors in the *Touch* production. There are currently 12 *Project Trust* sites throughout the United States.

In addition to training sessions, workshops and plays, SAPP has developed numerous educational materials on prevention for children, professionals and parents, including a film adaptation of *Touch*. Today Illusion Theater serves as a national clearinghouse for information and referral on prevention education, resources and programs.

In 1984, Illusion Theater collaborated with

Illusion Theater ensemble in a scene from No Easy Answers

WCCO-TV, a Minneapolis-based, CBS-affiliated TV station, and other community programs on "Project Abuse." "Project Abuse" was a two-week public service program designed to educate viewers about sexual abuse victims, offenders, treatment and prevention. In addition to special reports, town meetings and service announcements, "Project Abuse" included a 24-hour hotline that referred over 1500 calls in two weeks from victims, offenders and concerned persons. Videotapes of *Touch* and *No Easy Answers* were broadcast into participating classrooms and over 425,000 students watched the plays. Currently, "Project Abuse" is being syndicated across the country.

The Prevention Program is expanding its focus to include work on the prevention of violence. In addition to its newest prevention piece *For Adults Only*, the Theater is currently developing preventive materials in the area of child abuse and neglect.

The key factor in Illusion Theater's success, and the key factor in setting up a prevention program, is networking. This includes human service professionals, treatment and education systems, health care providers and parents in both planning and education efforts. Each member of the network is essential regardless of the size of the community. In all of its work, Illusion Theater staff has called upon the local communities to network among themselves, and use their own resources as well as Illusion Theater's to educate the constituents.

Sexual Abuse Prevention Project, Illusion Theater, 304 Washington Avenue North, Minneapolis, MN 55401, (612) 339-4944.

Soap Box Players Program
Coalition for Child Advocacy
Bellingham, Washington
Audience: Preschool–12, developmentally delayed, parents, educators, professionals, other interested adults

The Coalition for Child Advocacy is a private, nonprofit organization operating under the Whatcom County Opportunity Council, a community action agency located in Bellingham, Washington. In 1979 the Coalition began to focus on prevention of child sexual abuse. Drama was the educational tool selected by the Coalition, and the SOAP Box Players were organized (SOAP stands for Serious Overtures About People.)

The volunteer educational theater group began their presentations in October 1980. *The Touching Problem* and *SOAP Box Sense* demonstrate methods to use when talking with parents, teachers and children about sexual abuse prevention. The dramas are performed for parents, teachers and other professionals.

In *The Touching Problem,* the players enact skits that demonstrate profiles of a victim, an offender, a confrontation between a mother and her brother, a mother talking about touching problems with her son, and a teacher providing support for a child who has disclosed she is a victim.

In 1981 the SOAP Box Players and KVOS-TV adapted *The Touching Problem* for television. The docudrama shows how one child tries to deal with the unwelcome touch of a relative and how the problem is eventually resolved. The film presents facts, old and changing attitudes toward child abuse, and the consequences of abuse for children, the family and the community. It also shows steps parents can take to help their children avoid sexual abuse.

SOAP Box Sense is a 45-minute theater presentation using role play to teach protection skills to children; who and how to tell if they are victims of sexual abuse; how to say no to touch that is scary or uncomfortable; how to identify touching problems; how to tell someone about the problem; and who their community support system is. Parent and school staff orientation are provided, and classroom follow-up activities are suggested.

Feelings and Your Body, a preschool demonstration program, was initiated in 1984. Special programs for high and middle school students and developmentally delayed populations are also performed. The players perform for conferences and present workshops on various topics related to sexual abuse.

To date, the players have performed for over 50,000 adults and children. They have toured extensively throughout the states of Washington and Oregon and are available for performances upon request.

Soap Box Players Program, Coalition for Child Advocacy, P.O. Box 159, Bellingham, WA 98277, (206) 734-5121.

Talking About Touching Program
Committee for Children
Seattle, Washington
Audience: Preschool-grade 9, teachers, parents, principals, clergy, other concerned adults

Committee for Children in Seattle is a child sexual abuse prevention program specializing in curriculum development, teacher training, community education and research. Committee for Children was formed by a group of University of Washington researchers headed by Dr. Jennifer James. Dr. James' research, conducted from 1971-1981, documented a high incidence of sexual exploitation in the childhood histories of adult and teenage prostitutes. As a result of her research and a desire to promote prevention as a constructive next-step, Dr. James formed the Committee for Children in 1981.

Committee for Children believes that efforts to prevent child sexual abuse must become institutionalized through incorporation of personal safety materials into school curricula. This goal requires two conditions: (1) the availability of appropriate teacher-based prevention curricula, and (2) careful preparation of school personnel who use the material.

Committee for Children has developed several curricula and videotapes. The curricula are *Talking About Touching: A Personal Safety Curriculum* (K-5), *Talking About Touching with Preschoolers*, and *Personal Safety and Decision Making* (Grades 6-9). Each elementary and preschool lesson is based on a picture to be held up and shared with the class. The lesson plan and notes to the teacher appear on the reverse side. The junior high program contains five hours of case histories, mini-lectures, role plays and worksheets on decision making and assertiveness.

Yes, You Can Say No is an 18-minute videotape of a day in the life of an eight-year-old boy. With the help of friends, he learns the principles of assertiveness and seeking help. This video is the result of evaluation data pointing to weaknesses in student assertiveness skills.

Training tapes are available for schools that want to use the program but can't afford in-person training. These model tapes cover identification, reporting, responding to disclosure and effective use of *Talking About Touching*. A *Trainer's Manual* was developed to accompany Committee for Children's Train the Trainer Institute and contains background reading and specific material for setting up teacher and parent education sessions.

Two types of training models are currently offered by Committee for Children: a classroom teacher training and a training-the-trainer program. Teacher training is provided to staff from one or more schools. The average training is six hours and covers basic facts, identification, responding to disclosure, reporting and how to use *Talking About Touching*. Opportunities are provided for discussion, modeling, role play and problem solving in groups.

Train the Trainer grew from a need to impact large school districts in an efficient manner. A select group of school personnel are chosen from throughout a district to be trained over a three-day period. In addition to content on child abuse and prevention, these trainers learn about effective public speaking, the facilitation of meetings, conflict resolution and other training skills. This workshop is offered on request to schools throughout the United States and Canada during the school year. A five-day Train the Trainer Institute and an update session called Re-Train the Trainer are held in Seattle twice each summer.

Committee for Children has sold curricula to every state in the United States, throughout Canada, and in Great Britain, Norway and Sweden. An estimated 6,000 teachers have been trained directly by Committee for Children staff since 1982, while 550 trainers have impacted thousands of additional teachers. An equal number of parents have attended the session that accompanies each teacher training. It is likely that close to one-half million children have been influenced by the *Talking About Touching* program. The average cost to a district for training and materials is less than $1 per student.

The most recent evaluation of the elementary curriculum indicated significant effectiveness

A teacher goes over Talking About Touching *with her class*

in three areas: knowledge of personal safety rules and guidelines, problem-solving ability when faced with a personal safety dilemma, and assertiveness skills (including the ability to seek help). The weakest increase in skill level was associated with the measures for assertiveness.

The success of this organization is attributed to many factors. First, the insistence of parents on personal safety training for their children has been a critical factor. Committee for Children does not provide training to teachers without offering an evening session to parents. The support and enthusiasm of parents are vital to the success of a program.

Second, Committee for Children provides materials designed with the needs of teachers in mind. Curricula are self-contained and durable. Supersize lessons and Spanish/English editions are available and lessons are sequenced for use from year to year.

Third, Committee for Children believes that children need a little, not a lot, of information about sexual abuse, and that parents and teachers are the best people to provide it.

Fourth, *Talking About Touching* is designed to be taught in the context of safety education. While believing family life education to be equally important, Committee for Children does not consider it a prerequisite to personal safety training.

Fifth, Committee for Children approaches prevention of child sexual abuse as a human issue. All people, regardless of gender, religion, race, vocation or residence are affected by the exploitation of children, and the solution lies in the hands of all. Committee for Children employs male and female trainers to model that

men are also part of the solution to child sexual abuse.

Talking About Touching Program, Committee for Children, P.O. Box 15190, Seattle, WA 98115, (206) 322-5050.

Teen Acquaintance Rape Project
Alternatives to Fear
Seattle, Washington
Audience: Teenage boys, teenage girls, parents, teachers and youth leaders

Alternatives to Fear is a private, nonprofit agency organized in 1971 to provide community education on the prevention of sexual assault. The Teen Acquaintance Rape Project was developed and implemented in 1983. Its focus is acquaintance rape because 40-65 percent of teen girls who are victims of sexual abuse are assaulted by someone they know, often a date or boyfriend.

The program is divided into four components that can operate either independently or interdependently. Each component is directed to a different group: teen girls, teen boys, parents, and teachers and youth leaders.

The program encourages participants to examine the differences between ordinary, socially acceptable boy/girl activities (mainly in a dating or predating setting), and acquaintance rape. The development of skills in both boys and girls that will promote clear, honest communication about touching and other forms of intimacy is stressed. In addition, the program tries to give boys better goals than "scoring," and to provide girls with skills to evaluate potentially dangerous situations and protect themselves when clear communication is not enough.

The support of parents and the community makes programs for youth more accessible and effective. The parent and teacher programs provide adults with an understanding of the problem and concrete methods for promoting change.

All the programs present the same basic information tailored to meet the needs of the particular group. Each program provides the following information.

- General information about sexual assault, and then more specifically, incest and acquaintance rape
- Information about self-protection: prevention strategies, awareness, avoidance, escape and resistance
- Specific examples of acquaintance rape with emphasis on analyzing the dynamics involved and understanding why traditional prevention strategies may not be effective
- Typical dating behaviors, compared with the danger signals for acquaintance rape
- Suggestions for using emotional intimacy as a guide for physical intimacy, with a look at how peer pressure encourages sexual experience without intimacy
- Exploration of individual touching patterns with same sex friends, opposite sex friends, family members and nonfamily adults
- Assertiveness training for talking about touch with friends and relatives

The teen girl program stresses protection strategies, ways to respond to danger signals in a potential acquaintance rape situation, and methods of dealing with hostile or discomforting reactions to assertive behavior. The teen boy program suggests the benefits of changing stereotypical behavior patterns, and feelings and responses to others' (girls') assertive behavior. Boys also explore the differences between persuasion and coercion, ways to open communication, how to recognize and respect boundaries, victim reactions to sexual assault, and methods of being supportive to friends.

Parent sessions cover methods of communication with teenagers; exploration of family patterns that reinforce or inhibit teens' abilities to deal with touching and intimacy; ways parents can support teens' strategies for avoidance and self-protection; support for boys who resist peer pressure; responses to sexual coercion and assault of a child, including legal responses; and special concerns of fathers and teen daughters. Parents have an opportunity to discuss the conflict between parents' concerns about teen sexuality and their concern about safety from sexual assault. This discussion includes the particular problems of parents who are former victims of sexual assault.

Alternatives to Fear works with community agencies and schools to custom design training programs for the development of acquaintance rape prevention programs.

Teen Acquaintance Rape Project, Alternatives to Fear, 1605 17th Avenue, Seattle, WA 98122, (206) 242-4874.

Appendixes

An Overview of Reporting

GAYLE M. STRINGER

Educators are a part of the every day lives of children. They are often respected and trusted by children and are, by virtue of that trust, among the most critical participants in the life of the child. It is for this reason that reporting suspected child abuse is so important.

The involvement of school personnel in the reporting of child abuse is a part of federal standards and regulations, state laws and local policies and procedures. At the federal level and in all fifty states, educators are encouraged or mandated to report suspected abuse. There are specific practices and procedures in each of the fifty states and in the majority of school districts in the nation as well. An overview of procedures common to most reporting practices is provided below.

The development of reporting laws was motivated by a concern that children at risk be identified as soon as possible. Laws most often mandate a specific agency or agencies to receive and investigate reports of suspected abuse. The reporting laws, when in place, make it possible for service providers to deliver appropriate intervention and treatment to identified children and families.

An important and common element in state statutes is that they do not require the reporting person to be certain the child has been abused. The report is a request for investigation based on "reason to suspect" a child has been or is being abused.

Elements commonly found in reporting statutes are:
- a definition of child abuse
- who must report
- to whom abuse must be reported
- content of the report

Every educator must be informed as to the specific requirement of her/his state mandate. School districts should have a copy of state statutes and school policy. The following discussion will provide information about the commonalities in reporting laws.

How Is Child Sexual Abuse Defined?

Each state and territory has a definition of sexual abuse. These definitions vary widely but can generally be understood to mean: coercive or exploitative sexual contact for the sexual gratification of the abuser. It is aptly described as:

". . . . . .the forcing of sexual contact. When children are victimized, the sexual contact may involve handling of the child's genitals or requests for sexual handling by an older child or adult. Sometimes the contact is oral sex. Sexual contact includes attempts at penetration of the vagina or anus and, rarely, actual penetration. Some kinds of assaults involve no physical contact. A child may be forced to look at the genitals of an older child or adult, or the child may be requested to undress or otherwise expose her/himself" (Jennifer Fay, *He Told Me Not To Tell*, 1979).

Most states consider a minor child to be 18 years or younger and in need of protection by these statutes. A notable exception is Wyoming where the mandated reporting age is 16 years or younger.

Who Must Report Suspected Abuse?

In most states and territories, educators are specifically required to report suspected cases of child abuse. School personnel most often included in the "educator" category are teachers, principals, administrators, school nurses, counselors and pupil personnel workers. Both public and private schools fall under this requirement. Additionally, staff of licensed day care centers and child care institutions qualify as educators under these statutes as do administrators of summer camp facilities for children.

An educator who reports a potential case must have a "reason to believe" that abuse is occurring. If the report is made in good faith and the educator's intent is to ensure the safety of the child, she/he is protected by law from liability. (If an educator were to wait until absolute proof is available before reporting, a child may be in jeopardy of further abuse. It may not be possible to get proof of abuse as there is often a lack of physical evidence in cases of sexual abuse.) In reporting a suspected case of abuse the educator is simply asking that an investigation be made. Trained investigators will ascertain whether abuse has, in fact, occurred.

To Whom Should Suspected Abuse Be Reported?

Once an educator becomes aware or sus-

pects that a child is being abused, she/he must report within a specified time. This time limit varies from state to state although it is commonly 24 to 48 hours.

Every state specifies the agencies that are to receive reports of child abuse. It is important to be aware of appropriate reporting agencies in your area. Most often it is a division of the local department of social services called Child Protective Services (CPS). Trained workers take the report, record it, and determine the action to be taken. Local law enforcement or juvenile court officers may be authorized to take such report.

What Information Is Requested in a Report?

Reporting child sexual assault is fairly straightforward. The intake worker will ask for specific information. It generally is as simple as giving the child's name, parents' or guardians' names and address and the circumstances that led the reporting person to believe abuse has occurred. States vary in the provision of confidentiality for those who report. Even if the state provides anonymity, it may be helpful for the social worker to be able to contact the reporter again for further information. (It is common for those who have reported a case of child abuse to be concerned about possible reprisals from offenders. In reality such reprisals are extremely rare.)

State laws can only go so far to stop the incidence of child abuse. Ultimately, the responsibility for the safety of children rests with the entire community. In order to insist on the responsibility of educators, social workers, therapists, physicians and others with whom children work closely, most states impose a penalty for the failure to report suspected sexual abuse. The possibility of fines and/or a jail sentence exists in most jurisdictions. The point at issue is the "willful" failure to report.

Do's and Don't in Reporting Suspected Abuse

DO document any incident or discussion that leads you to suspect the abuse. Date, time and description of the incident or discussion is useful to those investigating the report.

DO build trust and ensure confidentiality. Though an educator must report to specific people, most other teachers, administrators and parents need not know. The child will feel less violated if the report is made on a need-to-know basis only.

DO reassure the child that she/he is not to blame. Under no circumstances is the abuse the fault or responsibility of the child. This is especially important when abuse is reported. The child often takes on the responsibility for the trouble in the family and the feelings of self-blame can be severe.

DO NOT investigate. Once you have reason to believe that abuse has occurred, report it to the proper authorities. Their personnel are trained to investigate the incident(s). (If you try to investigate, your actions could jeopardize the child's safety as well as any legal action pending as a result of the abuse.)

DO take care of yourself. Recognizing and reporting an incident of sexual abuse is stressful. Educators have a special role that often brings them emotionally close to children. Recognizing that a child with whom one has a relationship has been sexually abused is painful. If you find that you would like or need support be sure to seek it out. Your local rape crisis center is equipped to support you confidentially.

The abuse of children can only be stopped if the entire community works together. Exploitation of a child must not be tolerated and when exploitation does occur there must be swift intervention and protection from further abuse. Perhaps 16-year-old Susan, an incest survivor, best expresses the reason for reporting: "All I wanted was for it to stop, so I told my teacher. She believed me and we told the police. It was hard because it seemed like everybody got mad for a while. But it stopped and that made it all worth it."

Gayle M. Stringer is Education Coordinator for King County Rape Relief, Renton, WA.

178

What Happens When A Report Is Made?

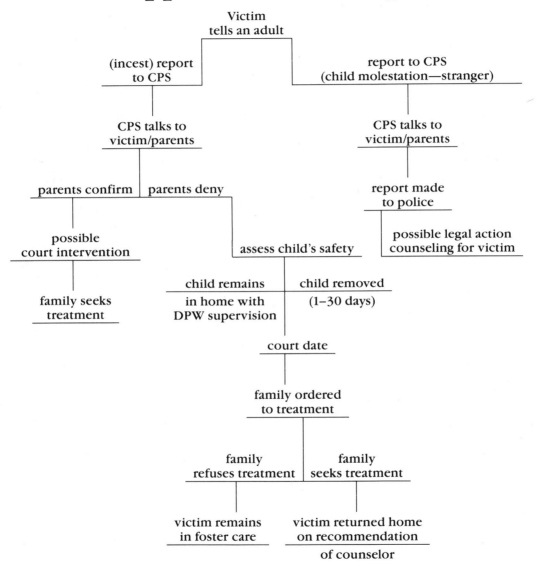

Reprinted with permission of Learning Publications from *Preventing Sexual Abuse* by Carol A. Plummer, copyright 1984.

Definitions

Child sexual abuse is the term most often used by professionals in the field to describe any sexual contact or activity between a child and an adult. *Sexual victimization* and *sexual exploitation* are used in the same broad sense. Other more limiting terms are *sexual assault, child rape, sexual molestation and sexual harassment*.

Thus, a stranger who exposes himself in front of a child is committing child sexual abuse. So is a father who has sexual intercourse with his daughter. Most sexual abuse of children falls somewhere between these two extremes. The categories of child sexual abuse are incest, pedophilia, exhibitionism, molestation, statutory rape and rape, child prostitution and child pornography.

Categories of Sexual Abuse[1]

Child pornography is the arranging, photographing by still, video or film production of any material involving minors in sexual acts including other children, adults or animals, regardless of consent given by the child's legal guardian, and the distribution of such material in any form with or without profit, and the exhibition of such material, with or without profit. The 1982 landmark decision of the Supreme Court held that the twenty states with laws outlawing child pornography did not infringe on First Amendment rights of freedom of the press. Thus any state can now take the steps needed under criminal law to ban and prosecute all those involved in the child pornography industry, from producer to buyer. It may require time to evaluate the effect of this ruling but, importantly, the court held that acts need not be "obscene," a vague term, but that all materials depicting sexual activities involving children are unlawful.

The estimate of American children involved in prostitution and pornography is 300,000. The majority of older youngsters involved in prostitution and pornography do so to provide themselves with money for food, clothing, drugs and liquor. Actually they may turn over most of their money to a pimp. In either case, they feel no hope of changing their lifestyle. Testimony at one congressional hearing revealed that in Los Angeles a 12-year-old boy can earn as much as $1,000 a day in prostitution.

Child prostitution involves children in sex acts for profit and generally with frequently changing partners. This widespread practice involves boys as well as girls. Although the children are sometimes acting on their own, adults (and parents) often manage their activities and receive the profits.

Exhibitionism (indecent exposure) involves the exposure of the genitals by an adult male to girls, boys and women. The purpose for the exhibitionist is to experience sexual excitement from the encounter (he may masturbate as well as expose himself) and to register the shock or surprise of the onlooker. Although he may talk or call attention to himself, he does not usually make any other approach.

Incest is defined as any physical sexual activity between family members. Blood relationship is not required: the term "family" is used in its broad social connotation as well as to describe the actual living arrangement of the involved persons. Thus, stepfathers or stepmothers and non-related siblings living together, often as a result of their parents' previous marriages, are included in the definition of incest. So are other relatives who do not permanently live with the child—uncles, aunts and grandparents, for example.

Molestation is a rather vague term that usually includes other vague terms such as "indecent liberties." Molestation includes such behaviors as touching, fondling or kissing the child, especially in the breast or genital areas, engaging in masturbation of the child, or urging the child to fondle or masturbate the adult. These activities may progress to mutual masturbation or to oral-genital contact. It is an unsatisfactory term because its limits are not defined.

Pedophilia (literally "love of child") denotes the preference of an adult for prepubertal children as the means of achieving sexual excitement. Either girls or boys may be the sexual object with some variations in the patterns or preference for each. The range of actual activity may include any of the forms of sexual abuse since the term "pedophilia" really indicates not a kind of activity but the fact that a child must be the participant-object in the activity.

Statutory rape and rape*. Sexual intercourse (statutory rape) with a child of either sex, including fellatio (oral-genital contact), sodomy (anal-genital contact), or penile-vaginal intercourse, may occur without physical violence through seduction, persuasion, bribes, use of authority or other threats. The lowest limit at which a child is presumed to be able to give legal consent to intercourse varies from state to state from ages 12 to 18. Except for legal consequences, age of consent is of much less significance than the meaning of the individual experience for the child or adolescent involved.

Rape is defined as sexual intercourse or attempted intercourse without consent of the victim. Even very young children (under 6 months) have been objects of rape but the majority of victims are over 5 years of age. The perpetrators are generally younger men under 35 years of age. Rapists tend to approach child victims because they are less threatening to the rapist's self-confidence and are unlikely to have the strength to resist.

Alcoholic intoxication is often blamed for the occurrence of rape and certainly the incidence of intoxication or being "under the influence" is high. Alcohol merely acts as a trigger, reducing inhibition against impulses which are present but which might not be indulged so readily without alcohol. Alcohol does not "cause" rape: it makes its commission easier.

Rape often occurs with deliberation and planning when the perpetrator is not under the influence of alcohol or drugs, and repetition of rapes, as a pattern of aggressive behavior towards females, is a common finding. Nor is forcible rape confined to female victims. Male children and adolescents, in their own neighborhoods and especially in penal institutions, are often subjected to forced oral sex and sodomy. In the former setting, the victim may be assaulted once; in a closed environment, forced rapes may continue over years and involve many partners.

A significant number of child rapists have also practiced exhibitionism and it is this fact that has led many to reexamine long-held beliefs that divided violent from nonviolent offenders. Further, many children under age 15 who have been involved in incest or childhood rape are also victims of intrafamilial physical abuse, which may have gone undetected in the past and which is brought to light only when sexual abuse is discovered.

*Editor's Note: ***Acquaintance or date rape*** is a form of abuse that occurs most often among adolescents. It is any forced, tricked or manipulated sexual intercourse by someone the victim knows, often a date or boyfriend. It may involve verbal manipulation by the offender based on the victim's inexperience and lack of information about sexuality and her own rights in a dating situation. Figures from King County Rape Relief in Renton, Washington indicate that 40-60% of teenage girls who are sexually assaulted are victims of acquaintance rape.

1. Material used with permission from *The Common Secret: Sexual Abuse of Children and Adolescents* by Ruth S. and C. Henry Kempe. New York: W.H. Freeman and Company, 1984.

Indicators of Sexual Abuse in Children

The following physical and behavioral characteristics may be signalling that a child is a victim of sexual abuse. As with other lists of symptoms, some of the same signs may indicate other types of problems. Until recently, sexual abuse was not often considered as a possible reason for erratic or problem behavior. It is important to recognize that sexual abuse is a possibility when a child/adolescent exhibits several of the following behaviors.

Physical Signs:

Bruising, bleeding or infections in the genital/anal area. Physical symptoms may be manifested as difficulty in walking, sitting or urinating; scratching or tugging at clothing around the genital area; torn, stained or bloody clothing; genito-urinary complaints or infections.

There may be no physical indicators that a child is being abused.

Behavioral/Attitudinal Signs:

- Eating, sleeping and eliminating disturbances
- Recurrent physical complaints
- Withdrawn or aggressive behavior
- Tired, lethargic, sleepy appearance
- Fearful or suspicious of adults
- Sexually explicit language or behavior not appropriate to the child's age
- Regressive behavior such as whining, excessive crying, thumbsucking, wetting or soiling self
- Aversion to a particular person, place or situation
- Change in school performance, truancy
- Fear, worry, overly serious, depressed
- Anger toward or dislike of adults, authority figures
- Running away from home
- Suicide threats or attempts
- Behavioral defiance, sexual promiscuity, prostitution
- Shy, withdrawn, overburdened appearance
- Substance abuse that is more than experimental
- Reluctance to undress for physical education
- Stealing, shoplifting
- Pregnancy wishes
- Interest in early marriage
- Attraction to older men or dislike of men
- Excessive hand washing, bathing
- Unreasonably restricted social activities or overly protective father
- Poor self-image, low self-esteem
- Fantasies about victimization or violence
- Alienation from family members, rejection of typical family affection
- Fear of strange men and/or strange situations
- Fear of being alone
- Overly clinging or dependent behavior
- Extreme avoidance of touch
- Abrupt change in behavior or personality
- Extreme over-achiever

Bibliography

The following resources were selected from *Sexual Abuse Prevention Education: An Annotated Bibliography* compiled by Kay Clark and available from Network Publications, Santa Cruz, CA. This bibliography is a comprehensive listing of over 200 resources published since 1980. Materials published before 1980 are included if they are considered to be classics in the field of child sexual abuse.

Names, addresses and, when possible, telephone numbers are listed with each item under the sections entitled "Booklets, Pamphlets and Miscellaneous Teaching Aids" and "Curricula and Leader Guides." Distributors for the audiovisual materials appear at the end of the bibliography. Book entries cite the publisher, city and year published. All publications were available at printing, but they may not all be listed in *Books in Print* or available through local bookstores because many are distributed through small publishing companies. Contact the publisher for purchase or information about books.

Books for Adults

Adams, Caren and Jennifer Fay. *Nobody Told Me It Was Rape*. Santa Cruz, CA: Network Publications, 1984.

Designed to help parents educate their adolescent about acquaintance rape and offer guidelines and skills to prevent sexual exploitation. Educators presenting units on rape and sexual exploitation will find the book informative and valuable in promoting discussion activities in the classroom.

Adams, Caren and Jennifer Fay. *No More Secrets: Protecting Your Child From Sexual Abuse*. San Luis Obispo, CA: Impact Publishers, 1981. Distributed by Network Publications, Santa Cruz, CA.

An expanded version of *He Told Me Not To Tell*, this 90-page paperback includes detailed dialogs, games and other tools to help parents teach their children ages 3-12 how to prevent sexual exploitation.

Adams, Caren, Jennifer Fay and Jan Loreen-Martin. *No Is Not Enough: Helping Teenagers Avoid Sexual Assault*. San Luis Obispo, CA: Impact Publishers, 1984.

A guide for parents to help teenagers become aware of factors that contribute to victimization. Includes information about acquaintance rape, exploitation by adults, media influence and peer pressure.

Ageton, Suzanne S. *Sexual Assault Among Adolescents*. Lexington, MA: D.C. Heath and Company, 1983.

This comprehensive study provides data on adolescents who have been victims, and information about offenders. Victim reactions are assessed for up to 3 years after the assault. Theoretical model of adolescent sexual assault is developed and tested, and adolescent vulnerability to sexual assault is explored.

American Association for Protecting Children, Inc. *Highlights of Official Child Neglect and Abuse Reporting, 1983*. Denver: The American Humane Association, 1985.

Statistics about child abuse, including child sexual abuse. An updated profile of officially reported child maltreatment in the United States. Focuses on the characteristics of reporting to child protective services agencies, the characteristics of the cases and the nature of the response to reported cases.

Armstrong, Louise. *Kiss Daddy Goodnight: A Speakout on Incest*. New York: Pocket Books, 1978.

A study of over 150 incest victims, their experiences and their responses. A first in the field.

Bass, Ellen and Louise Thornton, eds. *I Never Told Anyone: Writings by Women Survivors of Child Sexual Abuse*. New York: Harper and Row, 1983.

Accounts by survivors of sexual abuse by fathers, friends, relatives and strangers. Accounts are in the form of prose vignettes and poetry. Includes a forward by Florence Rush, a state-by-state listing of treatment and prevention programs, and a recommended reading and audiovisuals list.

Bateman, Py and Gayle Stringer. *Where Do I Start? A Parent's Guide for Talking To Teens About Acquaintance Rape*. Seattle, WA: Alternatives to Fear, 1984.

Information and specific "how to" tips for parents about discussing sexual exploration, sexual exploitation and acquaintance rape with their teenager.

Brady, Katherine. *Father's Days: A True Story of Incest*. New York: Dell Books, 1979.

A true story told by a victim of incest, about the incident and her perception of how it affected her life. One of the first real-life documentaries on the subject of incest.

Bulkley, Josephine, Jo Ensminger, Vincent J. Fontana and Roland Summit. *Dealing with Sexual Child Abuse*. Chicago: National Committee for Prevention of Child Abuse, 1983.

This booklet from the National Committee for Prevention of Child Abuse provides information about sexual child abuse through a series of essays by the authors, all of whom are active in the field. Subjects include child sexual abuse and the law, the medical professional, the social worker and the psychotherapist.

Burgess, Ann Wolpert, A. Nicholas Groth, Lynda Lytle Holmstrom and Suzanne M. Sgroi. *Sexual Assault of Children and Adolescents*. Lexington, MA: D.C Heath and Company, 1978.

An interdisciplinary approach to child sexual abuse prevention. Includes essays by each author on offenders, victims and services. Designed as a handbook for people who work with either the victim or offender. Themes are the human dimension, community program planning and interagency cooperation.

Colao, Flora and Tamar Hosansky. *Your Children Should Know*. New York: Bobbs-Merrill Company, Inc., 1983.

An assertiveness training program for parents to teach their children. Written to help give children the skills to pinpoint suspicious behavior and safely escape it. Uses a series of verbal exercises to practice with children, to give them a sense of control over their environment. Includes physical self-defense section.

Conte, Jon. *Social Work and Child Sexual Abuse*. New York: Haworth Press, Inc. 1982.

A multi-faceted perspective on child sexual abuse by researchers and clinicians. For social workers, health professionals and others who work with sexually abused children and their families.

de Young, Mary. *The Sexual Victimization of Children*. London: McFarland and Company, Inc., 1982.

A look at incest and pedophilia from a clinical point of view. Uses a sample of victims, offenders and nonparticipating family members to study the victimization of children.

Finkelhor, David. *Child Sexual Abuse*. New York: The Free Press, 1984.

Presents new theory and research on the subject of child sexual abuse, and suggests possible future directions in the field.

Finkelhor, David. *Sexually Victimized Children*. New York: The Free Press, 1979.

A study of sexual experiences that occur between children and adults. Includes theories about why child sexual abuse happens, presents findings of a study and discussions of issues raised by the study. Comprehensive and useful material about child sexual abuse.

Fortune, Marie Marshall. *Sexual Violence: The Unmentionable Sin*. New York: The Pilgrim Press, 1983.

Examines the social and religious roots of sexual violence and the responsibility of the church to deal with the consequences of silence. Useful to anyone attempting to respond to victim or offender, particularly counselors and/or ministers.

Forward, Susan, and Craig Buck. *Betrayal of Innocence: Incest and Its Devastation*. New York: Penguin Books, 1978.

One of the first books for lay people about incest. Discusses varieties of incestuous relationships and the effects on victims and offenders. Uses case studies.

Groth, Nicholas. *Men Who Rape*. New York: Plenum Press, 1979.

Examines the psychological and emotional factors that predispose a person to react with sexual violence to situational and life events. Based on 15 years of clinical experience with 500 sexual offenders. Includes a section on the sexual abuse of children.

Hechinger, Grace. *How To Raise a Street Smart Child*. New York: Hechinger, 1984.

A comprehensive guide for parents about safety. Includes practical information about muggers, thieves, gangs, bullies and child molesters. A realistic and useful tool for modern families.

Herman, Judith. *Father-Daughter Incest*. Cambridge: Harvard University Press, 1981.

Uses a clinical study of forty incest victims and interviews with mental health, child protection and law enforcement professionals to develop a composite picture of the incestuous family. Combines a clinical approach with a feminist analysis of the issue of incest.

Horowitz, Robert M. *The Legal Rights of Children*. Monterey, CA: Shepard's McGraw-Hill, 1984.

Written for lawyers who work with children, this book is also a useful reference handbook for counselors, agencies and educators in the area of child sexual abuse prevention. Many useful sections on abused children and the law including exploitation, the child witness, and child protection and reporting laws. Cites references for further information.

Hyde, Margaret O. *Sexual Abuse: Let's Talk About It*. Philadelphia: Westminster Press, 1984.

A chatty book that discusses child sexual abuse in a nonthreatening, nonjudgmental way. Uses case histories and discusses model prevention programs. Very readable overview on the subject of child sexual abuse.

Justice, Blair and Rita Justice. *The Broken Taboo: Sex in the Family*. New York: Human Sciences Press, 1979.

A study of incest: what it is, who commits it, why it happens, effects and signs, and suggestions for dealing with the problem.

Kempe, Ruth S. and C. Henry Kempe. *The Common Secret: Sexual Abuse of Children and Adolescents*. New York: W.H. Freeman and Company, 1984. Distributed by Network Publications, Santa Cruz, CA.

An introduction to child sexual abuse, particularly incest. Uses case examples from the authors' practices. An overview for students, nurses, physicians, teachers, ministers and priests, lawyers, legislators and all concerned lay people who want to learn about the subject.

King County Rape Relief. *He Told Me Not To Tell*. Renton, WA: King County Rape Relief, 1979. Distributed by Network Publications, Santa Cruz, CA.

A collection of ideas for talking to children about sexual assault. Designed to be incorporated into parents' general teachings about personal safety.

Kraiser, Sherryl L. *The Safe Child Book*. New York: Dell Publishing Co., 1985.

A book for parents who want specific suggestions for dealing with the problem of child sexual abuse prevention. Stresses that children need to be able to protect themselves, and outlines a comprehensive program for teaching them how.

Meiselman, Karin. *Incest: A Psychological Study of Causes and Effects with Treatment Recommendations*. San Francisco: Josey-Bass Publishers, 1978.

Provides information about the effects of incest in childhood upon psychological functioning in later years. Also summarizes findings of previous studies over the last 50 years. Mainly for mental health professionals.

Mrazek, Patricia Beezley and C. Henry Kempe, eds. *Sexually Abused Children and Their Families*. Oxford and New York: Pergamon Press, 1981.

A comprehensive and multidisciplinary book for experts in the field of child sexual abuse. Includes sections on definition and recognition, sexual child abuse and the law, psychodynamics and evaluation, treatment, and prognosis and outcome. References and audiovisual materials with critique.

National Center on Child Abuse and Neglect. *Sexual Abuse of Children: Selected Readings*. Washington, D.C.: DHHS Publication No. (OHDS) 78-30161, 1980.

Selected readings by authorities who represent a variety of disciplines. Includes articles on the sexual abuse of children, offenders, the law, incest, treatment and interviewing techniques. Although much has happened in the field since this book was published, it still offers insights and important basic information.

Porter, Ruth, ed. *Child Sexual Abuse Within the Family*. The Ciba Foundation. New York: Tavistock Publications, 1984.

A group of essays presented during a special study group on child sexual abuse from 1981-1984. The book provides guidance to professionals in the management of sexually abused children and their families. Much of the information is treatment oriented, but there is an excellent chapter on prevention and education.

Rush, Florence. *The Best Kept Secret: Sexual Abuse of Children*. New York: McGraw-Hill, 1980.

Traces the history of child sexual abuse to show possible reasons why it is as extensive and pervasive as it is in our society. One of the first to speak out strongly against blaming the child victim in any way. A classic in the field of child sexual abuse.

Russell, Diana E.H. *The Secret Trauma: Incest in the Lives of Girls and Women*. New York: Basic Books, 1986.

A comprehensive analysis of incest based on the literature and on the author's own random study of 930 women. Focuses on trauma, effects, prevalence, differences and comparisons of victims of abuse by biological and stepfathers, brothers, brothers-in-law. Includes a section on female perpetrators.

Russell, Diana E.H. *Sexual Exploitation: Rape, Child Sexual Abuse and Workplace Harassment*. Los Angeles: Sage Publications, 1984.

An integration of the existing literature on the subjects of rape, child sexual abuse and sexual harassment in the workplace. Useful to students and professionals. Includes Russell's random sample survey of 930 San Francisco women.

Sanford, Linda. *Come Tell Me Right Away*. Fayetteville, NY: Ed-U Press, Inc., 1982.

A short version of the popular book *The Silent Children*. Offers concrete and effective suggestions to teach children how to protect themselves from sexual abuse.

Sanford, Linda. *The Silent Children: A Parent's Guide to the Prevention of Child Sexual Abuse.* New York: McGraw-Hill, 1980.

> A detailed and practical program designed for parents. Includes comprehensive information about abuse, offenders and how to make children less vulnerable to abuse. A useful section of contributions by parents with special needs: Blacks, Asians, Hispanics, native Americans, single parents and parents of children with disabilities.

Seattle Rape Relief. *Choices: Sexual Assault Prevention for Persons with Disabilities.* Seattle, WA, 1985.

> Three separate self-help workbooks for persons with visual impairments, physical disabilities or hearing impairments. Activities, information and exercises address individual needs in terms of self-protection and prevention of sexual assault. The workbooks are available in braille, large print and regular print for maximum accessibility. Also to be used by teachers.

Soukup, Ruth, Sharon Wicker and Joanne Corbett. *Three in Every Classroom.* Bemidji, MN: Sexual Assault Program, 1984. Distributed by Network Publications, Santa Cruz, CA.

> A book for teachers. Facts about child sexual abuse and suggestions for dealing with a child victim in the classroom, identifying symptoms and reporting abuse. Bibliography and resources included.

U.S. Department of Health and Human Services. *Child Sexual Abuse: Incest, Assault and Sexual Exploitation.* Washington, D.C.: DHHS Publication No. (OHDS) 81-30166, (Revised) 1981.

> An overview of the problem of child sexual abuse. Includes definitions, effects on children and families, intervention, legal aspects, prevention, treatment and bibliography.

Books for Children

Amerson, Ruth. *Hi! My Name is Sissy.* Sanford, NC: Department of Social Services, 1984.

> Sissy is a 6-year-old girl whose Uncle John touched her in a way she didn't like. She tells her mother and they go together to get help.

Bass, Ellen. "I Like You to Make Jokes With Me, But I Don't Want You to Touch Me." In *Stories for Free Children.* Pogrebin, Letty Cottin, ed. New York: McGraw-Hill, 1982.

> A story that affirms a child's right to say no to touch that's confusing. Without specifically mentioning sexual abuse, the theme acknowledges confusing touch and stresses the child's absolute right to say no.

Basset, Kerry. *My Very Own Special Body Book.* Redding, CA: Hawthorne Press, 1980.

> Written to children. Emphasizes that each child is special and has rights. Frank language mentions specific forms of sexual abuse that might occur, and the importance of telling a parent or grown-up friend.

Bateman, Py. *Acquaintance Rape: Awareness and Prevention for Teenagers.* Seattle, WA: Alternatives to Fear, 1982.

> A workbook for adolescents, explaining the concept of acquaintance rape. Uses case stories to illustrate definition and talks about prevention in terms of self-knowledge, defining limits and gaining and keeping control in a potentially dangerous situation.

Bateman, Py. *So What if You're Not an Expert—You Can Still Take Steps to Protect Yourself Against Sexual Assault.* Seattle, WA: Alternatives to Fear, 1984.

> Specific and practical advice in self-protection for teenagers. Encourages teens to take assertive action to assure safety, from locking doors to fighting back.

Bateman, Py and Bill Mahoney. *Macho? What Do Girls Really Want?* Seattle, WA: Alternatives to Fear, 1985.

> A guide for boys to develop non-aggressive

dating habits. A frank discussion about the confusion boys face in trying to be successful in dating.

Berg, Eric. *Stop It*! Santa Cruz, CA: Network Publications, 1985.

This booklet for children focuses on the principle that children have a right to say no, and reinforces acting on that right. Also includes information about touches, intuition, secrets, body rights and telling someone. Delightful illustrations. Companion parent/teacher guide available.

Berg, Eric. *Tell Someone*! Santa Cruz, CA: Network Publications, 1985.

This booklet focuses on the concept that sexual abuse is not the child's fault and that a trusted adult(s) should be told if someone touches the child in a way that feels strange. Also includes information about touch, intuition, body rights and saying no. Delightful illustrations. Companion parent/teacher guide available.

Berg, Eric. *Touch Talk*! Santa Cruz, CA: Network Publications, 1985.

A booklet about touch to be read to young children in grades K-2. Delightful illustrations help explain that the way the child feels about a touch is what makes it good, bad or confusing. Also includes secrets, saying no, telling someone and body ownership. Companion parent/teacher guide available.

Berry, Joy. *Alerting Kids to the Dangers of Sexual Abuse*. Waco, TX: Word, 1984.

For parents/teachers to read to children. Delightful illustrations. Text includes sections on private parts, sexual abusers, sexual intercourse, guilt, ways offenders trick children into participating, talking with an adult, and ways to avoid abuse. A special section for parents/teachers appears in the back of the book.

Booher, Dianna Daniels. *Rape: What Would You Do If. . .?* New York: Julian Messner, 1981.

A book to teach teenagers how to avoid assault, and how to survive if assaulted. Specific, daily situations in which women might be threatened and suggestions about prevention through awareness.

C.A.R.E. *Trust Your Feelings*. Surrey, BC: C.A.R.E. Productions, 1984.

Explains different touches and their relationship to feelings, encourages children to trust intuitive feelings about touch, talks about private parts (the parts that are covered by a bathing suit), offers suggestions for saying no, telling someone you trust and body ownership. Multi-ethnic illustrations.

Chetin, Helen. *Frances Ann Speaks Out: My Father Raped Me*. Stanford, CA: New Seed Press, 1977.

Information for teenagers in the form of a play. Frances Ann and her grandmother tell Frances Ann's story—she has been abused by her stepfather from a very young age. She is removed from her home and sent to live with her grandmother when the authorities discover her stepfather has raped her.

Coalition for Child Advocacy. *Touching*. Bellingham, WA: Whatcom County Opportunity Council, 1985.

A storybook for children from preschool through elementary to share with adults. About touching, warning feelings and secrets that should be told. Illustrations by Jody Bergsma.

Dayee, Frances S. *Private Zone*. Edmonds, WA: The Chas. Franklin Press, 1982.

A book for parents to read to children. Focuses on body rights of children. Defines areas of body that only the child can touch, and encourages children to "yell and tell" if an adult violates a "private zone."

Ezrine, Linda. *Anna's Secret*. Baltimore: Harvey S. Spector Publishing Co., 1985.

A story about Anna's family and how they react when Anna discloses that a young man who babysits for Anna and her brother has been sexually abusing Anna. Includes information about contacting authorities and a counselor.

Freeman, Lory. *It's My Body*. Seattle, WA: Parenting Press, Inc., 1982. Distributed by Network Publications, Santa Cruz, CA.

A book for parents to read to very young children. Presents the basic concepts of prevention education in easy language with delightful illustrations.

Gordon, Sol, and Judith Gordon. *A Better Safe Than Sorry Book*. Fayetteville, NY: Ed-U Press, Inc., 1984. Distributed by Network Publications, Santa Cruz, CA.

A book for children ages 3-9. Provides basic information about sexual abuse. Focuses on reassuring children that adults will believe and support them if they communicate about abuse. Illustrations include multiethnic children and adults.

Hindman, Jan. *A Very Touching Book*. Durkee, OR: McClure-Hindman, 1983.

Talks about the basic concepts of abuse prevention, such as touching, feelings, secrets, saying no and telling. Teaches correct names for body parts and general sex information as well as information about sexual abuse. Illustration by Tom Novak are explicit.

Hutchingson, Barbara Zandlo, and Elizabeth Anne Chevalier. *My Personal Safety Coloring Book*. Fridley, MN: Fridley Police Department, 1982.

A coloring book developed to use in conjunction with a comprehensive personal safety program for elementary schools. Explains touch and telling a trusted adult. Needs an adult to direct and explain information.

King County Rape Relief. *Top Secret*. Renton, WA: King County Rape Relief, 1982. Distributed by Network Publications, Santa Cruz, CA. Cruz, CA.

Designed to teach teenagers the basic facts

about sexual exploitation. Focuses on acquaintance rape, what it means and how to avoid it. Stresses that sexual abuse is *never* the fault of the victim. A separate, detailed discussion guide is available for adults. (See Curricula and Leader Guides.)

Krause, Elaine. *For Pete's Sake, Tell*! Oregon City, OR: Krause House, 1983.

For discussion with youngsters ages 7-12. Teaches parents how to teach children to be aware, alert and assertive about sexual abuse. Each page of the text for children includes suggestions and hints for parents to guide the adult reader through the teaching experience.

Krause, Elaine. *Speak Up, Say No*! Oregon City, OR: Krause House, 1983.

Uses cartoon character ("Penelope Peabody") to help parents teach children to distinguish between different kinds of touch ("okay" and "not okay"). Each page includes parent tips, providing facts about child sexual abuse and prevention suggestions.

Kyte, Kathy S. *Play It S.A.F.E.* New York: Alfred A. Knopf, 1983.

A book for children about crime, including sexual abuse. Tips to teach children how to be less vulnerable to crime. Teaches them to be alert, to listen to and trust their instincts and to be confident that they can take steps to protect themselves.

Mackey, Gene and Helen Swan. *Dear Elizabeth*. Leawood, KS: Children's Institute of Kansas City, 1983.

A fictional diary of a 14-year-old incest victim. Three sections chronicle the disclosure, crisis treatment and long-term therapy stages of her healing process. For use by therapists or by a young victim as a self-help tool.

Mackey, Gene and Helen Swan. *The Wonder What Owl*. Leawood, KS: Children's Institute of Kansas City, 1984.

A book to read to young children (ages 3-7)

about sexual abuse. A delightful story that offers openings for parents to discuss and explain touch, secrets, telling a trusted adult and private body parts. A natural and non-threatening story. A guide for parents is included.

Marvel Comics and National Committee for Prevention of Child Abuse. *Spider Man and Power Pack*. New York: Marvel Comics Group, 1984.

This prevention tool in the form of a comic book teaches children how to protect themselves from sexual abuse and what to do if it happens. Talks about abusers who are acquaintances and about uncomfortable touch.

McGovern, Kevin B. *Alice Doesn't Babysit Anymore*. Portland: McGovern & Mulbacker Books, 1985.

This story about a baby sitter who systematically abuses her charges reassures that this type of situation can happen to anyone, that children can and should tell other people if it happens, and that it is never the victim's fault. Designed to be used as a communication tool for making children aware of the possibility of abuse by someone they know and trust.

Montgomery, Becky, Carol Grimm and Peg Schwandt. *Once I Was a Little Bit Frightened*. Fargo, ND: Rape and Abuse Crisis Center, 1983.

Based on a work by Joy Williams, this booklet was designed for use by parents, teachers or professionals with kindergarten through third grade students. To be used to discover and deal with possible sexual abuse.

Morgan, Marcia K. *My Feelings*. Eugene, OR: Equal Justice, 1984. Distributed by Network Publications, Santa Cruz, CA.

A coloring book for children, emphasizing that children's intuitive feelings about touch are usually accurate. Encourages children to listen to and trust warning feelings, and to share those feelings with a trusted adult. A for-adults section offers background information and suggestions about how to supplement the material in the coloring book.

Newman, Susan. *Never Say Yes to a Stranger: What Your Child Must Know to Stay Safe*. New York: Putnam Books, 1985.

A series of stories for parents to read with children. Each story illustrates a situation where a child is interacting with a stranger. Teaches tips to avoid being caught in a dangerous situation. Focuses on stranger abuse.

Palmer, Pat. *Liking Myself*. San Luis Obispo: Impact Publishers, 1977.

A book for young children about self-esteem. Teaches children to pay attention to, trust and act on their own feelings.

Palmer, Pat. *The Mouse, the Monster and Me*. San Luis Obispo: Impact Publishers, 1977.

Assertiveness tips for young children. Stresses children's rights and teaches them to say no.

Polese, Carolyn. *Promise Not to Tell*. New York: Human Sciences Press, 1985.

A fiction book about a child who is sexually abused. For teachers, parents, psychologists and child welfare advocates to use for both prevention and treatment. Explores the conflicting emotions that often prevent children from telling about sexual abuse.

Porteaus, Trace. *Let's Talk About Sexual Assault*. Victoria: Women's Sexual Assault Center, 1984.

A book for young women about sexual abuse: what it is, why it happens, what to do if it happens and how to reduce the risks of becoming a victim.

Stowell, Jo, and Mary Dietzel. *My Very Own Book About Me*. Spokane: Lutheran Social Services, 1982.

A book for parents, teachers, child therapists and children. To teach children about the basic concepts of abuse prevention: touching, telling, saying no. Talks about various "touching problems" of sample children, and how those children handled the situation. Parents' guide included. Therapists' guide and teachers' guide available.

Sweet, Phyllis E. *Something Happened to Me.* Racine, WI: Mother Courage Press, 1981. Distributed by Network Publications, Santa Cruz, CA.

A book for children who have been abused. Designed to be used by those who work with children. A child discusses her experience in story form, stressing the rewards of talking about her abuse to a caring and trusted adult.

Terkel, Susan Neiburg and Janice E. Rench. *Feeling Safe Feeling Strong.* Minneapolis: Lerner Publications Company, 1984. Distributed by Network Publications, Santa Cruz, CA.

Six fiction stories for and about young people who encounter confusing and difficult situations involving abusive or potentially abusive situations. Each story is followed by commentary discussing and explaining the story. Good communication tool for parents or teachers.

Wachter, Oralee. *No More Secrets for Me.* Boston and Toronto: Little, Brown and Company, 1982.

A book for children to read alone or for parents to read with their children. Four stories about children whose rights have been abused in some way, and what they did about it. Stories involve both girls and boys and incidents range from uncomfortable situations with a baby sitter to inappropriate touching by a father.

White, Laurie A. and Steven L. Spencer. *Take Care With Yourself.* Michigan: DayStar Press, 1983.

This book about young people includes the basic concepts of sexual abuse prevention—trusting intuition, saying no, tell someone and body rights. Also includes assurances that sexual abuse is never the fault of the one who is abused. Illustrations include a broad ethnic representation.

Williams, Joy. *Red Flag, Green Flag People.* Fargo, ND: Rape and Abuse Crisis Center of Fargo-Moorhead, 1980.

A coloring book for young children, outlining the prevention principles by categorizing touch according to red and green. Discusses telling, getting away, obscene phone calls, and provides a place for the child to write names of adults they can tell about confusing touch. Designed to be used with Red Flag, Green Flag People Program Guide (see Curricula and Leaders Guides), but can effectively be used alone.

YWCA of Greater Flint. *You Belong to You.* Flint, MI: YWCA Domestic Violence/Sexual Assault Service, 1980.

A coloring book to be used as a teaching tool to promote a positive self-image, children's rights to their own thoughts, feelings and bodies. Includes sections on private parts, touching, secrets, and telling. Originally designed as part of a 45-minute presentation offered by the Greater Flint YWCA.

Booklets, Pamphlets and Miscellaneous Teaching Aids

ABOUT INCEST
Channing L. Bete Co., Inc., South Deerfield, MA, (413) 665-7611.

A booklet for parents, physicians, police, school counselors, teachers, nurses and other professionals who work with children. Background information about incest, including types of incestuous relationships, effects, signs, reporting and support programs.

ADULT'S GUIDE TO STOP IT
ADULT'S GUIDE TO TELL SOMEONE
ADULT'S GUIDE TO TOUCH TALK
Network Publications, P.O. Box 8506, Santa Cruz,

CA, 95060, (408) 429-9822.

Three pamphlets designed to accompany the series of books for children, *Stop It, Tell Someone*, and *Touch Talk*. Each pamphlet offers information for adults about sexual abuse, and a page by page guide to using the children's book.

ALTERNATIVES TO FEAR: A BOARD GAME IN SELF PROTECTION
Alternatives to Fear, 101 Nickerson, Suite 150, Seattle, WA 98109, (206) 282-0177.

A game to be used by teenagers, adult women or volunteers training to assist at rape crisis centers.

ANA FAMILY
West River Sexual Abuse Treatment Center, Child and Family Guidance Services, P.O. box 1572, Rapid City, SD 57709, (605) 342-4303.

Anatomically correct dolls for use in prevention programs, or interviewing sexual abuse victims. Adult and child male and female figures. Instructional booklet included.

ARE CHILDREN WITH DISABILITIES VULNERABLE TO SEXUAL ABUSE?
Minnesota Program for Victims of Sexual Assault, 430 Metro Square Building, St. Paul, MN 55101, (612) 296-7084.

A 5-page brochure acquainting parents of children with disabilities with the problem of sexual abuse and outlining protection steps.

BASIC FACTS ABOUT SEXUAL CHILD ABUSE
National Committee for Prevention of Child Abuse, 332 S. Michigan Avenue, Suite 1250, Chicago, IL 60604-4357, (312) 663-3520.

This pamphlet includes definitions, types of offenses, statistics, reporting, and more. A lot of information in this compact publication.

CHILDREN NEED PROTECTION
Carver County Program for Victims of Sexual Assault, 401 East 4th Street, Chaska, MN 55318.

This booklet offers guidance to adults who want to know more about sexual abuse and how to protect children by talking with them about it. Includes a series of "What If" and "No" games to play with children.

FOR PARENTS: CONCERNING YOUR CHILD'S PERSONAL SAFETY
Council on Child Sexual Abuse, 708 South G Street, P.O. Box 1357, Tacoma, WA 98401, (206) 593-6624.

A pamphlet for parents includes the answers to questions like why and what to tell children about sexual abuse, and other ways to help insure the safety of children. Some information only applicable in local area.

HOW TO TALK TO YOUR CHILDREN ABOUT SEXUAL ASSAULT: A GUIDE FOR PARENTS
Human Services, Inc., Mental Health Division, Sexual Assault Services, Washington County, MN, (612) 777-5222.

Adapted from *Children Need Protection*. Illustrations include multi-ethnic children. Some information specific to local area.

IF SOMEONE TOUCHES YOU
National Crime Prevention Council, The Woodward Building, 733 15th Street NW, Washington, DC 20005, (202) 393-7141.

Poster to illustrate the principles "Say no," "Tell someone," and "It's not your fault." Colorful, 29" x 22" poster featuring McGruff, the Crime Prevention Dog.

THE KEY TO HAVING FUN IS BEING SAFE
The Safety and Fitness Exchange, Inc., 541 Avenue of the Americas, New York, NY 10011, (212) 242-4874.

A pamphlet that includes information about sexual abuse and safety tips for parents to teach children. Includes a list of children's rights, games to play and information for teaching children how to get help. Available in Spanish.

A MESSAGE TO PARENTS ABOUT CHILD ABUSE
Children's Hospital National Medical Center, 111 Michigan Avenue NW, Washington, DC 20010, (202) 745-4100.

A helpful booklet for parents with information to prevent assault as well as descriptive information and suggestions about steps to take if a child is abused.

NATURAL DOLLS

Migima Designs, P.O. Box 70064, Eugene, OR 97401, (503) 726-5442.

Anatomically correct dolls are available in adult and child male and female figures. Available in two skin colors.

POSTERS

Cleveland Rape Crisis Center, 3201 Euclid Avenue, Cleveland, OH 44115, (216) 391-3914.

Full color posters for children about sexual abuse prevention.

PRESCHOOL SEXUAL ABUSE STUDY CARDS

Sexual Assault Program, Beltrami County, Box 688, Bemidji, MN 56601.

A series of cards designed to illustrate touch types to small children.

PREVENTING SEXUAL ABUSE: A NEWSLETTER OF THE NATIONAL FAMILY LIFE EDUCATION NETWORK

National Family Life Education Network, P.O. Box 8506, Santa Cruz, CA 95061-8506, (408) 429-9822.

Quarterly publication includes background articles, resources, research updates and program descriptions in the area of child sexual abuse prevention.

PROTECTIVE PARENTING

Minnesota Criminal Justice Program. 658 Cedar, St. Paul MN 55155, (612) 296-8337.

A booklet for parents including information about facts, preventive measures, signs of abuse, reporting and the law. Section on the law is locally oriented (Minnesota law).

PUBLIC CONCERN AND PERSONAL ACTION: CHILD SEXUAL ABUSE

Children's Hospital National Medical Center, 111 Michigan Avenue, NW, Washington, DC 20010, (202) 745-4100.

This 12-page booklet is a very comprehensive discussion of child sexual abuse. It includes information about victims and offenders, the family, effects, general feelings and responsibilities, criminal proceedings and prevention.

PUPPETS

Krause House, P.O. Box 880, Oregon City, OR 97045, (no phone).

Peabody Mouse and Mother Mouse puppets (18" tall). From the program that includes the book for children, *Speak Up, Say No*, and the filmstrip/videotape of the same name.

SAFE, ADVENTUROUS AND LOVING

Protective Behaviors Anti-Victim Training for Children, 1005 Rutledge, Madison, WI 53703, (608) 257-4855.

This booklet outlines a 4-step anti-victim training process for adults to teach children. The four steps include talking to children about being safe, trust, networking and persistence. Includes pictures for children illustrating the four concepts, and text for adults explaining the concepts.

SAFETY KIDS SET

Brite Music Enterprises, Inc., 6111 Ernest Drive, Godfrey, IL 62035, (618) 466-1442.

A musical approach to teaching children how to safeguard themselves against sexual abuse, assault and kidnapping. The basic set includes a cassette, a sing-along coloring book, a membership card and an official safety kids club certificate. Also available are song books, posters and badges.

SAY NO, GET AWAY AND TELL SOMEONE

Minnesota Program for Victims of Sexual Assault, 430 Metro Square Building, St. Paul, MN 55101, (612) 296-7084.

Informational brochure on sexual abuse designed for persons with limited reading ability.

SEXUAL ABUSE: A GUIDE FOR YOUR CHILD'S SAFETY

Sexual Abuse Prevention Project, Alamance-Caswell Mental Health/Mental Retardation Program, Burlington, North Carolina. Distributed by Children and Youth Services, 407 South Broad Street, Burlington, N.C. 27215, (919) 228-0581.

A booklet for parents and other adults, giving background information about child sexual abuse and tips for talking with children about preventive measures. Includes signs of sexual abuse and a reference section. Illustrated with multi-ethnic photographs.

SEXUAL ABUSE AND YOUR CHILD
C.A.R.E. Productions, Box L #8—12th Street, Blaine, WA 98230, (604) 581-5116.

This information pamphlet includes definitions, facts for adults and children, signs of abuse, and other suggestions for parents.

SEXUAL EXPLOITATION: WHAT PARENTS OF HANDICAPPED PERSONS SHOULD KNOW
Seattle Rape Relief Developmental Disabilities Project, 1825 South Jackson, Seattle, WA 98144, (206) 632-7273.

A brochure to provide information about sexual abuse to parents of handicapped individuals, special education personnel and others who provide service to individuals with disabilities and their families.

SO WHAT IF YOU'RE NOT AN EXPERT?
Py Bateman, Alternatives to Fear, 1605 17th Avenue, Seattle, WA 98122, (206) 328-5347.

Part of a larger project to educate teenagers about sexual assault, this 19 page booklet outlines steps adolescents can take to prevent assault and what to do if it happens.

STREET SURVIVAL
Diane Robbins and Jennifer James, Seattle Institute for Child Advocacy, Committee for Children, P.O. Box 15190, Seattle, WA 98115, (206) 322-5050.

A book for young people who have run away from home, or are thinking about it. Sections on the pitfalls of street life, sexually transmissible diseases, birth control, runaways and the law, and getting off the street.

TALKING ABOUT CHILD SEXUAL ABUSE
Cornelia Spelman, National Committee for Pre-

vention of Child Abuse, 322 S. Michigan Avenue, Suite 1250, Chicago, IL 60604, (312) 663-3520.

A comprehensive pamphlet that discusses various aspects of child sexual abuse, including offenders, whether to report child abuse, and suggestions for talking with children.

THE TALKING AND TELLING ABOUT TOUCHING GAME
Safety Time Games, P.O. Box 6, Akron, OH 44308-0006.

A colorful game in the form of a fold out poster, to be used by teachers and parents to open discussion and teach facts and prevention techniques to children. Includes a parent and teacher guide.

TOUCH CONTINUUM STUDY CARDS
Cordelia Anderson in collaboration with the Illusion Theater, Minneapolis, MN. Network Publications, P.O. Box 8506, Santa Cruz, CA 95061-8506, (408) 429-9822.

Twelve laminated cards that depict many of the basic sexual abuse prevention principles, including different kinds of touch, trusting feelings, forced or trick touch, sexual abuse without touch, helping, and talking to someone.

TOUCH AND SEXUAL ABUSE
Illusion Theater, Minneapolis, MN. Distributed by Network Publications, P.O. Box 8506, Santa Cruz, CA 95061-8506, (408) 429-9822.

A general information pamphlet designed for parents, professionals and other adults, including agencies. Includes tips on what to say to children about sexual abuse, verbal and non-verbal messages and reporting information.

TOUCHING CAN BE FUN!
Women Organized Against Rape, Philadelphia, PA 92150, (215) 922-3434.

A pamphlet to read to children about sexual abuse. Talks about touching (good, confusing, bad), ways someone might try to trick a child, and who to ask for help.

WHAT EVERYONE SHOULD KNOW ABOUT THE SEXUAL ABUSE OF CHILDREN
Channing L. Bete Co., Inc., South Deerfield, MA 01373, (413) 665-7611.

A booklet that describes and discusses various forms of child sexual abuse, preventing and reporting suggestions, notes about offenders and why children are abused, effects and how to help if a child is abused.

WHAT PARENTS SHOULD KNOW ABOUT CHILD SEXUAL ABUSE
Tower, Cynthia Crosson and Susan Russell McCauley. National Education Association of the United States, P.O. Box 509, West Haven, CT 06516, (203) 934-2669.

A pamphlet for parents outlining information about facts, and how to react if a child is sexually abused.

WOULD YOU KNOW IF YOUR CHILD WERE BEING SEXUALLY MOLESTED?
Council on Child Sexual Abuse, 708 South G Street, P.O. Box 1357, Tacoma, WA 98401, (206) 593-6624.

A pamphlet for parents about child sexual abuse. Includes a section with word-for-word "script" on what to say to a child about touches, feelings, sexual abuse, saying no, secrets, telling, and a test to determine what the child has learned. Some information specific to local area.

Curricula and Leader Guides

C.A.R.E. KIT
Child Abuse Research and Education, Productions Association of British Columbia, P.O. Box 183, Surrey, B.C., Canada V3T 4W8, (604) 581-5116.

For children ages 5-9. Includes teacher's guide; training manual; a book for parents, children and teachers; puppets; posters; cassette; instructional flip chart.

CAT AND MOUSE: SELF-PROTECTION PROGRAM FOR CHILDREN
Girls Club of Omaha, Nebraska, 3706 Lake St., Omaha, NE 68111, (402) 457-5517.

A prevention program to use in schools, clubs and other organizations. Includes curriculum guide. Training available.

CHILD SEXUAL ABUSE PREVENTION: HOW TO TAKE THE FIRST STEPS
Cordelia Anderson, Illusion Theater. Distributed by Network Publications, P.O. Box 8506, Santa Cruz, CA 95061-8506, (408) 429-9822.

A guide for developing and implementing a child sexual abuse prevention program. Provides advice and guidelines, and directs to resources and services available.

CHILD SEXUAL ASSAULT AND ABUSE: GUIDELINES FOR SCHOOLS
I. Lorraine Davis, Publication Department, Wisconsin Department of Public Instruction, P.O. Box 7841, Madison, WI 53707.

Resources and suggested curricula, prevention programs and techniques for developing school board policy, community networking, legal references, sexual abuse indicators and interviewing techniques. Developed by the Wisconsin Department of Public Instruction to help schools deal with child sexual assault and abuse.

FEELINGS AND YOUR BODY
Coalition for Child Advocacy, P.O. Box 159, Bellingham, WA 98227, (206) 734-5121.

A pilot project prevention curriculum for preschoolers. Outlines 5 daily lesson plans that emphasize feelings, the right to say no and telling a trusted adult about touching problems. Project evaluation included.

HAPPY BEAR
Kansas Committee for Prevention of Child Abuse, 435 S. Kansas, 2nd Floor, Topeka, KS 66003, (913) 354-7738.

A preschool child sexual abuse prevention program that teaches children about the sense of touch and how to recognize and protect themselves from sexual assault. Complete program includes presentation, teacher training workshop, instructor's manual and videotape.

INCEST PREVENTION PROGRAM

Pat Janowiak, Ravenswood Community Mental Health Center, 4550 N. Winchester, Chicago, IL 60640, (312) 878-4300.

Program for private and public schools, K-12 grade.

MAKING IT WORK: A COMMUNITY ACTION PLAN FOR THE PREVENTION OF TEEN ACQUAINTANCE RAPE

Alternatives to Fear, 1605 17th Avenue, Seattle, WA 98122, (206) 328-5347.

A step-by-step guide to involve a community in the prevention of acquaintance rape among teenagers.

NO EASY ANSWERS

Cordelia Anderson Kent, Illusion Theater. Network Publications, P.O. Box 8506, Santa Cruz, CA 95061-8506, (408) 429-9822.

Twenty lessons include detailed objectives, background information for teachers, suggested activities and handouts. Junior and Senior High School.

PERSONAL SAFETY AND DECISION MAKING

Ann Downer, Seattle Institute for Child Advocacy, Committee for Children, Seattle WA. Distributed by Network Publications, P.O. Box 8506, Santa Cruz, CA 95061-8506, (408) 429-9822.

A unit on prevention of sexual exploitation. Five day curriculum for junior high school students. Three and one day outlines also included.

PERSONAL SAFETY: CURRICULUM FOR PREVENTION OF CHILD SEXUAL ABUSE

Marlys Olson, Child Sexual Abuse Prevention Program, Tacoma School District Administration Building, P.O. Box 1357, Tacoma, WA 98401, (206) 593-6624.

Extremely comprehensive material includes bibliographic information and complete lesson plan for headstart, K-2, 3-4, 5-6, junior high school and high school.

PERSONAL SAFETY CURRICULUM: PREVENTION OF CHILD SEXUAL ABUSE

Geraldine A. Crisci, Franklin/Hampshire Community Mental Health Center, 50 Pleasant Street, Northampton, MA 01060, (413) 586-3663.

Teaches personal safety skills for the prevention of sexual abuse to preschool through grade six aged children. Emphasizes safety without engendering fear. Available in Spanish.

PREVENTING SEXUAL ABUSE

Carol A. Plummer, Learning Publications, Inc., Holmes Beach, FL 33510. Distributed by Network Publications, P.O. Box 8506, Santa Cruz, CA 95061-8506, (408) 429-9822.

Curriculum guides for grades K-6, 7-12 and students with developmental disabilities. Contains information for educators and other professionals to design programs to fit the needs of their students. Sections on involving parents, instructor guidelines, curricula and lesson plans, roleplay activities, test questions and references.

PREVENTING SEXUAL ABUSE OF PERSONS WITH DISABILITIES

Bonnie O'Day, Minnesota Program for Victims of Sexual Assault, St. Paul, MN. Distributed by Network Publications, P.O. box 8506, Santa Cruz, CA 95061-8506, (408) 429-9822.

A curriculum for persons with hearing or visual impairments, physical or developmental disabilities. Includes parent training, teaching guidelines, exercises and student handouts.

PROTECTIVE BEHAVIORS: ANTI-VICTIM TRAINING FOR CHILDREN, ADOLESCENTS AND ADULTS

Peg West, Protective Behaviors, 1005 Rutledge Street, Madison, WI, (608) 257-4855.

Practical physical and psychological strategies to teach children how to protect themselves from danger and abuse, including sexual assault.

RED FLAG GREEN FLAG PROGRAM
Rape and Abuse Crisis Center, P.O. Box 2984, Fargo, ND 58108.
Program includes a guide, a coloring book, and a videotape. Targeted at children in the third and fourth grades; adaptable to other age groups.

THE SAFE CHILD PROGRAM—A SCHOOL CURRICULUM
Health Education Systems, Inc., P.O. Box 1235, New York, NY 10116, (914) 365-1120.
Videotape trainings to teach children 1) prevention of abduction, 2) prevention of sexual abuse and 3) safety for children who stay alone. Presents sexual abuse prevention as part of overall personal safety training, without using explicit information about sexual abuse.

SAFETY, TOUCH AND ME: A SEXUAL ABUSE PREVENTION PROGRAM FOR UPPER ELEMENTARY GRADE CHILDREN
Montgomery County Health Department, 4210 Auburn Ave., Bethesda, MD 20814.
A loose leaf curriculum guide for grades 4-6.

SELF-PROTECTION: A CURRICULUM FOR THE DEVELOPMENTALLY DISABLED
C.H.E.F., 20832 Pacific Highway South, Seattle, WA 98188, (206) 824-2907.
Two kits to teach self-protection skills to disabled children. Level 1 for elementary ages 6-11. Level 2 for junior and senior high, ages 12-19. Comprehensive kits include audiotapes, pictures, supplemental stories and slide shows.

SEXUAL ABUSE PREVENTION: A LESSON PLAN
Sandra L. Kleven, The Coalition for Child Advocacy, P.O. Box 159, Bellingham, WA 98227.
Illustrated step-by-step teacher's guide to classroom discussion and activities teaching sexual abuse prevention skills to grades K-6.

SEXUAL ABUSE PREVENTION: A STUDY FOR TEENAGERS
Marie M. Fortune, United Church Press. Distributed by Network Publications, P.O. Box 8506, Santa Cruz, CA 95061-8506, (408) 429-9822.
A leader's guide for a course in 5 sessions for young people ages 12-18. Sessions on rape as violence, good/bad touch, incest, and the media. Designed to use in public schools and religious communities to respond effectively to sexual and domestic violence.

SEXUAL MISUSE OF CHILDREN: TOOLS FOR UNDERSTANDING
Kay Christy Holley, Pierce County Rape Relief, Allenmore Medical Center, Suite A105, 19th and Union, Tacoma, WA 98405, (206) 627-1135.
Background information for schools and parents outlining responsibilities in prevention education. Activities to use with students in grades K-12.

SEXUALITY AND SEXUAL ASSAULT: DISABLED PERSPECTIVE
Virginia W. Stuart and Charles K. Stuart, Southwest State University, Marshall, MN 56258, (507) 537-7150.
Ten 3-hour sessions to improve sexual awareness of persons with disabilities and to offer prevention education relating to sexual assault.

SOURCEBOOK FOR EDUCATORS: SEXUAL ASSAULT PREVENTION FOR ADOLESCENTS
Susan de Alcorn, Pierce County Rape Relief, Allenmore Medical Center, Suite A105, 19th and Union, Tacoma, WA 98405, (206) 627-1135.
Comprehensive materials for junior and senior high school prevention program planners. Includes sections on teacher preparation, classroom presentations and activities, background information, including legal aspects, and resources.

STRATEGIES FOR FREE CHILDREN: A LEADERS GUIDE TO CHILD SEXUAL ASSAULT PREVENTION
Sally Cooper, Yvonne Lutter, Cathy Phelps, In-

trepid Clearing House, P.O. Box 02084, Columbus, OH 43202.

> Comprehensive guide to develop, implement and maintain a community-based child sexual assault prevention project for elementary-age children. Includes detailed narratives of workshops for children and adults, including commonly asked questions and suggested answers.

TALKING ABOUT TOUCHING: A PERSONAL SAFETY CURRICULUM
Ruth Harms and Donna James, Committee for Children, Seattle, WA. Distributed by Network Publications, P.O. Box 8506, Santa Cruz, CA 95061-8506, (408) 429-9822.

> Designed to be integrated into health and safety curriculum of any elementary school class. Stresses independent thinking and decision making so that children will be able to protect themselves from sexual abuse.

TALKING ABOUT TOUCHING WITH PRE-SCHOOLERS: A PERSONAL SAFETY CURRICULUM
Adapted by Margaret Schonfield, Committee for Children, Seattle, WA., distributed by Network Publications, P.O. Box 8506, Santa Cruz, CA 95061-8506, (408) 429-9822.

> Developed to be presented as part of the safety program in a preschool or daycare setting. Teaches about fire, streets, water and sexual exploitation. Large, illustrated teaching aids included.

TALKING TO CHILDREN/TALKING TO PARENTS ABOUT SEXUAL ASSAULT
Lois Loontjens, King County Rape Relief. Distributed by Network Publications, P.O. Box 8506, Santa Cruz, CA 95061-8506, (408) 429-9822.

> Designed for short term, "one-shot" presentations to children in grades K-5 and their parents. Provides detailed, step-by-step guide for outside professionals or for teachers with time constraints.

THIS IS IT! TEEN ACQUAINTANCE RAPE INFORMATION AND PREVENTION ACTIVITIES

FOR GROUPS
Alternatives to Fear, 1605 17th Avenue, Seattle, WA 98122, (206) 328-5347.

> A 200-page book of background information and group prevention activities to prepare adults who work with teens in any group setting in the community.

TOP SECRET: A DISCUSSION GUIDE
Billie Jo Flerchinger and Jennifer Fay. Network Publications, P.O. Box 8506, Santa Cruz, CA 95061-8506, (408) 429-9822.

> A guide for teachers and youth leaders using *Top Secret*, a book for teenagers about sexual abuse (see Books for Children). Sections include additional information for leaders, and discussion and activities suggestions.

TRAINER'S MANUAL: PREVENTION OF CHILD SEXUAL ABUSE
Ann Downer, Committee for Children, P.O. Box 51049, Wedgewood Station, Seattle, WA 98115, (206) 322-5050.

> A 130-page manual for trainers includes information on training skills, working with parents, working with the community, background reading, identification, reporting, disclosure, offender and victim treatment resources, and education resources (books, pamphlets, film, curricula).

YOUTH HELPING YOUTH
Boys Town Center, Boys Town, NE 68010, (402) 498-1111.

> A project to bring together abused teenagers in a "self-help" setting and teach skills for recovery and prevention of future abuse.

Films and Audiovisual Materials for the Classroom

ACQUAINTANCE RAPE FILM SERIES
Motorola Teleprograms, Inc.

> Four films for junior and senior high school students. Designed to increase awareness

and knowledge about peer exploitation.

THE PARTY GAME
8 minutes, color.
Illustrates the concept of effective and ineffective communication.

THE DATE
6½ minutes, color.
Sex stereotypes and their role in acquaintance rape.

JUST ONE OF THE BOYS
8½ minutes, color.
Illustrates how peer pressure and labeling can contribute to acquaintance rape.

END OF THE ROAD
9½ minutes, color.
Discusses assertive behavior techniques and how these techniques can sometimes prevent acquaintance rape.

AWARE AND NOT AFRAID
Distributed by Migima Designs. Video, 20 minutes, color, young adults.

> Five teenagers discuss frightening situations they have been in, and how they successfully escaped. Available in ¾″ and ½″ formats.

BELLYBUTTONS ARE NAVELS
Multi-Focus, Inc., 16mm, 12 minutes, color, preschool—secondary students, teachers, childcare workers and parent groups,

> A grandmother reads a picture book to Jonathan (age 3) and Megan (age 4). Teaches her grandchildren the names for body parts including eyes, fingers, penis, scrotum, vulva, vagina, clitoris, buttocks, anus, legs and feet. Includes parent/leader guide with suggestions for discussion.

BETTER SAFE THAN SORRY I & II
Filmfair Communications, 16mm or videocassette, 14½ minutes.

> These two films are aimed at different age groups. The first is for 9-14 year-olds, II is for K-3. Both films present potential dangers of sexual assault and suggestions for how to avoid abuse. Spanish version available.

BETTER SAFE THAN SORRY III
Filmfair Communications, 16mm or videocassette, 19 minutes, color, junior and senior high school.

> Dramatization presenting situations in which teenagers are victims of acquaintance rape, incest and other sexual abuse. Common sense rules for personal safety and avoidance are suggested.

BOYS BEWARE and GIRLS BEWARE
AIMS Media, 16mm or videocassette, 14 minutes and 12 minutes.

> Two films to alert children ages 9-14 about the approaches of child abusers. Common sense precautions to avoid danger. Discusses the possibility of the offender being someone the child knows and the importance of telling about abuse.

BROKEN DREAMS: THE SECRET OF DATING VIOLENCE
Duluth Women's Coalition, 70-slide presentation with synchronized sound track and 18-page discussion booklet. High school.

> Explores the problem of acquaintance rape using student actors and narrators. Designed to open discussion about values and expectations in relationships.

BUBBYLONIAN ENCOUNTER: A FILM FOR CHILDREN ABOUT THE SENSE OF TOUCH
Kansas Committee for Prevention of Child Abuse, 16mm film, ½″ and ¾″ videocassettes, 27 minutes.

> Adapted from the play *Bubbylonian Encounter*, this film is for children in grades K-6. "Bub" arrives from another planet where people don't touch. She must learn about the different kinds of touching "from scratch."

CHILD ABUSE: DON'T HIDE THE HURT
AIMS Media, color, 16mm and videocassette, 12½ minutes, youngsters/pre-teens.

> Emphasizes the importance of reporting incidents of abuse to a responsible adult or a group of friends.

CHILD MOLESTATION: A CRIME AGAINST CHILDREN
AIMS Media, 16mm or videocassette, 11 minutes, color/sound.

> Helps intermediate and junior high school students identify incest. Interviews with some children who are victims.

CHILD MOLESTATION: WHEN TO SAY NO
AIMS Media, 16mm, 13½ minutes, color/sound. Grades 4-8.

> Situations presented that depict children being approached by strangers, neighbors, relatives. Suggests responses. Discussion provoking film.

CHILD SEXUAL ABUSE: A SOLUTION
James Stanfield and Company, 6 color/sound filmstrips or videotape.

> This series is designed for school child sexual abuse prevention programs. Two of the filmstrips are for teachers-administrators, one is for parents, and three are for children (preschool-1; 2-4; and 5-6 grades).

CHILD SEXUAL ABUSE: WHAT YOUR CHILDREN SHOULD KNOW
Indiana University Audio-Visual Center, videocassette and 16mm.

> Originally 5 TV programs produced by WTTW/Chicago. Provides techniques and information to help children and adults identify and avoid child sexual abuse. Each program is for a different level: parents, K-3, 4-7, 7-12 and senior high.

DON'T GET STUCK THERE
Boy's Town Center, 15 minutes, color.

> A film for helping teenagers who have already been abused. In the film, adolescents share their experiences.

FOR PETE'S SAKE, TELL!
Krause House, Filmstrip and audio cassette or ¾" ½" videotape, 6 minutes.

> Uses animation (a mouse) and rhyming narrative. Comes with teaching guide. Available in Spanish.

INCEST: THE VICTIM NOBODY BELIEVES
Motorola Teleprograms, Inc., color, 16mm and videocassette, 23 minutes, high school and adult.

> Three young women talk about their experiences as abused children. Good background information for teachers and parents.

INVESTIGATION OF RAPE
Motorola Teleprograms, Inc., color, 20 minutes.

> A dramatization to show the procedures after someone is raped: police and medical procedures, transportation to the hospital, the physical examination, collection and preservation of evidence.

IT'S OK TO SAY NO!
Migima Designs, videocassette, color, K-6.

> Children discuss situations involving inappropriate touch.

KILLING US SOFTLY
Cambridge Documentary Films, 16mm color film, 28½ minutes.

> Discusses how advertising's image of women perpetuates and promotes violence against women. Excellent film for making students aware of "hidden persuaders."

LITTLE BEAR
The Bridgework Theater, Inc., videotape, elementary.

> Adapted from the play by Bridgework Theater. "Little Bear" communicates information and skills to increase the ability of children ages 3-12 to recognize and deal with potential sexual exploitation. Uses the touch continuum, talks about saying no and telling a trusted adult.

MORE THAN FRIENDS
O.D.N. Productions, Inc., videocassette in sign language; 21 minutes, junior high school, senior high school.

> Sign language drama. Demonstrates how effective communication can prevent misunderstandings about sexuality. Engages the audience in discussions about personal

values, stereotypes, peer pressure and sexual assault.

NEGATIVE TOUCH: WAYS TO SAY NO
Society of Visual Education, color, filmstrip/audiocassette, 16 minutes.

Uses the touch continuum to teach children to identify negative touch and what to do about it if it happens. Shows children in potential abuse situations involving strangers, someone known to the child and incest.

A NIGHT OUT
O.D.N. Productions, Inc., videocassette in sign language, 10 minutes.

In American Sign Language. Describes a teenager's encounter with one version of acquaintance rape. Tom takes Julie out and pays for date. Fantasy evening turns into a violent confrontation. Good film for regular high school classes, as well as for hearing impaired.

NO EASY ANSWERS
Indiana University Audio Visual Center, ¾" videotape, 50 minutes.

Adaptation of the play *No Easy Answers*. Aimed at teenagers' questions about sexuality and sexual abuse prevention.

NO MORE SECRETS
O.D.N. Productions, 16mm color film, 13 minutes.

Four friends, ages 8-10, exchange confidences about personal experiences they've had with sexual abuse. Positive message about importance of sharing information.

NOT ONLY STRANGERS
Coronet Films and Video, 16mm and video, 23 minutes, color, senior high.

A teenage girl is raped by a classmate and decides to file criminal charges. The film details the procedure. Explicit language.

OUT OF THE TRAP
The Bridgework Theater, Inc., videotape, high school.

Adapted from the play by Bridgework Theater. Designed to communicate skills and information to secondary-school-aged students that will increase their ability to prevent and deal with sexual abuse. Accompanying guidebook.

RAPE: A NEW PERSPECTIVE
Motorola Teleprograms, Inc., color, 7 minutes.

Challenges old patterns of blaming the victim. Shows rape as a violent act and uses the cross-examination of a robbery victim being questioned as a rape victim sometimes is. Promotes discussion.

SHATTER THE SILENCE
Phoenix Films, Inc., Color, 16mm, and videocassette, 29 minutes, senior high and college.

Dramatic film rather than documentary. 20 open discussions about child sexual abuse in classes in psychology, mental health, family living, social studies.

SOME SECRETS SHOULD BE TOLD
Motorola Teleprograms, Inc., 16mm and video, 12 minutes, elementary.

Uses puppets to explain sexual abuse in a non-threatening way, and how to get help if it happens.

SOMETIMES I NEED TO SAY NO
Rape Crisis Center of Syracuse, 16mm, 35 minutes, elementary.

Adapted from a play for elementary school children, this film uses a privacy continuum to teach children they have a right to say no to unwanted touch.

SPEAK UP, SAY NO!
Krause House, color filmstrip/audiocassette, 6 minutes.

Uses cartoon characters to show children that sexual abuse is not their fault and to urge them to report incidents. Teacher's guide available.

STRONG KIDS, SAFE KIDS
Paramount Studios, videocassette, color, elementary.

Partially animated, with Henry Winkler,

John Ritter and Mariette Hartly. Presents different abusive situations and encourages children and adults to stop and discuss what they've learned.

TARGETS

Motorola Teleprograms, Inc., color, 16mm and videocassette, 18+ minutes, junior and senior high school.

A group of teenagers involved in an accident meet an angel between life and heaven. They are granted a reprieve from death if they will agree to go to "victim school," where they learn how they have allowed other people to write in their victim book. Teaches how to avoid being a victim.

THIS FILM IS ABOUT RAPE

Motorola Teleprograms, Inc., 16mm, color, 30 minutes, high school.

Introductory film about sexual assault for junior and senior high school students. Suggestions for responding physically and psychologically to an attack, and discussions about assertiveness, self-defense and rape crisis hotlines.

TOUCH

Motorola Teleprograms, Inc., 16mm or videocassette, 32 minutes, color/sound.

Adapted from the play by Illusion Theater Company and Media Ventures, this film talks to K-6 grade levels about good touch, bad touch, confusing touch, trusting and acting on intuition.

THE TRIAL, THE MARK, THE VOICE

Bridgework Theater, ¾" videotape, 60 minutes, color.

Videotape of a play by Bridgework Theater. Puts child sexual abuse on trial, emphasizes prevention and community responsibility.

WHAT TADOO

Motorola Teleprograms, Inc., color, 16mm, and videocassette, 18 minutes, primary and intermediate grades.

Frog friends What and Tadoo teach children four basic prevention rules—Say No, Get

Away, Tell Someone, and Sometimes Yell—to protect themselves from abuse by strangers and acquaintances.

WHO DO YOU TELL?

Motorola Teleprograms, Inc., 16mm or ¾" videocassette, 11 minutes, color, elementary.

Uses animation and films of discussions among children. Discusses a wide range of problem situations such as what to do if you're lost, if your house is on fire or if you are approached by a sexual abuser.

Films and Audiovisual Materials for Teachers, Parents and Professionals

BEST KEPT SECRET

Motorola Teleprograms, Inc., 16 mm and videocassette, 15 minutes.

Produced by ABC 20/20 News Magazine. Interviews with parents of children who were sexually-exploited at a Manhattan Beach, California preschool.

BREAKING SILENCE

Future Educational Films, Inc., color, 16mm and videocassette, 58 minutes.

A documentary film about incest, through the stories of victims, including male victims. Discussion pamphlet included with film.

CHILD ABUSE

AIMS Media, color, 16mm and videocassette, 29 minutes.

Legal aspects of three types of child abuse are explained by dramatizing each type: battered child, father-daughter incest and neglect. Points out key indicators and defines legal boundaries as they apply to officials' roles.

CHILD ABUSE

Society for Visual Education, Inc., color, sound filmstrips, 12 minutes each.

Three filmstrips to train teachers and counselors to recognize and deal with physical and behavioral indicators of abuse, neglect and sexual molestation. Includes filmstrips for students for teaching how to recognize abuse, how to get help, how to avoid abuse, and the right to say no. Comprehensive teacher's guide included.

CHILDHOOD SEXUAL ABUSE: FOUR CASE STUDIES
Motorola Teleprograms, Inc., color, 16mm and videocassette, 50 minutes.
Four clinical studies presented to facilitate discussion and analysis of techniques. Good for in-service training to help viewers prepare for emotional distress associated with abuse cases.

CRIME OF SILENCE
Portia Franklin, cassette recording, 120 minutes.
Set of two cassettes featuring a four-part series on the sexual abuse of children. Includes information on incest, child sexual abuse, reporting and factors contributing to abuse. Recently broadcast on National Public Radio.

DOUBLE JEOPARDY
Motorola Teleprograms, Inc., color, 16mm and videocassette, 40 minutes.
Designed to sensitize professionals to the emotional state of a child participating in the criminal justice system as a witness against the offender. For professionals in protective services, medical and law enforcement personnel. Also useful for teachers, clergy, social workers and others in the helping professions.

EVERY PARENT'S NIGHTMARE
Motorola Teleprograms, Inc., color, 16mm and videocassette, 15 minutes.
Documentary by ABC's 20/20 Series explores several prominent sexual abuse cases and the lobbying groups forming to tighten laws against offenders.

THE HIDDEN SHAME
Motorola Teleprograms, Inc., color, 16mm and videocassette.

Documentary by ABC's 20/20 series on the subject of incest: two sisters from the same family who were both abused by their father.

IF I TELL YOU A SECRET
Lawren Productions, color, 16mm and videocassette, 34 minutes.
A film for professionals about interviewing the child victim of sexual abuse. Useful to a variety of professionals, including social workers, law enforcement personnel, doctors and attorneys.

INCEST: THE FAMILY SECRET
Filmakers Library, Inc., color, videocassette, 57 minutes.
Women victims talk about childhood experiences. Includes a look at the role of the mother in an incestuous family, and testimony from an incestuous father.

INTERVIEWING THE ABUSED CHILD
Motorola Teleprograms, Inc., color, 16mm and videocassette, 22 minutes.
A training film showing a pediatrician, social worker and a teacher interviewing battered, neglected and sexually abused children.

THE LAST TABOO
Motorola Teleprograms, Inc., color, 16mm and videocassette, 28 minutes.
Six childhood sexual abuse victims testify about their experiences. Stresses importance of counseling programs.

MY VERY OWN BOOK ABOUT ME
Migima Designs, color, videocassette, 20 minutes.
To help teachers use the activity book *My Very Own Book About Me* (see Books for Children). Information about detecting and preventing abuse.

NOT IN MY FAMILY
Lawren Productions, color, 16mm and videocassette, 34 minutes.
Five mothers discuss their emotional responses and the steps they took to adapt after they learned their daughters had been

victims of incest. For community groups, parents and professionals. Discussion guide included.

PEDOPHILE
AIMS Media, color, 16mm and videocassette, 20 minutes.
> For educators, law enforcement personnel and parents. Theories about offenders: who are they, how do they gain the child's trust and why do they abuse.

SETTING LIMITS
O.D.N. Productions, Inc., videocassette, 24 minutes.
> In American Sign Language, a guide for teachers who use *More Than Friends* and *A Night Out*. Highlights important themes and suggests questions to use in leading group discussions.

SEXUAL ABUSE OF CHILDREN: AMERICA'S SECRET SHAME
AIMS Media, color, 16mm and videocassette, 28 minutes.
> Documentary about the methods of abusers. Practical information is presented with first-hand and expert testimonies.

SEXUAL ABUSE OF CHILDREN: A TIME FOR CARING: THE SCHOOL'S RESPONSE TO THE SEXUALLY ABUSED CHILD
Lawren Productions, color, 16mm, 28 minutes.
> For school personnel. Physical signs of abuse are discussed and illustrated.

THE SEXUALLY ABUSED CHILD
Lawren Productions, color, 16mm and video, 26 minutes.
> A model for handling cases of child sexual abuse at different levels of the criminal justice system. For law enforcement personnel, parents and teachers. May be used in conjunction with companion film *A Time for Caring*.

THE SEXUALLY ABUSED CHILD: IDENTIFICATION/INTERVIEW
Motorola Teleprograms, Inc., color, 16mm and videocassette, 10 minutes.
> Demonstrations of various interviewing techniques when child sexual abuse is suspected. Good training aid for professionals.

TALKING HELPS
O.D.N. Productions, color, 16mm and videocassette.
> A film to help educators, youth group leaders and parents teach sexual abuse prevention skills to children. To be used as a companion film to *No More Secrets*. (See Films and Audiovisual Materials for the Classroom.)

TALKING TO A CHILD ABOUT PREVENTING SEXUAL MOLESTATION
Migima Designs, slide-tape presentation, 20 minutes.
> Techniques for discussing good and bad touches with children, and how to talk with them about their private body parts.

A TIME FOR CARING
Lawren Productions, color, 16mm and videocassette, 28 minutes.
> Film provides information for teachers and parents about procedures when child sexual abuse is suspected. For professionals who work with domestic violence, the film offers ways of helping victims. May be used in conjunction with a companion film *The Sexually Abused Child*. Outline for workshop provided.

FILM DISTRIBUTORS

Aims Media
626 Justin Avenue
Glendale, CA 91201-2398
(818) 785-4111

Boys Town Center
Boys Town, NB 68010
(402) 498-1111

Bridgework Theater, Inc.
113½ East Lincoln Avenue, Suite 3

Goshen, IN 46526
(219) 534-1085

Cambridge Documentary Films
P.O. Box 385
Cambridge, MA 02139
(617) 354-3677

Duluth Women's Coalition
Box 3205
Duluth, MN 55803
(612) 646-6177

Filmfair Communications
10900 Ventura Blvd.
Studio City, CA 91604
(818) 985-0244

Filmakers Library, Inc.
133 East 58th Street
New York, NY 10022
(212) 355-6545

Future Educational Films, Inc.
1414 Walnut Street, Suite 4
Berkeley, CA 94709
(415) 540-0324

Indiana University Audio-visual Center
Bloomington, IN 47405
(812) 335-8087

James Stanfield and Company
P.O. Box 1983
Santa Monica, CA 90406
(213) 395-7466

Kansas Committee for Prevention of Child Abuse
435 S. Kansas, 2nd Floor
Topeka, KS 66603
(913) 354-7738

Krause House
P.O. Box 880
Oregon City, OR 97045
(no phone)

Lawren Productions
P.O. Box 666
Mendocino, CA 95460
(707) 937-0536

Migima Designs
P.O. Box 70064
Eugene, OR 97401
(503) 726-5442

Motorola Teleprograms, Inc.
Simon & Schuster
108 Wilmot Road
Deerfield, IL 60015
(312) 940-1260

Multi-Focus, Inc.
333 West 52nd Street
New York, NY 10019
(212) 586-8612

Multi-Focus, Inc.
1525 Franklin Street
San Francisco, CA 94109
(415) 637-5100

O.D.N. Productions, Inc.
74 Varick Street–Suite 304
New York, NY 10013
(212) 431-8923

Paramount Studios
5555 Melrose Avenue
Hollywood, CA 90038
(213) 468-5000

Phoenix Films, Inc.
468 Park Avenue South
New York, NY 10016
(212) 684-5910

Portia Franklin
P.O. Box B
Old Chelsea Station
New York, NY 10011

Rape Crisis Center of Syracuse
423 W. Oriandago Street
Syracuse, NY 13202
(315) 422-7273

Society for Visual Education
1345 Diversey Parkway
Chicago, IL 60614
(312) 525-1500

Contributors

CAREN ADAMS has worked in the field of sexual assault prevention since 1975. As director of King County Rape Relief in Renton, WA, from 1975-1979, she developed materials for parents on talking to children about sexual assault. She has lectured for parent groups and appeared on the "Today Show" and other TV programs focusing on child sexual abuse prevention. She has co-authored two books, *No More Secrets* and *No Is Not Enough*, and a booklet for parents, *Nobody Told Me It Was Rape*.

CORDELIA ANDERSON, MA, is Director of Illusion Theater's Sexual Abuse Prevention Program in Minneapolis. She also instructs and conducts therapy sessions for female prostitutes and victims of childhood sexual abuse. Before joining Illusion Theater, she was employed for three years in the Hennepin County Attorney's Office where she specialized in working with child victims. She coordinated the original Child Sexual Abuse Prevention Project and developed the play, *Touch*, with Illusion Theater. Ms. Anderson co-authored Illusion's prevention plays *No Easy Answers* and *For Adults Only* and developed and published other child sexual abuse resources. She has appeared on local and national media programs and has designed and conducted over 1,000 training sessions in sexuality, sexual abuse and abuse prevention.

JOSEPHINE BULKLEY, JD, is Director of the American Bar Association's Child Sexual Abuse Law Reform Project at the National Legal Resource Center for Child Advocacy and Protection in Washington, DC. Ms. Bulkley provided technical assistance to reform laws and legal procedures in four jurisdictions in South Carolina,

Ohio, Massachusetts and Maryland. She was project attorney for the ABA from April 1979 to April 1984. During that time she directed child abuse projects including a national survey and analysis of child sexual abuse laws; published three major child sexual abuse reports and legislative recommendations; provided technical assistance and spoke at national, state and local conferences; and produced a videotaped mock trial training package for juvenile court prosecutors. She has authored several articles and publications on child sexual abuse and served on the House Select Committee on Children, Youth and Families.

SANDRA BUTLER is the author of *Conspiracy of Silence: The Trauma of Incest* as well as articles about theoretical and clinical issues in the field of child sexual abuse. Since 1980 she has led groups for incest survivors using writing as a way to explore the relationship between the creative process and self-healing. She is a speaker, lecturer and seminar leader for human service workers around the country and is currently working on a book for survivors called *Healing Stories*.

JON CONTE, PhD, is Assistant Professor at the School of Social Service Administration at The University of Chicago and founding editor of the *Journal of Interpersonal Violence*. Dr. Conte is a frequent lecturer at national and international meetings. His current research includes the impact of sexual abuse on children, the etiology of sexual violence and the effects of programs to prevent the sexual victimization of children. A clinical social worker and researcher by training, Dr. Conte maintains a private practice working with victims of interpersonal violence and acts as a consultant to treatment providers and other private and public agencies.

GERALDINE A. CRISCI, MSW, is a clinical social worker in the area of child sexual abuse prevention. She directs the Personal Safety Program, a prevention project based in Hadley, Massachusetts, and is currently involved in evaluation research monitoring the effectiveness of prevention education with preschool children. She directed a child sexual abuse education and prevention project for children from rural and Hispanic communities and authored *Personal Safety Curriculum*, a prevention guide for children of preschool and elementary ages.

LYNN B. DAUGHERTY, PhD, is a clinical psychologist in independent practice in Roswell, New Mexico. She has worked at the Montana State Psychological Hospital and as Director of the Southeastern New Mexico Forensic Evaluation Team, a unit providing psychological services to the court system. Her extensive work with victims of child sexual abuse and sex offenders led her to write the recently published book, *Why Me? Help for Victims of Child Sexual Abuse*.

I. LORRAINE DAVIS is state supervisor for School Social Work Services, Wisconsin Department of Public Instruction. She is director of the Wisconsin Child Abuse and Neglect Training for Educators project, and a lecturer/preceptor at the University of Wisconsin School of Social Work. Ms. Davis has served as national consultant with several organizations, including the National Center on Child Abuse and Neglect, The National Council on Exceptional Children, and the National Association of Social Workers. Ms. Davis is presently on the Board of Directors of the following organizations: Parental Stress, Inc., The Children's Trust Fund (Child Abuse and Neglect Prevention Board), Protective Behaviors,

Inc. and The National Rural Coalition for the Prevention of Incest and Child Abuse.

ANN DOWNER, MA, is the Training Director for the Committee for Children in Seattle. She has been with the Committee for Children since 1981 and developed their well-known child sexual abuse prevention training program. She authored the program's *Trainers Manual*, the junior high curriculum, *Personal Safety and Decision Making*, and contributed to the development of other Committee for Children curricula.

JENNIFER FAY, MA, is a sexual abuse prevention educator, consultant and author. She began her work in this field in 1979 as Education Director at King County Rape Relief in Renton, WA. She is the author of the parent guide *He told Me Not To Tell* and coauthor of *No More Secrets, Top Secret, Nobody Told Me It Was Rape* and *No Is Not Enough*. She leads national workshops for parents, teachers, counselors and other professionals. Ms. Fay was featured in the PBS television series "Child Sexual Abuse: What Your Children Should Know."

DAVID FINKELHOR, PhD, is the Associate Director of the Family Violence Research Program at the University of New Hampshire. He is the author of two books on the subject of child victimization: *Sexually Victimized Children* published in 1979 and *Child Sexual Abuse* published in 1984. Finkelhor has received grants from the National Center for Child Abuse and Neglect and the National Center for Prevention and Control of Rape. He has authored over two dozen articles on child sexual abuse.

JEAN KILBOURNE, EdD, is a media analyst, lecturer and writer. She is the creator of two slide presentations, *The Naked Truth: Advertising's Image of Women*, and *Under the Influence: The Pushing of Alcohol via Advertising*. She has made two award winning films, *Killing Us Softly* and *Calling the Shots*.

CAROL PLUMMER, MSW, is the author of *Preventing Sexual Abuse*, a curriculum on child sexual abuse prevention for children and adolescents. Ms. Plummer provides trainings on child sexual abuse prevention throughout the nation for Learning Publications and for the United States Air Force's child care and youth center directors in Europe, the Pacific and the United States. In addition, she provides trainings for teachers and administrators of schools, day care centers, and migrant education programs on sexual abuse prevention.

FLORENCE RUSH is the author of the well known book, *The Best Kept Secret: Sexual Abuse of Children*, and has written numerous articles on the subject of child sexual abuse. She is a psychiatric social worker with 31 years of experience in the field. Since her book was published in 1980, she has appeared on national television and radio in the United States and Canada and lectured extensively at universities, service organizations and professional conferences.

ELAINE SCHERTZ has used her degrees in education and music in the Bridgework Theater, Goshen, IN, program since 1980. She has served as actor and program consultant and is currently Marketing Manager for Bridgework Theater.

ELLEN SHAMAN is Project Director of the Disabilities Project at Seattle Rape Relief. She has extensive experience in the fields of rehabilitation, public health planning and advocacy for persons with disabilities. She conducts trainings and consultations nationwide in the areas of sexual assault and disabilities.

MARY ELLEN STONE, MA, Director of King County Rape Relief in Renton, WA since 1979, has worked with women's issues, including sexual assault, domestic violence and health care, since 1975. She cochaired the Washington Coalition of Sexual Assault Programs from 1981-1983.

MARIA IDALI TORRES, MSPH, has participated in the planning, implementation and evaluation of health programs in Puerto Rico and Massachusetts since 1975. She worked as a health education specialist for the Child Sexual Abuse Education and Prevention Among Rural and Hispanic Children Project. She is presently conducting a research project focused on health issues of Puerto Rican women and children.

DON YOST founded and is now the director of Bridgework Theater, Goshen, IN. He has worked in the social services as counselor and administrator since 1976. He has written plays commissioned by the Indiana State Board of Health, the Center for Community Justice and the Mennonite Church. His work with child sexual abuse prevention began in 1980. He provides prevention consultation to schools and theater groups.

Program Index

Bridgework Theater, Inc., p. 149
113½ East Lincoln Ave.
Goshen, IN 46526
(219) 534-1085

The Child Assault Prevention Project (CAP), p. 150
CAP Project National Office
P.O. Box 02084
Columbus, OH 43202
(614) 291-2540

Child Assault Prevention Project, p. 152
Junior High Boys' Program
West Contra Costa Rape Crisis Center
2000 Vale Road
San Pablo, CA 94513
(415) 236-7273

Child Assault Prevention Project, p. 153
Casa de Esperanza
P.O. Box 56
Yuba City, CA 95992
(916) 674-5400

Child Sexual Abuse Prevention and Treatment
Program, p. 154
Council on Child Sexual Abuse
P.O. Box 1357
Tacoma, WA
(206) 593-6624

Children Need to Know Personal Safety Program,
p. 155
Health Education Systems, Inc.
P.O. Box 1235
New York, NY 10116
(914) 365-1121

Children's Creative Safety Program, p. 157
Safety and Fitness Exchange
541 Avenue of the Americas

New York, NY 10011
(212) 242-4874

Children's Self-Help Project, p. 158
170 Fell Street, Room 34
San Francisco, CA 94102
(415) 552-8304

Community Education Program, p. 159
King County Rape Relief
305 South 43rd
Renton, WA 98055
(206) 226-5062

Disabilities Project, p. 160
Seattle Rape Relief
1825 So. Jackson, Suite 102
Seattle, WA 98144
(206) 325-5531

Project PAAR-Plus, p. 161
Green County Prosecutor's Office
Xenia, OH 45385
(513) 376-5087

Project S.A.A.F.E., p. 162
Jackson Mental Health Center
969 Lakeland Drive
Jackson, MS 39216-4699
(601) 982-8811

Rape Crisis Network Children's Program, p. 164
Lutheran Social Services
North 1226 Howard Street
Spokane, WA 99201
(501) 327-7761

Red Flag Green Flag Program, p. 164
Rape and Abuse Crisis Center
P.O. Box 2984
Fargo, ND 58108
(701) 293-7298